SPI

MUSSOLINI

His Part in My Downfall

Edited by
Jack Hobbs

PENGUIN BOOKS

This book is dedicated to Erin Pizzey in her lonely fight to stop brutal
physical and physiological violence on women and children

PENGUIN BOOKS

Published by the Penguin Group
Penguin Books Ltd, 80 Strand, London WC2R 0RL, England
Penguin Group (USA) Inc., 375 Hudson Street, New York, New York 10014, USA
Penguin Group (Canada), 90 Eglinton Avenue East, Suite 700, Toronto, Ontario,
Canada M4P 2Y3 (a division of Pearson Penguin Canada Inc.)
Penguin Ireland, 25 St Stephen's Green, Dublin 2, Ireland (a division of Penguin Books Ltd)
Penguin Group (Australia), 250 Camberwell Road, Camberwell, Victoria 3124, Australia
(a division of Pearson Australia Group Pty Ltd)
Penguin Books India Pvt Ltd, 11 Community Centre, Panchsheel Park, New Delhi – 110 017, India
Penguin Group (NZ), 67 Apollo Drive, Rosedale, Auckland 0632, New Zealand
(a division of Pearson New Zealand Ltd)
Penguin Books (South Africa) (Pty) Ltd, Block D, Rosebank Office Park,
181 Jan Smuts Avenue, Parktown North, Gauteng 2193, South Africa

Penguin Books Ltd, Registered Offices: 80 Strand, London WC2R 0RL, England

www.penguin.com

First published in Great Britain by Michael Joseph 1978
Published in Penguin Books 1980
Reissued in this edition 2012
009

Copyright © Spike Milligan Productions Ltd, 1978
All rights reserved

Printed in England by Clays Ltd, Elcograf S.p.A.

ISBN: 978-0-241-95812-4

www.greenpenguin.co.uk

MIX
Paper from
responsible sources
FSC
www.fsc.org   FSC® C018179

Penguin Books is committed to a sustainable
future for our business, our readers and our planet.
This book is made from Forest Stewardship
Council™ certified paper.

Clive James, in a review of one of my war books, quoted it as "an unreliable history of the war". Well, this makes him a thoroughly unreliable critic, because I spend more time on getting my dates and facts right than I did in actually writing. I admit the way I present it may seem as though my type of war was impossible and all a figment of a hyperthyroid imagination, but that's the way I write. But all that I wrote *did* happen, it happened on the days I mention, the people I mention are real people and the places are real. So I wish the reader to know that he is not reading a tissue of lies and fancies, it all *really happened*. I even got down to actually finding out what the weather was like, for every day of the campaign. I've spent a fortune on beer and dinners interviewing my old Battery mates, and phone calls to those members overseas ran into over a hundred pounds. Likewise I included a large number of photographs actually taken *in situ*, don't tell me I faked them all, so no more "unreliable history of the war" chat.

I want to thank the following for their help with documents, photographs, maps, recollections which are included in this volume: Major J. Leaman, Lt. S. Pride, Lt. C. Budden, B.S.M. L. Griffin, Sgt. F. Donaldson, the late Bombardier Edwards, Bombardier H. Holmwood, Bombardier S. Price, Bombardier A. Edser, Bombardier S. Kemp, L/Bdr. A. Fildes, Gunner "Jam-Jar" Griffin, Bombardier D. Sloggit, L/Bdr. R. Bennett, Gunner J. Shapiro, Gunner H. Edgington, Gunner "Dipper" Dye, Driver D. Kidgell, The War Museum Picture Library, Mrs Thelma Hunt, Mrs P. Hurren, all of whom have helped to give you this "unreliable history of the war".

This volume ends up on a sad note, even for a born joker like me: the conflict caught up with me and I was invalided out of it. However, the rest of the book tells of what an unusual mob we were and have been ever since. The closeness of those years still exists in as much as we have two reunions a year, something no other British Army unit have. This book is a dedication to the spirit and friendship of "D" Battery, 56th Heavy Regiment, Royal Artillery.

S. M.
Bayswater
March 1978

Salerno

THURSDAY, SEPTEMBER 23, 1943

MY DIARY: STILL AT WAR! EARLY CLOSING IN CATFORD. READ LETTER FROM MOTHER SAYING CHIESMANS OF LEWISHAM ARE SO SHORT OF STOCK, THE MANAGER AND STAFF SIT IN THE SHOP MIMING THE WORDS "SOLD OUT".

Dear Reader, the beds in the Dorchester Hotel are the most comfortable in England. Alas! neither Driver Kidgell nor Lance-Bombardier Milligan are in a bed at the Dorchester – no! they are trying to sleep on a 10-ton Scammell lorry, parked on the top deck of 4,000-ton HMS *Boxer*, inside whose innards are packed 19 Battery, 56th Heavy Regiment, all steaming in the hold; from below comes the merry sound of men retching and it's all from Gunner Edgington. We are bound for Sunny Salerno. For thirteen days since the 5th Army landing, a ferocious battle had ensued on the beachhead. Even as we rode the waves we knew not what to expect when our turn came. The dawn comes up like Thinder. *Thinder*? Yes, that's Thin Thunder. "Shhhhhh," we all shout. The chill morning air touches the khaki somnam-

HMS Boxer, *which landed us at Salerno. This picture was taken after the war, when she'd been converted to a Radar Ship.*

bulists sleeping heroically for their King and Country. We are awakened by Gunner Woods in the driving cab, who has fallen asleep on the motor horn. A puzzled ship's Captain is wondering why he can hear the sound of a lorry at sea. Kidgell gives a great jaw-cracking yawn and that's him finished for the day. He stretches himself but doesn't get any longer. Deep in his eyes I see engraved the word, "TEA". "Wakey wakey," he said, but didn't. The ship is silent. The helmsman's face shows white through the wheel house.

"It is Dawn," yawns Kidgell.

"My watch says twenty past," I yawned.

"Yes! It's *exactly* twenty past Dawn," he yawned.

We yawned. Like a comedy duo, we both stand and pull our trousers on; mistake! he has mine and vice versa. The light is growing in the Eastern sky, it reveals a great grey convoy of ships, plunging and rising at the dictation of the sea. LCTs. LCTs, some thirty of them, all flanked by navy Z-Class destroyers. The one on our port bow is stencilled B4. Imagine the confusion of a wireless conversation with it.

"Hello B4, are you receiving me?"

PAUSE

"Hello B4 answering."

PAUSE

"Hello B4, why didn't you answer B4?"

"Because we didn't hear you before."

In the early light the sea is blue-black like ink. Kidgell is carefully folding his blankets into a mess, "I haven't slept that well for years."

"How do you know?" I said. "You were asleep."

He chuckled, "Well it *feels* like I slept well."

"Where did you feel it, in the legs? the elbows? teeth?" I was determined to pursue the matter to its illogical conclusion; I mean if *sane* people are going around saying "I slept well last night", what would lunatics say? "I stayed awake all night so I could see if I slept well"? I mean – we are interrupted by the shattering roar of aircraft!! "Spitfires!" someone said, and we all got up again.

"Thank God they weren't German," says Kidgell.

"Why thank him," I said. "He doesn't run the German air force, thank Hitler."

"Alright, clever Dick." He giggled. "This is going to sound silly – thank Hitler they weren't Germans."

The helmsman's face showed white through the wheel house.

I produce a packet of Woodbines. I offer one to Kidgell. I have to . . . he's got the matches. My watch says 12.20; that means it's about seven o'clock. We stow our gear into a lorry full of sleeping Gunners with variable pitch snoring; three of them are snoring the chord of C Minor. We decide to walk "forrard". The *Boxer* makes a frothy swathe as her flat prow divides the waters. The sky is turning into post-dawn colours – scarlet, pink, lemon. It looked like the ending of a treacly MGM film where John Wayne joins his Ghost Riders in the sky. (Personally I can't wait for him to.) It's chilly; we wear overcoats with the collars up. Kidgell looks pensively out towards Italy.

"I was wondering about the landing."

"Don't worry about the landing, I'll hoover it in the morning."

He ignored me, but then everybody did. "I've been thinking."

"Thinking? This could mean promotion," I said.

"I was thinking, supposing they land us in six foot of water."

"Then everyone five foot eleven and three quarters will drown."

"That's the end of me, then."

"I thought you were a champion swimmer!"

"You can't swim in Army Boots."

"You're right, there is not enough room."

"What *are* you talking about?"

"I'm talking about ten words to the minute."

A merry matelot approaches with a Huge Brown Kettle. "You lads like some cocoa?"

We galloped at the speed of light to our big packs and returned to meet the merry matelot as he descended from the Bridge. He pours out the thick brown remaining sludge. The gulls in our wake scream as they dive-bomb the morning garbage. We sip the cocoa, holding the mug with both hands to warm them. A change from holding the mug to warm the Naafi tea. Another cigarette, what a lunatic habit! "Here

9

we are," I said. "We go to these bastards who make this crap and we say 'We will give you money for twenty of those fags', we smoke them, we make the product *disappear*! Ha! Supposing you bought a piano on the same basis? Suddenly, in the middle of a concert it disappears, you have to belt out and buy another one to finish the concerto. It's lunacy."

In the deck-house, a red-faced officer scans the horizon ahead. "I wonder exactly where we are," says Kidgell.

"I think we're on the ancient sea of Tyrrhenum Sive Inferum." That finishes him.

"When we reach Sicily we will hug the coast to afford us air cover and the way things are, I'd say we could *just* afford it."

We are travelling one of the most ancient trade routes in history, Carthaginians, Greeks, Romans, Mamelukes, Turks and Mrs Doris Hare. "Fancy us being part of history," I said. "I don't fancy it," said Kidgell.

The Tannoys crackle. "Attention, please."

A Gunner faints. "What's up?" we ask.

"I thought I heard someone say please."

"Attention . . . This is the Captain speaking . . . (What a good memory he had) . . . In three minutes the Ack-Ack guns will be firing test bursts . . . this is only a practice, repeat, practice."

Soon the sky was festooned with erupting shells, black puffs of smoke with a red nucleus from the barrels of the multiple Pom Poms. The Tannoy again.

"Hello this is your – " a burst of amplified coughing follows.

"It's the resident consumptive," I said.

The coughing ceases. "Attention, that practice firing will be repeated every morning at – " Coughing – coughing – "at" – coughing . . .

The helmsman's face showed white through the wheel house.

"I feel a sudden attack of roll-call coming on," I said.

I was right. Sgt. King lines us up on deck. We answer our names and anyone's that isn't there; even if they called "Rasputin" a voice answers "Sah."

"Milligan?"

"Sah!"

10

"Devine?"

"Sah!"

"Edgington? . . . Edgington?"

From the deck below comes a weak voice "Sah!" followed by retching.

Britannia rules the waves, but in this case, she waives the rules. A roar of engines, the Spitfires return, we all get up again. They repeat roaring back and forth through the day, we get used to it, we get so used to it that when a Focke Wolfe shoots us up, we're all standing up, aren't we? Breakfast is happening in the galley.

"I have been a slave to breakfast all my life but breakfast *and* a galley slave never!" says Kidgell.

We lined up head on to a trio of Navy cooks, who doled out Spam Fritters, Bread, Marge, Jam and Tea and avoided looking at it when they did. We ate on top deck enjoying the sea breeze, the pleasant weather . . . were we *really* going to war or were we on our way to Southend for the day? As Kidgell is licking his mess-tin clean the klaxons go, submarine scare! Immediately the destroyers start circling, gun crews scramble to their mounts, the barrels trained down. . . . A false alarm! Curses! I wanted to see the Greeny wake as the missile raced from the U-boat, a sneer on the German Captain's lips, "Take zat, Englander." On the bridge of HMS *Dauntless*, Lt. Wynford-Beaumont-Plague turned his trim little craft towards the black periscope. "Full speed ahead." The words came through clenched teeth and fists. Too late, the Germans suddenly see the bows of the British destroyer slice through the conning tower, splitting the Kaiser's picture into a thousand fragments. "We didn't even get a depth charge," says Kidgell.

"My God," I said, "is there a charge on *depth* now?"

A long green groaning thing is approaching. The identity tags say "Edgington. 953271 C of E."

"Was that a Jerry sub?" he said.

"No, it was a false alarm," I said.

"Oh dear," he moaned, "I wanted something to cheer me up."

He managed a wry smile, opened a tin marked "Emergency Chocolate Ration", and took out a cigarette; never a stingy one he offered them round. The fact there was only one in

11

the tin left much to be desired. I desired it so I took it.

"You sod," he said. We shared it.

"You feeling any better?" I asked.

He groaned, "Argggggg. I'm no bloody good at sea."

"But you're *always* at sea, Harry."

"I've missed me bloody breakfast."

"We've just had breakfast, and believe me, you haven't missed anything."

Edgington's empty stomach rumbles loudly. "Spitfires," shouts Kidgell. We all get up again.

"What *was* for breakfast?" he said.

"We don't know," I said. "There's a court of enquiry this afternoon."

Mid-day, the sun is out, it's that perfect temperature, not hot not cold, like Naafi tea.

SEPTEMBER 23, EVENING

MY DIARY: SIGHTED NORTH WEST TIP OF SICILY!

If my geographical recollections were right, that would be Capo San Vito. It wasn't. In the evening light inland mountains seemed made of purple mist; on the sea was a green-grey seafret; to the primitive mariner it must have given birth to legends, to Gunner Liddel it gave forth to "I wonder what's for dinner." He watches a destroyer's evasive zig-zag course. "Driver must be pissed," he says.

He'd been a regular for eleven years and had risen to the rank of Private. He was sweating on being downgraded, I didn't think he could be, from where he was the only way was up. He had two great bunions on his feet, mind you, *he* didn't think they were great. They had promised to downgrade him 2B. I approached him, struck a Hamlet-like pose and said, "2B or not 2B." He tried to throw me overboard.

"It'll be my luck to get killed and next day it'll come through downgraded to 2B."

"That would be terrible," I said, "being killed is bad enough, but to be a corpse *and* 2B as well, that's too much."

The Cocoa-Pot Matelot introduces himself. He was Eddie Hackshaw and from what I hear, still is, a short squat London lad with a cheery smile. He has taken a fancy to me. He gave me a silver Arab ring for luck. He troops Kidgell,

12

Edgington and self down to see the engine-room. We meet the engineers, they are embalmed in oil and grease, all Liverpudlians.

"These are the Whackers who do the engines," he said.

"Ah, the famous Do-Whacker-dos." (Groans.)

They had been working long hours since "D" day, and looked desperately tired.

"It was bloody murder, two of our lads were killed on deck by Jerry artillery!"

We sat at their mess table, which *was* a mess.

"We haven't had time to scrub it since we did the landings."

We sat and talked, they gave us tea, grub, and handfuls of fags. A Big Liverpudlian, as I remember his name was Paul, said, "Did youse know the anagram of Salerno was 'Narsole'?"

"I thought it was the other way round."

The face of the helmsman showed white through the wheel house. Lunch was a mangled stew, lumps of gristle floating on the surface. Edgington said if you held your ear to it you could hear an old lady calling "Helppppp."

The curtain of night is falling as we pass Argonaut-like in the shadow of Sicily. The sun, like a scarlet Communion host, dips into a horizon that is gossamer with mist; the wave-tops catch the last pink fading light, and reflect like a million flashing indicators. The night comes: we heard the Tannoy.

"This is the Captain speaking, there will be no naked lights, matches or cigarettes during hours of darkness. We are travelling through a known U-boat area. Will all officers ensure this order is carried out?"

Dinner was lunch four hours later and several degrees colder. I went below and Hackshaw scrounged me a bottle of beer.

"Where you been?" says Kidgell.

"In the galley."

He leaps up, grabbed his mess-tins. "Is there more grub there, then?" he said, saliva pouring down his chin like Pavlov's dogs.

It may be an illusion but night seemed to make the sea sound louder and lovelier. It even made Kidgell sound louder and lovelier. It wasn't long before he was humming a little tune, and preparing his bed. Standing on top of his lorry made him look taller, it was the only thing that did. I had once asked him were all his family short, he said "Yes."

I said "Why?" and he said, "Because they were frightened of heights."

We watch a destroyer sending morse by lamp.

"Do you know," I said, "Gunner Liddel thinks that Ash Wednesday is a Fourth Division football team?"

We laugh.

"Stop that noise, do you want the bloody German submarines to hear us?" says the voice of Edgington.

"He was laughing in German," I explained.

We slide into our blankets. Doug and I converse on Cabbages and Kings, I can't recall the dialogue, but I know we discussed where Alf Fildes would be (he was on his way from Malta we learned later). We also discussed our fears about Salerno. Like an omen, as we spoke, came the first distant boom of gunfire.

"Hear that?" said Doug.

"Yes, I heard it."

Gradually, silences between exchanges became longer. I thought of home, would I see them all again? It all seemed so bloody mixed up. How did we ever let this happen? Had we challenged Hitler when he occupied the Saar, it would have been a pushover . . . too late now, chum, now he's every bit as strong as us. . . . Stronger.

SEPTEMBER 24, 1943

I was awake at first light, and I heard gunfire. I sat bolt upright, we were down to about three knots, very slow, granny-knots. We were pulling into the Bay of Salerno! All the beaches look remarkably peaceful. Good! we'd have a quiet landing. The still waters of the Bay were a carnival of ships, some 200, all shapes and sizes rode at anchor. The amazing American Amphibian DWKs were ferrying supplies ashore. Looming large among all this was HMS *Valiant* and HMS *Warspite*. Suddenly one let fly a devastating salvo which thundered around the bay and rocked the warship some fifteen degrees off her axis.

"That's not going to do Jerry any good," said a sailor and

14

Lorries and guns coming ashore at Red Beach, Salerno. Note the man in the foreground with two broken forearms – now going for broken legs to get his ticket.

added. "It's not doing the *Warspite* any good either."

In the morning mistiness we make out hyper-activity on the beaches – lorries, tanks, half-tracks, beach-masters waving flags, pointing, lifting, lowering, signalling, shouting – all involved in the logistics of the war. The shells from *Warspite* were bursting inland on the hills behind Pontecagnano, which dominated the landing beaches. Why wasn't Jerry replying? We drop anchor; immediately trouble, the chain has wrapped around the propeller shaft, fun and high jinks. We cheer as a diver goes down. A boat from the beach approached with a purple-faced Officer who shouted rude things through a bull-horn at our Captain, whose face incidentally showed white through the wheel house. To make it more difficult for our Captain, the destroyers lay a smoke-screen around us, and the Tannoy crackles: "Hello – click – buzz-crackle – it's – click-buzz-crackle – later." End of message.

"It's all getting a bit silly," said Harry. "All we had was the view and now that's been bloody obscured!"

Now is the time for action! I take my trumpet from its case. There must be men still alive who remember the sound of "The Last Post" from the smoke-shrouded *Boxer*. The Tannoy crackles.

"Whoever is playing that bugle, please stop," said a piqued Navy voice.

Salerno. 200 soldiers and sailors watch a lone black soldier pushing a lorry up the beach.

The anchor chain is finally freed. The smoke-screen lifts to show we are now facing away from the beach.

"They're takin' us back again," says Gunner Devine.

"Of course not, you silly Gunner, no, the Captain has turned his ship around in the smoke to show us how clever he is."

There are laconic cheers as the diver surfaces.

"Caught any fish?" someone says.

He holds up two fingers.

"Is that all?"

The engines start up again, the ship swings slowly round and points toward Italy, I mean he couldn't miss it. Sub-Section Sergeants are going around telling us to "Get ready to disembark." Drivers are unchaining the restraining cables that secure the vehicles to the deck. The day is now a delightful mixture of sun and a cool wind. The *Warspite* lets off another terrifying salvo. It thunders around the bay. We watch it erupt among the hills.

"That'll make the bastards sit up," says Sgt. "Jock" Wilson.

"I'd have thought", I said, "it would have the opposite effect!"

"Oh hello, Spike," he says. "How you bin enjoying the sea trip?"

"Well, Sarge, Yes and No."

"Wot do ye mean Yes or No?"

"Well, Yes I am, and No I'm not, but mostly No I'm not, otherwise, Yes I am."

He frowned. "You'll never get promotion."

Wilson was a Glaswegian, he was "Fitba" (Football) mad, and his family at home were hard put to it to send him all the news cuttings on the Scottish Matches*.

SEPTEMBER 24, 1943

REGIMENTAL DIARY: *HMS Boxer landed first party on Red Beach, Salerno Bay at 0940 hrs.*

The ship touched the beach very gently, so gently I suspect it's not insured. "Sorry about the bump, gentlemen," said a chuckling Navy voice on the Tannoy. A cheer arose from

*Scottish Matches = ones that won't strike.

17

the lads as the landing ramp was lowered. Another salvo from *Warspite*. At the same time an American supply ship starts to broadcast Bing Crosby singing "Pennies from Heaven" over its speakers. To our right, over the Sorrento peninsula, a German plane is flying very high; pinpoints of high bursting Ack-Ack shells trace his path.

Time 9.30. Sea calm.

The Tannoy crackles. Another coughing demo? No.

"Hello, is it on? – Hello, Captain Sullivan speaking."

"Give us a song, Captain," shouts Gunner White.

"Attention, will all men without vehicles, repeat, without vehicles, please disembark first?"

"I think I'm without vehicles," I said to Harry.

"How about you?"

"No, I haven't got vehicles, but they might be incubating," says Edgington, who is, now that the sea is calm, back to his cheery self; the roses haven't come back to his cheeks, but he tells me they're on their way. "They have reached my knees and are due in me navel area this afternoon."

The Tannoy: "Will men without vehicles disembark now?"

"We've been spoken for, Harry," I said as we trundle down the gangways to the "Floor" of the *Boxer*. We were about to set foot on Italy. The jaws of the *Boxer* are opened on to a sunlit beach.

"I could never have afforded all this travel on my own," I say. "It had to be the hard way, World War 2. I've always wanted to see Russia, I suppose that would mean World War 3."

I don't believe it, we were walking down the broad ramp on to the Salerno beaches, no bullets! no shells! and I didn't even get my feet wet, as I leave my first footprint in the sand. I shout loudly "TAXI!", and point in the direction it's coming from. "The woods are full of them," I add.

We move in a milling throng on to the beach. I start the sheep bleating and soon we are all at it, much to the amusement of the seamen watching from top deck. The scenery by L/Bdr. Milligan: the beaches are a mixture of volcanic ash and sand, the colour of milky coffee, it stretches left and right as far as the eye can see. Strewn along the beaches is the debris of a battle that had raged here; an occasional German long-range shell explodes in the bay. There are no hits. The beaches vary from twenty to thirty yards deep. Back from this is a mixture of pines, scrub, walnut trees and sand hillocks mounted with Tuffa grass. Bulldozers have made clearways flanked by white ribbons denoting them mine-free. There is activity the length and breadth of the shores. Great ammo dumps are, as we watch, getting higher and bigger. Just inland, Spitfires are refuelling and about to take off from a makeshift airstrip. American Aero-Cobras are revving their engines, turning into the wind and taking off in the direction of Naples.

We congregated by the sand hillocks, dumped our small kit and started to explore the area. Hard by was an American Lightning plane that had crash-landed half in the sea; a glimpse inside showed a blood-saturated cockpit. "He must be very anaemic by now," said Sherwood. There are slit trenches everywhere, water bottles, helmets, empty ammo boxes, and spent-cartridge cases by the hundreds.

"Must have been a hot spot," said Bdr. Fuller.

At the bottom of a trench I spot a Scots Guard cap badge, several pieces of human skull with hair attached, and a curling snapshot of two girls with an address somewhere in Streatham. I put it in my paybook intending to forward it to the address. We come across thirty or so hurried graves with makeshift wooden markers. "Private Edwards, E.", a number, and that was all. Fourteen days ago he was alive, thinking, feeling, hoping. . . . If war was a game of cards, I'd say someone was cheating.

We pause now for Gunner Edgington's recollections of the landing which go like this (stand well back). . . .

The scene as it met our eyes as we come up on deck very early that morning, with the ponderous old HMS *Boxer* leading the convoy and still some way off, the distant coast. It was barely dawn – mighty early – it was to be a fine day, though a touch of unaccustomed chilliness in the air. We had after all just come from North Africa – the sea calm, the elements indeed almost holding their breath – overhead the sky was fairly clear – but there, dead ahead of us was an awesome "Curtain up" setting of Salerno, a name which meant nothing to us at this juncture. [It did to me, *I* listened to the radio. S.M.] An hour later, the sun having fought his way into his kingdom [my God he's waxing lyrical. S.M.] the incredible sight of a beautiful flat broad sandy beach, fringed some way back by tall grass over low dunes. Behind that, a great half moon of meadow-land with here and there large wooded areas . . . a spot that in other times might have been a secluded quiet paradise of nature . . . and yet, here raged war! For, as far as the eye could see along the beautiful coastline, a veritable armada of ships stood hull-to-hull, their prows to the beaches, disgorging soldiers and endless waves of sophisticated war-making machines. The activity that swarmed in unbelievably unhurried fashion, reminiscent of Hampstead Heath and the fairgrounds at Easter, had, as its musical accompaniment, the roar of great guns, the incessant racket of powerful vehicles and the cheerful shouts of men with megaphones yelling leisurely instruc-tions to us all. As the *Boxer*'s great jaws opened slowly to the wondering gaze of us all standing within, we saw to our left a Spitfire [I thought it was an American Lightning] brewing up, flaming and smoking hideously, and past it on a grassy fringe a very tall slim flagpole, from its very top almost to its base a broad strip of red cloth fluttering . . . Red Beach!! [Well done, Harry, I'll take over now. There's a cheque in the post.]

We all stand well back far away from any work, and watch the confusion of unloading the vehicles. Officers and Sergeants are weaving back and forth saluting, shouting.

"What *are* they doing?" says Edgington.

"I think they're trying to win the war," I said.

"Why?" he said. "I'm satisfied with it as it is."

Kidgell's Scammell lorry is emerging from HMS *Boxer*. I ponder the logic that gives a driver five foot five inches a giant lorry to drive that necessitates him putting an orange box on the seat before he can see out. Gunner Devine has taken his boots and socks off and is paddling in the sea; an irate officer shouts at him, "Hey, you! What do you think you're doing?"

"I think I'm paddling, sir," was the reply.

"Paddling? This isn't bloody Blackpool."

"I know that, sir, Blackpool's in England."

"Get dressed at *once* and report to me!"

20

The officer stormed off. Well, almost! In turning he hurt his ankle. Next thing the khaki God of authority is hopping up and down, holding the injured limb, his face contorted with pain. He sees before him a sea of smiling gunners.

"You're al' on a charge," he screamed.

"I think that's a fair ending," said Edgington, grinning at the departing cripple.

My God! Edgington was holding a mug of *tea*! How did he do it? He pointed to a tin brewing over a derv fire. Sgt. Mick Ryan comes across. He is dripping with sweat – was it fear of work?

"Come on, youse bloody signallers!" he points to a Scammell and a jack-knifed 7.2 gun well down in the sand.

We take the drag ropes and pull. The rest of the morning is a repetition of this. "Heave, steady," etc. A naval officer in virgin-white uniform motors past in a jeep. He is tall, sun-tanned. He has the eyes of a man used to searching distant horizons, a handsome intelligent face and strong jaw and a mouth with the suggestion of a smile. The medals on his jacket told of his past heroisms. He was – how can I describe him? – a pain in the arse. Nice Lt. Budden is approaching.

"Hands up all the men who want to go to war!"

There is a massive negative response. He points at me.

"*You*. Milligan."

This was victimisation!

"There must be some mistake, sir. I'm eighty-six and a cripple."

He points. "Over there, 25-year-old liar."

I clamber on to Sherwood's bren carrier to be taken to a premature death. The carrier is overloaded, I perch on top. Budden sits in the passenger seat looking at maps. We roll across the sand hills; it's not easy for me to stay on, so with consummate skill I fall off.

"Stop being silly now, Milligan," says Mr Budden.

I remount. This time I jam myself between two kitbags. We reach a secondary road and – here comes the bonus – we pass the Temple of Neptune and Cerene, at Paestum, both looking beautiful in the sunlight. Strung from the Doric columns are lines of soldiers' washing. At last they had been put to practical use. If only the ancient Greeks had known.

What the ancient Greeks didn't know was that L/Bdr.

21

Milligan had fallen off again! I got back on. This time I removed the kitbags, I climbed into the hole and they lowered the kitbags on top, leaving my head and shoulders free. I had appealed to Sherwood to drive slowly past the Temples.

"Wot Temples?"

"You'll never get another chance to see them close at hand," I said.

"You're right," he says. "*You'll* never get another chance to see them again," and he drove on.

Mr Budden has heard all this.

"Bombardier Sherwood is not of a scholastic mind, Milligan. He is a son of the soccer field. Had you said, 'Slow down, Reading are playing the Mussolini Rovers', I'm sure it would have touched a part of his English soul that is forever football boot."

We have cleared the sand dunes, the minor roads, and have turned left on to the Battapaglia highway going north. We wait to allow some of the vehicles to catch up with us. There's no sign.

"I suppose they've stopped to see the Temples," grinned Sherwood.

The houses that line the road were two-storey, square, whitewashed. Hanging on the walls were strings of tomatoes. People sit outside on simple wood and rush chairs. The women were mostly bare-legged, wearing black clothes and wooden-soled sandals. Some pretty-faced girls look from the windows. A short fat middle-aged balding man runs across the road and gives us a bunch of purple grapes. He smiles and shakes his hand in a friendly gesture. "*Viva Englise*," he says. I chew grapes and spit the pips at the neck of Sherwood.

Twenty minutes later our little convoy is complete.

"We are to establish an OP, somewhere up there," Budden points to the mountainous country ahead.

I hated OPs; when they were quiet they were quiet, but when the shit was flying it was a dicey place. We pass several burnt-out tanks, mostly ours; that's the trouble, Jerry had better tanks. We were trying to get away with superiority in numbers, very unfair on our tank crews. We never had any armour to match the Tiger, or the Jag Panther. The shades of night were falling fast as we went through Battapaglia past the ruins of the Tobacco factory that had been a bloodbath

22

18 Battery negotiating a difficult road near Sipicciano; note sergeant in foreground, hoping lorry will run over him.

for both sides.

SEPTEMBER 24, 1400 HRS

MY DIARY: TRAVELLING UP NARROW MOUNTAIN ROAD, FREQUENT STOPS TO LET FARM CATTLE GO PAST. MOUNTAINS EACH SIDE TOWERING OVER US, LIKE DAUMIER'S DRAWINGS IN DANTE'S PARADISE LOST.

Not only is Dante's Paradise Lost, but *we* are bloody lost. Lt. Budden is looking studiously at his map, the wrong way up.

"It's upside down, sir."

"I *know* that, *I* turned it upside down for a reason."

"Sorry, sir, only trying to help."

"If you want to help, Milligan, act like a Basenji."

Basenji? He'd got me. What was Basenji? A platoon of

23

battle-weary soldiers are filtering past us to the rear. Their shoulder-flash reads QUEENS.

SEPTEMBER 24, EVENING

MY DIARY: OWING TO NON-ARRIVAL OF NO. 19 AND 21 WIRELESS SETS NO BATTERY OP CAN BE ESTABLISHED, ORDERED TO "STAND DOWN".

Now to let you have the boredom of the Official History of the Regiment.

Their (19 Bty) position lay at the foot of Monte Mango, and was approached by means of roads little better than mountain tracks, worse indeed than any encountered in Africa. Yet by evening after a day of feverish activity [see? they even make the poor buggers work with a temperature. S.M.] *and some quite unprincipled borrowing of equipment (cigarettes, chocolate, etc.) they were in action, and were immediately given the attention of Stukas.*

Now Gunner Edgington recalls the first gun position. Action! Lights! Cameras!

I recall travelling on one of the Scammells as we went into action. We travelled fourteen miles I remember "The Dean"* saying, yet we found out later the "bridgehead" was only two miles in depth – it had been started just two weeks before, and though we didn't know it then, Jerry was well advanced on the task of chucking us right out. One man, a certain Sergeant of our Battery by name of Michael "Bullprick" Ryan, was to completely reverse the situation almost single-handed!

We didn't get moving till late in the day and then crept along an interminable, winding, tortuous course, until long after nightfall we came into an earth road between the giant trees of what seemed like a forest, except that they were set strangely in very orderly straight rows. There were smaller trees between them – apples? – lemons? – and running suspended along all of them, grapevines – all of them loaded with their fruit, fully ripe, for it was September.

No light but Budden's torch – everyone inhibited from

*Bdr. Spike Deans

any noise that was avoidable – a hissed instruction, and the driver swung his wheel, the huge vehicle grinding slowly into the vines tearing great lengths of them away. The torches showed great puddles of what seemed like blood in the soft ryecorn-sprouting earth.

Trees – these giants carried masses of very fine walnuts – were dragged down by two Scammells arranged fan-wise to a particular tree with a powerful steel hawser running from one front winch-gear round the tree to the other's front winch – a line of fire was cleared! Next morning, a raid – Spike and "Dook", shaving, dive under a Scammell. Fire orders kept coming and kept getting cancelled. We could see Monte Stella through the trees – like a kid's drawing of an alp – watched our infantry struggling on it –

19 Battery about to fire on Monte Stella, on which Jerry is perched. Man firing gun in off-white vest is Gunner Devine.

The moment after firing; idiot photographer failed to capture shell exploding on peak. Note driver with steering-wheel of bus lorry – the rest was stolen by Italians

25

then the most incredible "shoot" of them all – Mick knocked the top clean off it with two rounds, sighting through the barrel a 7.2 howitzer aimed like a pistol!! Suddenly a great ragged mob of Hun fighter planes interceded, surging over the nearest crest, bellying down right over our tree tops, cannons going, though whether at us I know not.

Yes. I remembered being Stuka-ed, the evidence of this was a six-foot-deep trench at the bottom of which looking up white-faced and saying "Tell Hitler I'm sorry" was Lance-Bombardier Milligan. What *did* Basenji mean?

My slit-trench was in the angle of a farm-hut wall and a raised bank. All day Jerry 155mm shells were passing over our positions.

"They're after the 25-pounders in the field behind us," says Sgt. Ryan.

"Behind?" I said, turning yellow. "Christ, we're far forward for heavies."

"Forward?" he giggled. "We had bloody Nebelwurfers in this field this afternoon."

Ryan had excelled himself. In the absence of an OP he had aligned his gun on Monte Mango by looking up the barrel, elevating it a bit above that, and by God, he was actually dropping the shells right on target.

I was surplus to requirements so I spent the afternoon writing letters, and eating handfuls of purple grapes that grew above my trench. I'd read about Conquerors partaking of the spoils of war. What I hadn't read about was the terrifying attack of the shits that followed.

Dear Mum, Dad and Des.
We've been moved, I'm not allowed to say where. We had spaghetti for lunch. The lunacy continues and has every chance of becoming a way of life unless we stop it soon. Men are getting so used to wars that the Psychiatric wing of the RAMC are planning how to break the news to the men when the war is over.

I am keeping well, we don't go hungry in this war, the Compo Rations are very good, that's if you get to the box first – this is the first day in this country, so I haven't caught anything yet. I would welcome any books, periodicals and newspapers, preferably ones that say the war is over, and believe me the war is over . . . over here. I'm writing this in a hole in the ground, it's convenient, because if you get killed, they just fill the hole in and sell it as a cemetery. That's all the cheery news, will write again when the situation is a little less fraught.

Loving son, Terry.

I lit up a cigarette and lay back. Mind a blank. The guns roar, the night comes. Grapevine message, "Dinner", across the field with mess-tins, I am walking on a field that has been laying fallow for a few years. One still feels the furrows where the plough once moved. In the corner of the field under some walnut trees, a heavily camouflaged cookhouse is operating, and by the screams they are operating without an anaesthetic. In the queue I find Kidgell and Edgington.

"Where you been hiding?" is the merry greeting.

"Hiding? *me* hiding? that's a malicious rumour, I haven't been hiding. I have been standing on the peak of a mountain, swathed in a Union Jack, with a searchlight beaming on me and I have been crying 'Come on you German swines, and feel the taste of British steel!' Do you call that hiding?"

"That's a load of cobblers."

"Talking of cobblers," says Kidgell, "wot are those terrible things floating in the stew?"

"Mines," says our cook. "But don't worry, they're ours."

It is a Maconochie Stew, and it tastes bloody marvellous. We sit with our backs against a bren carrier. The odd gun falls silent as the gun-teams take turns for their meal. It's dark now, all around the unending roar of artillery. Odd rumours.

"They say he's starting to pull out and our patrols are on the outskirts of Naples."

"Cor, Naples, eh?"

We would all like to be in Naples. It would be the first European city since we left England nearly two years ago. We've all been warned of the "dangers". If the brochure was telling the truth, venereal disease was walking the streets of Naples and one could contact it just by shaking hands with a priest. The BQMS has passed a message we won't be getting any mail for a week, he says things like that to cheer himself up. Amid the gunfire we hear a droning, a lone plane, it's Jerry, he drops a green flare. It was so pretty we all cheered when it came on.

"Milligan???? Milligan????" A voice is calling.

"Is that you mother?" I reply.

It's Bombardier Fuller, he is saying, "Pack enough kit to last forty-eight hours, you're goin' up the OP."

Enough to last forty-eight hours. Wearily I climb into Bdr. Sherwood's bren carrier, already in it and waiting are Captain Sullivan, Signaller Birch and Bombardier Edwards. In a second carrier are Lt. Budden, Sig. Wenham; I cannot recall the Driver.

MY DIARY: GOT ON TO NARROW ROAD TO MANGO, ROAD JAMMED WITH VEHICLES, TWO TRUCKS AHEAD STRUCK BY JERRY MORTARS. STUCK FOR NEARLY TWO HOURS.

Progress is slow, road jammed with vehicles, very dark now, ahead is a glow of a large fire. Lt. Budden dismounts, he is coming towards us with a face that says Confusion Unlimited, and he appears to be the Managing Director.

"That's the mountain there," he points to a mountain that is so big it doesn't need pointing to. Still I take his point. "We've got to get up that."

"We need a ladder, sir."

"How we going to get a bloody bren carrier up there?" says Birch.

"Post it."

He tried to hit me.

"I'll miss him."

"Who?" says Birch.

"A helmsman whose face showed white through the wheel house."

It's really dark. We can hear the small arms fire. The crump of mortars is endless. What *was* Basenji? There is now a nose-to-tail traffic jam along a narrow walled lane; the red glow ahead is getting larger, and now owns the sky. Some walking wounded are squeezing past us on their way back.

28

"Wot's happening?" I said to one of them.

"Jerry mortars, they set fire to the ammo truck – any minute now."

He had hardly said it when there was an explosion and the random fireworks of the ammo going off showered the sky with sparks; it was great fun, and costing us a fortune. A Military Policeman is coming down the convoy.

"Back up, if you can," he says, and laughs. We pass the message down the line, half an hour later we start to move backwards. A Despatch Rider is riding up from down behind us calling out "Any 19 Battery here? . . . Any 19 Battery here? . . ."

Birch says "Yes."

Silly sod! *Never* answer anything in the Army, too late now. It's Don R. Lawrence. He tells us we have to take the bren carrier and go back to pick up a wireless set which has just arrived from the beach, and Captain Sullivan on another truck is going to the OP, so we breathe a sigh of relief, we start extricating the bren carrier from the congestion, marvellous, when we've almost got it out the bloody thing breaks down, we struggle and manage to push it on to its side to allow the traffic through. Budden tells us, "We'll have to walk to HQ and get fresh orders."

I tell him I don't need fresh orders, I'm perfectly satisfied with the ones I've got.

"Please, Milligan," says Budden, "*try* and be a soldier."

We finally reach RHQ. It's off a walled lane in an Italian farmhouse, built around a forecourt two storeys high; an exterior staircase leads up to the first floor, which is surrounded by a balcony. The farm is blacked out except the room where *our* HQ is, that is a mass of light chinks coming from windows and doors like an early *Son et Lumière*. Several vehicles are parked in the forecourt. The drivers are asleep in the back. Twenty minutes pass. Mr Budden appears, he smells of Whisky, the khaki after-shave for men. He is much happier.

"We are not needed, Milligan," he says.

"Does that mean for the duration?"

We both walk back to the gun position, which is easily found. We just followed the loudest bangs.

29

SEPTEMBER 24, 1943

MY DIARY: COOL NIGHT, A TOUCH OF AUTUMN CHILL IN THE
AIR. HAD VERY DISTURBED SLEEP. KEPT WAKING UP IN A COLD
SWEAT, TOOK SWIG AT WATER BOTTLE, HAD A FAG. WHAT A
BLOODY LIFE. I FINALLY DROPPED OFF INTO A BLACK SLEEP,
LIKE DEATH. AM I THE BLACK SLEEP OF THE FAMILY?

SEPTEMBER 25, 1943

I awoke at first light, sat up, yawned. I felt as tired as
though I had not slept. A morning mist is rapidly disappear-
ing. It swirls around the head of Monte Mango. I start the

*Loading a 7.2 – to the right, Monte Stella; to the left, Monte
Mango*

30

ritual of folding my blankets. A voice calls, "Hey, Terry." Terry? I hadn't been called that since I turned khaki. It was Reg Lake, a Captain in the Queen's Regiment. He had been sleeping about thirty yards away. Reg was the pre-war manager of the New Era Rhythm Boys, one of the best semi-pro bands in London. He was the one who gave me my first break as a "crooner". Last time I had seen him was on a 137 bus going from Brockley to Victoria.

"My God, Terry, what are you doing in this God-forsaken place?"

"I'm helping England win the war." What a silly bloody question. "Reg," I said, "or do I call you sir?"

"How long you been here?" he said.

"Came yesterday – I thought it was a day trip."

"I was here on the landings, you missed all the fun."

"I'll try and make up for it."

It was difficult to make conversation. I couldn't say, "Where's the band playing this week?" I asked what had happened to the boys in the band.

"All split up."

"That must be painful."

"Most of them are in the services – remember Tom the tenor player with only one lung? They took him."

"They took me and I've only got two."

He was called away by a Sergeant. I never saw him again, I've no idea if he survived the war. If he reads this book, I hope he gets in touch.

A voice is calling across the land, "Bombardier Milligan."

"Bombardier Milligan is dead," I call in a disguised voice. The voice replied, "Then he's going to miss breakfast."

Good God! it's nearly nine! I just get to the cookhouse in time to have the remains of powdered eggs, bacon and tea that appears to have been all cooked together.

"You slept late," says Edgington.

"I'm training for sleeping sickness."

We are now gathered around the Water Wagon doing our ablutions. Edgington is at the lather stage, peering into a mirror the size of a half crown propped on a mudguard. He was moving his face clockwise as he shaved. I had stripped to the waist, which brought cries of "Where are you?" I had my head under the tap enjoying the refreshing cascade of chlorinated cold water, at which time, twelve FW 109s are enjoying roaring out of the sun, guns hammering, there's a God-awful scramble, we all meet under a lorry. I caught a glimpse of the planes as they launched their bombs on the 25-pounder regiment behind us.

"Look out," warns Edgington, when the planes were half way back to base. He hurled himself face down. "All over." We stand up. Edgington presented a face, half lather, dust and squashed grapes.

What was *I* laughing at? One moment I was well. Next moment I was on my knees vomiting. It was unbelievable. I became giddy, kept seeing stars and the Virgin Mary upside down.

"Report sick," says Bombardier Fuller.

"You're so kind," I said.

They took me to the Doc, who said I had a temperature of 103.

"What *have* you been doing?" he said.

"I was washing, sir."

Having a temperature of 103 allowed you to stop fighting. No but seriously, folks, I was ill! Oh I *was ill*!! The war would have to go on without me! In a bren carrier they took me shivering with ague to the Forward Dressing Station. It was a small tented area off a rough track; a Lance-Corporal, tall, thin with spectacles, took my details, tied a label on me, I think it was THIS WAY UP.

"That stretcher there," he said.

So, they were going to stretch me! I felt a bit of a fraud. Around me were seriously wounded men. Some were moaning softly. A chubby Catholic Priest, about forty-five, red faced, blond hair going grey, walked among us.

"What's wrong with you, son?"

"I got fever."

"Fever?"

"Yes. Disappointed, father?"

He grinned, but it didn't wipe the sadness off his face. He told me they were awaiting the arrival of some badly wounded men from the Queen's.

"They were trying to take that." He nodded towards Monte Stella.

Three jeeps arrive with stretcher cases. Among them is a German, his face almost off. Poor bastard. There was a trickle of wounded all afternoon, some walking, some on stretchers, some dead, the priest went among them carrying out the last rites. Was this the way Christ wanted them to go? The most depressing picture of the war was for me the blanket-covered bodies on stretchers, their boots protruding from the end. For my part I kept falling into a delirious sleep, where I told General Montgomery to sing "God Save America" with his trousers down. When I awoke it was evening. I'd been lying there about four hours.

"Are they going to take me?" I asked an orderly.

"Yes, you're next, Corporal," he comforted. "We had a lot of badly wounded, we had to send them off first."

With the sun setting, and the tent sides turning pink in the light, I was loaded aboard an ambulance in the top bunk. The top bunk! It all came back to me, the top bunk, that's the one my parents always put me in during those long train journeys across India on the old GIP* Railway . . . all seemed so long ago. . . . The ambulance bumped and jolted through the narrow mountain roads. I recalled those bright sunlit Indian days, as a boy, where every day *was* like a Kipling story. . . .

"Like a drink of water, Corporal?"

"Yes."

The attendant poured water into a tin mug. I gulped down two, it tasted like nectar.

It was four stretchers to an ambulance; in between with his back to the driving cab sat an orderly. The inside was painted white. The vehicle smelt new. A blood plasma bottle was attached to the soldier on the lower bunk, his chest swathed in bandages. The orderly constantly checked the flow of the plasma. The German kept groaning. It all seemed to be coming to me through a heat charged mist. I was hovering twix delirium and reality. I doze off.

The ambulance stops, near-by artillery are banging away, the doors open, it's dark, voices mixed with gunfire, I am being unloaded. I'm on the ground, from there a large municipal building with a flat roof is silhouetted against the

*Great Indian Peninsula.

night sky. Covered with ivy, it looks like the setting for *Gormenghast*. I am carried up stairs along corridors, more stairs, and finally into a dim-lit ward of about thirty beds, all with mozzy nets down. I am placed on the floor.

"Can you undress yourself?" says an overworked orderly.

Yes, I can.

"The pyjamas are under the pillow," he points to a bed.

My God, it looked good, already turned down, white sheets and pillows, TWO PILLOWS, being ill was paying dividends. I pulled on the standard blue pyjamas.

"Where's the karzi?" I said weakly.

He pointed out the door. "Dead opposite."

I wasn't quite dead but I went opposite; that journey over, I pulled my body under the sheets. I was desperately tired and feverish, but stayed awake to enjoy the luxury of sheets. Another orderly; they all wear gym shoes so you don't hear them coming, he took my pulse, temperature, entered them on a board that hung on the foot of my bed.

"Like some tea?" He spoke Yorkshire.

"Aye," I said in Yorkshire.

"Anything to eat?"

"Yes, anything."

He came back with a plate of tomato soup and bread. On the tray were four white tablets.

"Take these when you dun, they'll help bring temperature down."

"I don't want it down, I want it up for the duration."

I gulped it down. Took the tablets, brought them all up. Who said romance was dead? So much for my first forty-eight hours in Italy.

Interior of B.R. military hospital, post Salerno days

SEPTEMBER 26, 1943, 0600 HRS

Awakened by a nurse. A *female* nurse, all pink and scrubbed in spotless uniform smelling of Pears soap.

"Darling, I love you, marry me," I said.

"Good morning," she said, threw back the mozzy net and before I could answer had stuffed a thermometer in my gob.

"It's down," she said.

"What's down?" I said.

"You're only a 100."

She bent over the next bed, and showed two shapely legs, one would have been enough. I felt my temperature go up again. I really was ill. I fell asleep, an orderly woke me up with breakfast. The ward was coming to life, I wasn't; orderlies were taking down the last of the black-outs, those patients who could were putting the mozzy nets up, trailing out to the ablutions, others were swallowing medicines, here comes mine, four white tablets, what are they? The orderly doesn't know.

"I don't have to," he says, "then if you die it's not my fault."

Cheerful bugger. For the first two days my temperature goes up and down, and so I'm not alone, I go with it. At night it was worst with delirium and terrible dreams. However, gradually I start to recover. The nurse (I wish I could remember her name) tells me of an incident. In the officers' section there's a Colonel from the RAOC; he's due for a hernia operation, the matron has been given the job of shaving him, she knocks on the door.

"Come in," says the Colonel.

The matron throws back the bed clothes, lathers all around his "willy", shaves him and starts to leave. The Colonel says, "Pardon me, matron, but why did you bother to knock?"

In the next bed is a Marine Commando, Jamie Notam. He's in with our old friend "Shell Shock", received during the landings around Marina. He was forty-one, a bit old for a Commando.

"I used to be a Gentleman's Gentleman," he's speaking with a broad Scots accent.

Jamie is sitting on the edge of his bed, he is in his battle dress, his boots highly polished, a hangover from his gentleman's gentleman days. His bed was immaculate, his eating irons and mess-tins shine like silver. He basically wanted to *do* things; if he folded a newspaper it was always perfectly square, but there the creation stopped. He could never *make* anything. It was always *do* but what he did was perfect. He must have been the ideal servant. It's eleven o'clock of a morning. Outside the sun shone, that autumnal light more silver than gold, it beamed through the windows of our ward, favouring the beds who were on that side.

In the centre of the ward are three trestle tables loaded with books, periodicals and newspapers. On one is an old Italian wireless set plugged up to a ceiling light. From it issues music from Allied Forces Network in Algiers. It's mostly danceband music and singers like Crosby, Sinatra, Dick Haymes, Vera Lynn, Ann Shelton and Evelyn Dall (who?). The ward is big, high ceiling, plenty of light. All the bedside lockers have a water jug and glass. If you wished, you could have orange or lemon juice flavouring. In the locker were those tortuous pieces of porcelain, the bed-pan and the pee bottle. The attempt to make the place look homely, small tins with a few wild flowers, was very much appreciated. Since my admission, the sounds of artillery had daily receded. It was now reasonably quiet, save for the sound of planes passing overhead.

Some of the patients sat up in bed, some writing letters, some reading newspapers with headlines like: AMBASSADOR KENNEDY TELLS PRESIDENT BRITAIN IS FINISHED (if he meant *after* the war he was spot-on). Some soldiers had donned their dressing-gowns and were seated on other patients' beds, talking, smoking, or playing cards. The sick ones lay still, some asleep, some staring at the ceiling. We aren't a casualty ward so we don't have any blood or bandages. The lad in the bed on my right is very ill and in an oxygen tent; he has pneumonia and looks ghastly. My temperature was down to normal in the day, up to a hundred at night.

"How'd you get into the Commandos at the age of forty-one?"

"I told 'em I was thirty."

"Why didn't you say thirteen, you'd have got out altogether."

"I wanted adventure."

"Call this adventure?"

He shows me photographs of himself outside his master's Manor House somewhere in Scotland.

"You left all that to come here?"

He nodded ruefully. "I must ha' been bloody mad," he said.

Well he was now. He was interesting company even though

36

he was on tranquillisers and occasionally fell down. I sent
him on errands like scrounging fags, getting my breakfast
tray, bringing extra cups of tea, he loved it, he was back "in
service" again, and I took every advantage of it.

"Shall I gie yer boots a clean?" he'd say and I would say
"Yes," wouldn't I?

I felt well enough to write my first letter home from Italy.

My dear Mum, Dad and Des,

*I am officially somewhere else, that somewhere else is
where I am, I am not at liberty to say, the whole of this land
we have arrived in is now TOP SECRET, in fact no one is
allowed to know where it is, even the people who live in it are
told to forget they are here, however, the bloody Germans
know where it is, and don't want to let us have it (Spaghetti). I've been here about a certain number of days
(Spaghetti) and we all arrived here by certain transport and
landed at a certain place at a certain time, of all these facts
I am dead certain (Spaghetti). We are allowed to mention
the sky, so I'll say that we have in fact got one, it's directly
overhead and high enough to allow you to stand up. The
weather, well it was nice and warm when we landed but is
turning cool, as are the natives, and now there is rain every
other day, I am not with the regiment at the moment, no,
I have had an illness called sandfly fever, it's caused, as
the name suggests, by getting sand in your flies, which
immediately sends your temperature soaring, so despite the
cold weather I'm quite warm thank you, in fact my temperature got so high, walking patients used to sit around
my bed at night to keep warm. (Spaghetti). However, I'm
better now, I've still got a temperature but it's normal.
Next I'll be sent to a bloody awful Reinforcement Camp,
where all the mud is sent to be slept on by unclaimed
soldiers. So far the Battery have not sustained any casualties except me. (Spaghetti). With the censorship as it is it's
pointless to write any more, all I want you to do is to write
and tell me where I am (Spaghetti).*

Your loving Son/Brother/Midwife
Terry

SEPTEMBER 28, 1943

MY DIARY: THE NEWS SAYS JERRY'S EVACUATED NAPLES.
HEAVY RAIN.

A Scottish, sandy-haired, freckle-faced Doctor is at the
foot of my bed, he looks at me, smiles, looks at my board.

"Temperature's down then."

"Is it, sir?"

"It's ninety-nine. How do you feel?"

"I feel about ninety-nine, sir."

I slept most of that day, waking up for meals. It was all
very pleasant, the service, the sound of the rain, the bloke in
the next bed dying. That evening they took him out for some
kind of an operation and he never came back. I remember
the name on his chart was Parkinson ACC, he was a cook
aged forty-five, and he'd snuffed it. Poor bugger; still, he
was an army cook, and killed quite a few in his time.

What news! there's an ENSA Concert Party in the Big
Hall this evening!

"What's ENSA?" says Jamie.

I told him, "Every Night Something Awful."

The Hall was packed. There is a proper stage; on the
curtains are the faint outlines of the Fascists' emblem, which

*British troops' triumphal entry via the side streets while the
Americans take the main roads.*

38

has been unravelled in a hurry. A Sergeant is in the pit on a lone upright piano, he strikes up a merry medley of tunes, "Blue Birds over the White Cliffs of Dover" (and why shouldn't they be white with all those birds flying over?). The curtains part and there are three men and two girls in evening dress, they were the "squares" of all time, they are all singing "Here we are, Here we are, Here we are again!" Which was an outright lie as we'd never seen 'em before. We give them a good hand. A short red-faced male with a fierce haircut and popping eyes comes forward and starts to wrestle with the microphone to bring it down to his height.

"Thank you! Thank you!" he gushes. "Well, as we say, here we are again."

He tells a series of terrible jokes, we roar with laughter, he announces the Something Twins, on come two girls dressed as Shirley Temples, they sing "On the good ship Lollipop", and we wish they were, they do a very simple tap dance. Storms of applause, next a male about fifty sings "The Bowmen of England", as if all their strings were slack, he finishes, storms of applause! On come the two girls dressed as sailors – loud whistles. They sing "All the Nice Girls Love a Sailor". The third male comes on, he's everything a comic should be except funny, about forty-five, rotund, evening dress, a flat cap, a glove on one hand, after each joke he transfers the glove to the other and says "On the other hand", he ends up with a song that I forgot even as he sang it. He left an indelible blank on my mind. The pit pianist then plays "The Stars and Stripes". . . . Storms of cheers, what liars we are. So it goes on; a brave attempt to cheer the lads up, and we all appreciated it, it was as well we didn't have to pay. We wander back upstairs to our ward, it's night now, the black-outs are up, dinner is on its way.

"They're letting me out tomorrow," says Jamie.

"You going back to your unit?"

"No, I'm going before a medical board, they're going to downgrade me."

"You lucky sod."

"Aye, I don't think I'd like any more fighting, I should have stayed at home."

So ended Jamie Notam's dream of high adventure. I wonder what happened to him.

THURSDAY, SEPTEMBER 30, 1943

I'm up and about, I'm OK, I'm cured, I'm normal again, I feel fine, I'm ready to be killed again, he's fit, send him back, etc. etc. Yes. The Scots doctor on his rounds.

"So you're leaving us, Mirrigen."

"Yes, sir."

"How do you feel?"

"Very ill, sir, very, very, very ill."

He smiles. "Well, Mirrigen, all good things come to an end."

Was *I* the good thing? Help!! Two new patients arrive, and are dumped in the bed each side. Both are coughing like consumptives, what luck, if I hang around I might get it. Shall I kiss one? I wonder where the Battery are and what they are doing, going Bang! I suppose. There is a barber among the patients, Rifleman Houseman.

"Anyone want a haircut?"

There is no reply.

"Free," he adds, and is knocked down in the rush. I let him loose on my head, when he showed me the result in the mirror, I nearly fainted.

"Howzat?" he said.

"Out," I replied.

My head looked like someone had set it on fire.

"It was all for free," explained Rifleman Houseman.

BRILLIANT RECOVERY FROM SANDFLY FEVER BY HUMBLE L/BOMBARDIER

So the headlines should have run, all I got was a Lance-Corporal suffering from incurable stupidity, who said, "Bombardier Millington?"

"That's almost me," I said.

"You are to be discharged tomorrow."

"I understand that my name is now Millington and I am to be discharged as fit."

"Yes, RTU*."

RTU? That had me, so I sang it to a Novello tune "R T U again whenever spring breaks through." (Groans).

*Return to Unit.

40

He blinked and made me sign a piece of paper that in as many words said, "We have tried to kill this man but failed."

"You will be ready by 0830 hours and take the unexpired portion of your day's rations."

Unexpired rations? The mind boggled. I started a series of farewells and looked deeply into the eyes of all the nurses with a look that said quite positively, "You're lucky I never screwed you," and they looked back with a smile that said, "When you've been promoted to Captain, knock three times."

OCTOBER 1, 1943

It's a mixed day, a souffle of sun and cloud. Outside the 76th General a 3-tonner truck is waiting like a wagon at the Knacker's Yard. A short squat driver with a squint in his left eye "finds" and calls our names out from a bit of tacky paper. "Lance-Bombardier Mirrigan?"

"Yes, that's me," I said. "Lance-Bombardier Mirrigan."

He calls out the names of several more soldiers of the King, who at the sight of them would abidicate. I enquire where we are being taken.

"Corps Reinforcement Camp." He pronounced the word "Corpse". An Omen.

We all climb over the back of the tailboard, there's no roof, only the supporting struts. So started a journey of much boredom. Come, let us start.

I look at the vacant stares of my travelling companions, all infantry men, they have my sympathy. We drove for half an hour, during which they never said a word.

"Like a fag," I said to one.

"Ta," he says.

That's half his vocabulary gone, I thought. He was Irish. The roads are tired and dusty, tanks have ground away the surface, after half an hour we pass through Battapaglia.

"We're going South!" I said.

Still no sign of animation from my companions. The buildings we pass are all much like I originally described, the colours usually white, pale blue, deep blue, sometimes a light pink, clusters of shops, small one-man affairs, all look-

41

ing pretty run down and shabby. There are goods for sale but none luxury. There's bread, vegetables, seasonal fruit, apples, walnuts, grapes, figs; "Casa de Scarpa" show a poor variety of shoes, looking very pre-1939, what was I talking about? *I* was a pre-1920 model myself.

What was I doing in this war? it's only three years old, I'm *older* than the war! it's not fair! how can a three-year-old war understand a man of twenty-five? We are passing fresh-painted army signs, Base Ordnance Depot, Town Major, REME Workshops, and what's this? VD Clinic? So soon? Isn't love a wonderful thing? What isn't a wonderful thing is sitting in this bloody lorry with seven Australopitheci. British PoWs didn't give information when tortured by the Gestapo because they didn't know how to talk.

"Dat town was called Battapaglia," said the Irishman.

The act of speaking five consecutive words so exhausted him, he laid down. We pass Italian Military Policemen, looking scruffy and unshaved; they were performing helpful tasks like guarding German PoWs, whose arses they kicked in revenge, but they were getting weary of repeated insults from allied soldiers giving Fascist salutes with cries of "Mussolini – Spaghetti!" Suddenly the sky blackens, great thunder clouds congregate, the temperature lowers, spots of rain fall. The Irish soldier then makes an incredible prediction.

"I tink it's goin' ter rain."

Immediately a deluge started.

"See?" he triumphed.

With no cover, we sat huddled in our greatcoats.

"Are you alright in the back there?" came a voice from the cab.

"Come on in the water's lovely," I said.

The journey seemed endless. "Where in God's name are they taking us?"

"I tink", said the Mick, "dey are just querying us."

As quick as it started the rain stopped, the sun came out. Soon we were all steaming like wet laundry. At mid-day the lorry arrives at a field of tents, fronted by a farmhouse; there is a sign: Corps Reinforcement Unit. We are shown into the HQ office. A Corporal seated behind a desk:

"Name? Number? Religion? Regiment?" He tells us,

"You are here to await pick-up by your regiments."

"How long will that take?" I said.

He frowns. I've broken the code! "Well, I don't exactly know, so far no one has picked up anybody, we've only been 'ere for a week, so it will take a while for 'em to find the location. There are tented lines, two men to a bivvy. Part 2 Orders are posted on the board outside."

We walk along the line of muddy tents. I find an empty one. I see men walking rapidly with empty mess-tins; food! I follow. We arrive at a field kitchen. Food??!! Two slices of cold bully beef, a carrot, a boiled potato. A mug of tea, two biscuits. No mess tent, eat where you stand. I see an intelligent face, his shoulder flashes, HAMPS.* We get talking, name Arrowsmith, was on the landings, shell shock. He looks a little like Ronald Colman, slim, about five foot seven, intelligent, sensitive.

"It's simple arithmetic, the longer you are alive in action, the nearer you are to getting to your lot. You see, I think, I rationalise, and that way you see only too clearly your death approaching. If I go back to my mob, I'll never see Blighty again. I came ashore with B Company. At the end of three days, me, the sergeant and one private were all that was left. We were given replacements; two days later, me and two of the new replacements are all that's left. I mean, it's on the cards; one night we are on patrol, we brush with a Jerry patrol, a grenade explodes on a tree next to my head, I don't remember any more till I wake up in an ambulance. The quack says it's concussion and I'll soon be alright. Alright? The cunt! He's talking about the outside! what about up in *here*?" He taps his head with his spoon, it sounded hard-boiled. "That's where it all happens, and inside me it says *no go*."

We go back to our tents.

"Can't sleep in this bloody thing," says Arrowsmith surveying his muddy bed.

I suggest we look around for a dry place.

"Dry?" He laughed.

"You don't know what Basenji means do you?"

"What?"

"Never mind."

*2/4 Hampshire.

43

We squat in our tents, smoke and talk. At this Camp there was a morning roll-call at 7.00, breakfast from 7.30 to 8.30, then Parade at 9.00, the rest of the day you did what you could with a muddy field and two hundred tents. There was no transport, no entertainment, no money. The boredom was unbelievable. I mean, if a man sneezed, it was considered entertainment. The camp was about three hundred yards from Red Beach, Salerno. For the next three days Arrowsmith and I just foraged around, collecting walnuts and looking for war souvenirs. We had the occasional bathe, but the water was getting that first autumnal chill that made swimming nippy.

The Pioneer Corps were on the beaches collecting war salvage, all middle-aged men. We talked to them. Why did they join up?

"Anyfink ter git away from the bleedin' wife."

They are all old soldiers, some from World War 1, they are well organised. At lunch they light a fire on the beach, and are soon frying eggs and bacon.

"Like some grub?" says their Sergeant.

"Christ, yes," I said.

The Sergeant is a Londoner, he's about fifty, big, burly and

Salerno Beach. Soldiers treasure-hunting.

44

used to be a fish porter at Billingsgate.

"I wos gettin' fed up, so I fort, 'ave a go in the Pioneer Corps. When they knowed I bin a sergeant in World Woer I, they makes me a sergeant right away, so strite on I'm orl rite fer lolly."

He tells us about the "perks".

"The CO 'e says, go orf and get some salvage, so we takes a day's rations, bully bread cheese an' all that, we piss orf somewhere and swop the bully and cheese fer Iti eggs or chickens, an' we live like fightin' cocks, but", he giggled, "we don't do no fitin'."

For two days we met them on the beach and gave them a hand picking up empty ammo boxes, shell cases, and were rewarded with marvellous grub; the last day they brought three bottles of white Chianti, we got back to the Camp that evening very merry. We had also solved sleeping in the mud. Three hundred yards east of our camp in a field, I spotted a small hut on legs; these are apparently farmhands' resting places during the hot harvesting season, made of straw, with wooden slats for the supporting skeleton. It was lovely! dry and warm. We slept very cosy that night.

But all good things come to an end, in this case a cigarette end; we set fire to the place. The glow drew the attention of the enraged farmer and we had to grab our belongings and, wearing only our socks and shirt, run like hell for the camp. We were stopped by the sentry, who had us taken to the guard room. The guard Sergeant asked what we were doing "runnin' round half bloody naked".

"Our grass hut caught fire," explained Arrowsmith.

I couldn't speak for suppressed laughter.

"What grass 'ut?" says the Sergeant.

We had to tell the story and he put us on a charge for absenting ourselves from the camp. Next morning he forgot all about it. Well, not exactly, during the night he was convulsed with terrible pains in his side, he had a perforated appendix and was hurried to the hospital, so next morning I presume he had forgotten us. The subsequent guard commander said, "Piss off." The boredom was getting me down. One grey morning I asked to see the OC.

"What for?" said the Corporal.

"It's about Basenji."

"Wait here."

He knocked on a door. A very crisp voice shouted, "Come in."

Opening the door the Corporal said, "There's a Lance-Bombardier Mirrigan wishes to see you, sir."

I was ushered in. The OC was a Major. He was a bright red. He wore his hat. Under a bulbous nose was a pepper and salt cavalry moustache. His chin was a mass of small broken veins, he blinked at twice the normal rate, and from time to time sniffed what was a running nose. He would be somewhere between thirty-eight and ninety-seven, it was hard to tell. He was writing an aerograph letter which, on my approach, he hurriedly covered with a blotter. Silly sod.

"What do you want?" he said curtly.

"This will come as a surprise to you, sir, but what I want is a job."

He looked at me, blinked and sniffed.

"A *job*?" He stressed the word and said it again. "*Job?*"

"Yes, sir."

"Being a soldier *is* a job."

"Well, I want a job on top of that job."

"What kind of a job?"

"*Any* kind, sir, it's the boredom here, it's driving me mad."

"You think you're alone? What's your army trade?"

"Wireless operator."

"Well, I'm sorry we don't have a wireless set for you to play on——"

"Any job, sir, otherwise I will desert."

"Desert? Look, go to the Q stores, see Bombardier Logan, tell him the Major says you are to help him."

I saluted and left him to his aerograph. As I closed the door behind me, I heard him give a gigantic sneeze and say, "Bugger!"

Bombardier Logan turned out to be a Scot; he didn't have a face, just an area under his hat. His eyes, mouth and nose were all in conflict as to who should be in the centre. It turns out he was an ex-boxer. By the look of his face, every punch had got through. His ears were mangled fragments of gristle and skin. He was partially deaf, but then he was only

46

partially human. He was from Glasgow, and spoke with an accent no one understood, not even himself. He walked stooping forward, his arms hanging ape-like, a square head with real corners on it.

From eight in the morning to eight at night I worked. There was nothing else to do, if there had been I'd have done it. He took pity on me and said,

"Ye karn harve some T chaists tae mak yer sael a baed." ("You can have some tea chests to make yourself a bed.")

He permitted me to sleep in the same room. It was dry and had three hurricane lamps in, so at least one could read in bed. Having nothing to read didn't help. By day he talked to himself in Scots gutteral – interspersed with snatches of Scottish folk songs – it nearly drove me insane.

The Scotts have taught the bagpipes to the Canadians, the Australians, the Indians, the Gurkhas, the South Africans, the Rhodesians; even the Chinese! they've got a lot to answer for. This Bombardier couldn't converse – saying hello to him had him completely baffled. Every night he regaled me with stories of his boxing prowess. He'd had two hundred fights. I asked him how many he'd won, he said "Seven." He showed me a picture of his wife. She looked like she'd had two hundred fights as well; she had – with him. What he really needed was a head transplant.

Suddenly, with no warning we have to move. A back-breaking twenty-four hours loading stores on to lorries, again in the pouring rain. The Major (his name escapes me, but I think it was Castle) must have felt pity, for as the Bombardier and I sat in the empty storeroom, soaked, he brought in a bottle of whisky, and poured a liberal amount into our tea mugs.

"You've worked very well, Millington, I appreciate it, it's been a bloody hard boring time setting up this unit, we've had bugger all co-operation, all the stores, etc., have all been rushed up to the front lines, that's why the food's been so bloody awful, but this place we're moving to, things will be much better."

Well, that was nice. First comforting words I had had for weeks. Before he left he said, "Before we leave tomorrow, any questions?"

"Yes sir," I said. "What's Basenji?"

He frowned. Walked back a few paces towards me. "What's what?"

"Basenji, sir, what's it mean?"

"I've no idea . . . is it an Italian word?"

"I don't know, sir."

He stood a while, then turned and left in silence. The Scottish Bombardier drained his mug. "It's an Afrrrrrican dog," he said.

"What is?"

"Basenji . . . it's an Afrrrrican Dorg . . . it can nay bark."

My God . . . *he* knew what Basenji meant! "How did you know?" I said, desperate to find out.

"I wus bitten by one in South Afrrica."

"Where?"

"I tod yer, South Afrrrrica."

OCTOBER 10, 1943

We Move to a New Depot

The new depot was at the north end of a coastal town called Castelemare di Stabia. We were to occupy a great railway repair depot, now deserted. It had been hammered by our planes, but two-thirds remained intact. There were plenty of empty goods wagons which we immediately used for store-rooms and billets; They were ideal, about six men to a wagon. Now it was hard to go "off the rails".

I spent two days putting up shelves and organising the stores. If I'd waited for the Scots lunatic we'd have been still doing it, he constantly kept getting lost amid the maze of railway lines. "Aw the bludee Carrrrriages luke the sam tae me." We had to draw a white cross on our wagon so he could find it. Alas, those with a sense of humour painted white crosses on another twenty wagons, and he was lost for days. The Major's promised improvement in living standards never materialised, it got worse, no guarantee of our seven a day cigarette ration, I went four days without a cigarette, I got withdrawal symptoms. The pupils of my eyes dilated to pinpoints; my night manipulations increased until the skin was rubbed off and I spoke in a high strained voice on the verge of a scream.

OCTOBER 14, 1943

MY DIARY NOTES: DISGRACEFUL! I HAVE SEEN THE RSM
WITH A FIFTY TIN, AND HE TOLD US NO FAGS WERE IN STORE.
THEY ARE IN STORE . . . HIS BLOODY STORE. FOOD TERRIBLE,
BULLY BEEF AND HALF A MUG OF TEA FOR BREAKFAST, HERE
WE WERE NEARER TO INDIA THAN ENGLAND, AND ONLY HALF
A MUG OF BLOODY TEA.

There was a revenge party on the RSM's wagon. In the
small hours, when he slept in nicotined bliss, the sufferers
had pushed his wagon a mile out of the depot into a siding.

OCTOBER 15, 1943

Thank God!! "You are being transferred," said the RSM,
whose name was Death. (What happened if he was killed in
Action? We regret to announce the death of Death?) "You
are being transferred to the CPC."

I envisaged another endless lorry journey, but no!!! It was
in the same marshalling yard. I wrote home and told my

British infantry rowing boat up street in search of a river.

49

folks I was now serving under Marshal Yard. This time I was billeted on the edge of the Complex. It was a building, one-time offices, I was in a basement with windows at ground level. Outside, the River Sarno ran past the window, looking left I could see the beach, and offshore the Isola Revigliano with the remains of a Roman lighthouse. Just what I needed! The difference in the lifestyle here was great. Regular fag issue, and good food, I even noted down the Menu!

MENU

Breakfast: Bread, 1 pint tea
                  Sausage bacon onion and fried bully
                  Porridge
                  Biscuits. Marg and jam

Lunch: Cheese
                  Beans and tomato sauce
                  Potatoes (creamed)
                  Bread and jam

Dinner: Meat rissoles. Fried potatoes
                  Spaghetti and tomato
                  Fried onions
                  Mashed potato
                  Peas
                  Fruit and cust.
                  Tea and biscuits

and it never lessened in its constancy. Seven cigs a day and matches. Fifty fags from Naafi once a week (not free).

Towering above the countryside, with vines growing on its lower slopes, was the ominous shape of Vesuvius, like me it smoked heavily. At night, from my bed, I could see the purple-red glow from its throat, it looked magnificent. At one time it had looked so to those doomed people, the Pompeians, but I wasn't a Pompeian, I was Irish, how could Vesuvius wipe out Dublin? No, I was perfectly safe, but Vesuvius wasn't. I discovered that Pompeii was but three miles as the crow flies. This incredible relic of a Roman city free of camera-clicking tourists was a situation I had to thank Hitler for. Thank you, Hitler!

HITLER: You hear zat, Goebbels? Milligan is visiting Pompeii. Keep all tourists out, and zer ruins *in*!"

After roll-call, accompanied by a Private Webb, we hitched and walked till we arrived at the gates. There was no one about, save a sleepy unshaven attendant, who said he had no tickets and charged twenty lire to go in, which he put straight into his pocket. It was a day I shall treasure, a day I met the past, not only the past but the people from it, be it they were now only plaster casts. I had read Pliny the Younger's account of that terrible day of destruction, *Gells Pompiana* and several text-books, so I was reasonably well informed. We had gone in the entrance that opened on to the amphitheatre and the Grande Palestra on our right. The excitement it generated in me was unbelievable, and it stayed with me all day. I don't think there are many sights as touching as the family who died together in the basement of their home, off the Via Vesuvio, the mother and father each side of three little girls, their arms protecting them this two thousand years. There were the lovers who went on banging away even though being suffocated. He *must* have been a Gunner. What a way to go!

All through that warm dusty day I wandered almost in a dream through the city, now almost deserted save for an occasional soldier.

It was late evening when we finally arrived at the Porta Ercolano that led into the Via de Sepolcri. We sat in the mouth of one of the tombs and smoked a fag. Webb was knocked out.

"Bloody hell," he said. "I never heard of the place, I never knew it existed, they don't say a bloody word about places like this at school. Alfred the Great, Henry the Eighth, Nelson, Queen Victoria and that's the bloody lot."

I discovered that the Americans had actually bombed it! They believed German Infantry were hiding in it! Not much damage had been done, museum staff were already at work trying to repair it. Bombing Pompeii!!! Why not the Pyramids, Germans might be hiding there? Or bomb the Astoria Cinema, Wasdale Road, Forest Hill, that's an ideal hiding-place for Germans? Or bomb Mrs Grollick's boarding house, Hagley Road, Birmingham?

Webb afforded me amusing incidents during the day; we approached the front of a house in the Via de Mercurio, another shabby unshaven attendant was standing outside. He looked like a bag of laundry with a head on. He indicated a boxed partition on the wall. "*Vediamo questo?*" he said, and the innuendo was that of something "naughty".

"*Si,*" I said fluently.

We gave him ten lire each, and with a well-worn key he opened the door. It revealed a male figure dressed as a Roman soldier; holding up his kilt from under it was an enormous phallus that rested on a pair of scales, the other scale held a bar of gold. Very interesting, but the point of it all escaped me.

"Wot's 'ee weighing 'is balls for?" said Webb, the true archaeologist.

"I think it's something to do with wartime rationing."

The Italian explains the message, the man is saying, "I would rather have my prick than a bar of gold." Wait till he's sixty, I thought.

Another diversion is the Lupanarium.

"'Ere, isn't that a man's prick sticking out over the door?"

"Well, it certainly isn't a woman's."

It was a monster made of concrete and about a foot long.

"What's it doin' up there?" says Webb.

I demonstrate by hanging my hat on it.

"A hat-stand? Get away."

"Well, it's a stand of some kind," I explained, "and this is a house of ill repute."

Webb grinned from ear to ear. "Ahh, that's why they got that bloody great chopper sticking out, then."

"You should have been a Latin scholar," I said.

The Lupanarium: around the walls were paintings, or rather a catalogue of the various positions that the clients could have; there was everything but standing on the head. I observed that the cubicles the ladies had to perform in were woefully small, one would have to have been five foot four or a cripple. It must have been an interesting sight that day of the eruption, all fourteen cubicles banging away and suddenly Vesuvius explodes, out the door shoot men with erections and no trousers followed by naked screaming tarts.

"Screwsville – Pompeii": when we got there the girls had gone.

You don't get that stuff in the film versions.

The sun was setting when we retraced our footsteps. I was loath to leave but I was to return here again in exciting circumstances. We hitched back on several lorries including one American with a coloured driver, yellow.

"Ain't you limeys got any fuckin' transport?" he said.

"Yes, we have lots of transport, trams, buses, but they're all in Catford."

He didn't know what I was talking about and he said so. "What are you talkin' about, man?"

He hated me. I hated him. It was a perfect arrangement. We were just in time for dinner. I took mine to the billet (the walk did it good) and ate it in the semi-reclining position; when in Rome. . . . Another occupant of our billet

53

stumbled in. Corporal Percival, he's smelling of beer.

"Where have you been?"

"I been to Naples," he said.

Naples wow! The big time! The Catford of Italy.

"I went to the Pictures, I saw . . . Betty Grable and Cesar Romero in *Coney Island*. Bai she's got lovely legs."

"What about his?"

"Fook off."

"Of course, I'll pack at once."

Percival was a North Country lad, all "Eeeee bai Gum". He doted on Gracie Fields.

"Gracie Fields," I guffawed, "she's as funny as a steam roller going over a baby."

"You must be bludy thick, she's a scream."

"Yes, I scream every time I hear her sing."

"Ooo do you think is foony then?"

"W. C. Fields, Marx Brothers."

"Oooo?"

He'd never heard of them.

"I bet they're not as foony as Gracie, you put 'em next to her and she'd lose 'em."

The mind boggled, Gracie Fields meets the Marx Brothers! Help! I tried to demonstrate to him how Groucho walked.

"Wot ee walk like that fur? It looks bludy daft."

"It's supposed to, you Nana, look! North Country humour is *all* bloody awful, all Eeeee bai Gum, flat hats and boiled puddens. I mean, you must be all simple to think George Formby's funny, I get the same feeling from him as if I'd been told my mother was dead."

The onslaught silenced him, then he spoke. "Milligan? That's Irish isn't it."

"Yes, well I'm half Irish."

"That's bludy truble . . . that's what keeps you simple minded."

"Bernard Shaw and Oscar Wilde were Irish."

"What bludy good did they do?"

"They were recognised as great writers."

"Not by me, fook 'em."

"Listen, mister, the worst thing in life I can think of is being tied to a post and forced to listen to George Formby. . . ."

54

"Alright, 'oo do you think is a gud singer?"

"Bing Crosby."

"'Im? 'ee sounds like 'ee's crapped 'imself and it's sliding down wun leg."

"Yes . . . he *would* sound like that to you; I suppose you think Gigli is a load of crap as well."

"Gigli? Who's she?"

"*He*'s a great opera singer."

"Gracie Fields could sing opera standing on her head."

"If she did, it would be the first time I'd laugh at her."

Arguments like this were frequent, there seemed to be a love-hate relationship between the North and South, the South loved themselves and the North hated them for it. Percival had been down with sandfly fever like myself.

"Were you on the landings?"

"Nay, we cum in ten days after to lay Sumerfield Track for fighter planes ter land on, but ship with the stoof on were soonk by Jerry radio-controlled bomb."

Percival had once brought me to the verge of tears; one night, he came in pissed as usual.

"Ever seen a white-eared elephant?" he said.

No, I hadn't. Whereupon he pulls the linings of his two trouser pockets out, opens his flies and hangs his willy out. I cried with laughter, who in God's name invented these tricks? and all the others like the swan flies East, sausage on a plate, sack of flour, the roaring of the lions, there was a touch of obscene genius about them all.

Life at this camp was very cushy, but I discovered that there was no guarantee of me getting back to my Battery and this really shook me. I wrote to Major Jenkins saying if I wasn't taken back soon, I'd desert. Back came a letter from the Battery Office. "Don't desert, truck on way." Signed Bdr. Hamer (Battery Clerk). One morning after roll-call, I was exploring the environs of the camp when I discovered the remains of what had been a large bonfire. The surviving pieces were interesting: Fascist uniforms worn by school-children during indoctrination training, *Bambini della Lupa* (Children of the Wolf), and along with them were little wooden rifles and kindergarten books praising Mussolini, *Il Duce nostra Buona Padre* . . . etc. etc. How in God's name can adults do this to children? To pervert their minds, and

55

yet even today the indoctrination goes on. China. Russia. Our own democracies corrupt with pornography and Media Violence. As my father once said, "It will only last for ever." Among the ashes are numerous erotic photos of pictures of statues from Pompeii and Herculaneum. Altogether a very strange mixture.

OCTOBER 17, 1943

Nice sunny day, not too hot. Roll-call at 7.30. Good breakfast. EGGS!!! It was this day Lance-Corporal Percival says, "Ah feel like a shag, I got an address of a safe place, do you fancy a nibble."

"Not me," I said, "I don't fancy a bird that half the 5th Army has been through."

"It'll do you gud, lad, loosen yer braces and stiffen yer socks."

I decline. "We'll come and wait, then we can go for some grub in town.'

The walk into Castelemare is a dead straight road, dusty, and flanked by unending walls, like walking down a corridor with no roof on. Percival stops.

"Ah, this is the place," he said, looking at an address.

It wasn't exactly a brothel, it was rather like a middle-class block of those bloody awful 1930s faceless flats. We go up polished stone steps to the third floor. We ring a doorbell, it opens revealing a fat fifty-ish woman. She wears a loose cotton dress to her knees, bare legs and rope slip-on sandals, she has a typical brown Southern Italian skin, her black greying hair is pulled back behind her head in a bun, she is absolutely unattractive but has magnificent huge brown eyes.

"*Ah Vengo*," she says with a broad smile, and ushers us in.

I couldn't help notice Percival respectfully take his hat off, or was he starting to undress? She walked ahead, rattling off a stream of Italian in Neapolitan dialect, she takes us to what looks like a dentist's waiting-room.

Before we had time to sit down, another door opened and in came a young girl, about nineteen, very plain, bobbed black hair, a short denim skirt and a white blouse, bare legs and high-heeled cork-soled shoes. She was a little on the Junoesque side. She smiled and nodded her head in the direction she came. Percival left his hat on the chair, went all soppy, and followed her out of the room. The door closed and I heard the key turn in the lock. The fat lady, I now noticed, had her left hand and wrist bandaged.

"*Tedescho, boom boom*," she said, and made like a pistol. "*Tedescho Molto Cativo*," then she sat down in the chair opposite, lifted her skirt and showed me her fanny, which had so much hair on it looked like a black poodle on her lap.

I had never had such a thing happen to me before, and I was nonplussed. She stayed like it and smiled. "*Jig a Jig*," she said.

Unable to rise to the occasion I said, "No, me no Jig a Jig, I Roman Catollica", she burst into laughter and pulled her frock down and left the room laughing, with one hand over her mouth.

She came back again, lifted her skirt up (My God she was proud of it), "*Non Costa Niente*," she was telling me it wouldn't cost me anything, so I told her that may be so, but it would cost *her* ten thousand lire.

She had a good sense of humour, with her figure she needed it, and she laughed heartily as she realised that she wasn't going to get it. She left me. I picked up a paper from the centre table, *Corriera della Sera*, a dramatic front-page drawing of Italian Paratroops attacking "La Armata Inglise in Tunisia", it was full of such heroic drawings, why didn't our papers have some like that? Valiant British Troops eating Bully Beef. Heroic British Troops shaving, etc.?

It's all over, Percival comes into the room, much redder than I'd seen him before, the girl's demeanour hadn't changed. She indicated that I was next, I said, "No gratizia, Io Molto stanco." I might just as well have had it away with her because Percival now borrows a hundred lire off me to pay her! "Is this still your North Country bloody humour?" I said.

He grinned. "I'll pay thee back – right now I'm bludy 'ungry."

"That's you isn't it? The three Fs."

"Three Fs?"

"Fucking, Food and Fags."

Postcard of Castelemare

We set off and as we leave, the fat lady gives my arm one last squeeze. "*Per Niente,*" she whispered.

"After the war," I said.

We approach the town proper, a modest seaside resort, a Blackpool of Italy, but more elegant. We trudge around the streets looking for a reasonable cafe. We find one on a wide one-time populous street, now rather run down, on it is a Trattoria Tuscano, "Alied Solders Welcomes". Inside, about twelve tables, all covered in white paper, sparsely laid out with cutlery. A few tables are occupied by what look like potential Mafia recruits, all huddled over their tables talking in low voices, an act of great self-control for Italians.

MY DIARY: HAD THE FOLLOWING: SPAGHETTI, FISH AND CHIPS, MEAT AND VEG, WINE AND GRAPES ALL FOR FIFTY LIRA (2/6!) ABSOLUTE BARGAIN. HOW DO THEY MAKE A PROFIT?

During the meal an old Italian in shabby clothes and a greasy felt hat shuffled in, and sat at a chair just inside the door (he had a guitar wrapped in a cloth). He smiled a sad tired smile at us, tuned the guitar with his ear on the side of the instrument, then launched into "*O Sole Mio*". I even remember the key was F; this was lovely, I'd never had a meal to musical accompaniment before. He next played "*Oh Za Za Za Maddona Mia*", and finally "The Woodpecker's Song". All his harmonies were meticulously correct.

"George Formby cud play 'is bludy 'ead off," says Percival.

The thought of a headless George Formby fills me with delight.

"Ask 'im ter play 'In the Mood'."

"You ask him."

"Aye, banjo player, sonari 'In the Mood'." He then sings several bars of unrecognisable crap.

The old musician smiles and shrugs his shoulders.

"Silly bouger, 'e don't recognise it."

"Listen, Glen Miller wouldn't recognise it."

"Gid aht of it," he's getting pissed now. "Ah use ter play in t'local dance bund."

He got thoroughly nasty, I paid the bill and left him asking the old man to play "When the Poppies Bloom Again". I for one didn't want to see him again till they did. I walk back in the cool dark evening, and just my luck, a jeep with two redcaps pulls up.

"Where you going, Corporal?" They smell of recently consumed whisky, I suppose this was their post-piss-up Let's-go-out-and-do-somebody trip. I tell them I'm walking back to the CPC.

"Where's your paybook?"

To their dissatisfaction I produce it.

"Where's your unit?"

"Lauro."

"Where's that?"

"Italy."

"Don't be funny with us, sonny," says the second one, who has to angle his head back at forty-five degrees to see out from under the peak. The first one smiles with triumph.

"You haven't signed your will," he beams.

"How silly of me," I said.

"Sign it at once."

I wrote my name painstakingly across the will "Corporal Hugh Jympton".

They roared away breaking the speed-limit. It was a delightful surprise to reach the billet to find their jeep in the ditch, upside down, and an ambulance loading on the two redcaps. I find the billet empty save for Webb.

"Where's all the lads gone?"

"Lorry arrived this morning and took them away. Some kind of draft."

I slept well that night; as I blew out my little oil lamp, it started to rain, it poured, it deluged, and lightning played about the crown of Vesuvius. . . .

OCTOBER 19, 1943

I was getting twitchy, doing nothing positive for so long. I had started talking to myself, and I wasn't satisfied with the answers. I had rearranged my billet so many times that my bed had been placed in every position except the ceiling, and I was working on that. There were days when I'd try and see if I could get both legs into one trouser leg, and both feet into one sock. I was carrying out this exercise when Percival comes in.

"There's a bloke in a truck waiting fer you."

"Is he wearing a white coat?"

"He looks bloody daft so he must be from your mob."

I couldn't believe it. I packed my humble belongings and dashed outside. There was my Cinderella's coach in the shape of a 15-cwt truck. The driver is Ted Wright, a short, very dark, good-looking lad with large brown eyes, and eyebrows so perfectly arched that they looked as though Jean Harlow had drawn them on him.

"I've come to take you home," he said with a grin.

In sheer delight I give him five cigarettes.

"What's this for?"

"That's for picking me up, Ted."

"I must pick you up again."

"You saved me from going mad."

He put the truck in gear and off we drove. It was an overcast day, with an occasional peep through by the sun. We are driving along the narrow coastal road. It takes us through small towns – Torre Annunziata, Torre del Greco, Resina,

60

Portici – all built on the new coastline formed by the earth-shaking disaster of AD 79, possibly by those very people who fled Pompeii, Herculaneum, Oplontis and other dead cities not yet discovered. It was easy to imagine these short swarthy inhabitants as their direct descendants. Wright gives me news of the mob.

"We've had our first casualty."

At once I prayed that it wasn't my mate Harry. "Who was it?"

"Rumble, he was killed. . . ."

"How?"

"Very unlucky really – "

"Yes, it is unlucky to be killed."

"He was writing a letter home* when suddenly Jerry sent over one lone shell, it burst behind him, a piece went in the back of his head, he died at once."

"Poor bugger. . . ."

Strangely, I didn't feel that moved. Had it been peacetime and I'd been told he was killed by a tram, I'm sure I'd be desperately sad; somehow in wartime all those feelings were reduced. Strange.

"We've all been flooded out."

"Weak bladder?"

"Shut up or I'll take you back; no, we're all dug in on a plain in front of a river, what's it called, the – er – Vallerbo or something – "

"Volturno," says clever.

"Yes, well, you know that bloody thunderstorm we had last night."

"Personally," I said.

"Well, the bloody lot fell on us, the river flooded, and Christ, in ten minutes all the dug-outs were like sunken baths!"

Coming down the road towards us are two tank transporters. The front one is carrying an almost intact fuselage of a FW 109, and the one behind, a Mark IV Tank with a neat hole drilled in the turret.

"Wonder where they're takin' them," says Wright.

"I think they test them out for information, then they send

*Some say he was having a wash.

them for exhibition in London."

"Christ, I wish they'd put *me* on exhibition in London."

We ride in silence. We go through the Salerno Gap, and are soon nearing the outskirts of Naples. Lots of pretty girls. Soon we are in the thick of the Via Roma traffic, we move at a snail's pace. People are as thick as flies, some thicker. It takes us nearly an hour to get through the chaos.

"Never think there was a war on here, would you, shops full of stuff, all the squaddies buying knickers for their birds, mind you the prices are going up like lightning. It's the Yanks, they pay anything for stuff, they're loaded with money." He stopped, and said, "Cor, I forgot," he started to feel in his map pocket. "Got some mail for you."

Mail! MAIL! I hadn't had any for a month. It was like being five years old on Christmas morning. Ten letters! I read my mother's first. My father has now been transferred to the Command RAOC Depot, Reigate, where he has decided that the standard Infantry ammunition pouches are useless. They helped win Alamein but that's not good enough for father. He has designed some strange things that are strapped round the leg that, my brother later told me, made it impossible to walk or run. In other words you could carry twice as much ammo but had to stand still all the time.

Thank God he wasn't running the war like he wanted to. My mother was apparently doing little for the war effort except pray for the death of Hitler. If he didn't die soon, her knees were going to give out. My brother has won the South London Poster Design prize, for which he got a certificate saying "You have just won the South London Poster Design Prize." After six dusty hours we arrive at an Italian farmhouse near the village of Cancello just across the Volturno on the 46 Div. front. It's dark and I can't get a picture of the lay-out, looming around are vehicles draped with camouflage nets, looking like strange grotesque monsters. It started to drizzle. The Wagon Lines are billeted in various buildings, the central one being the farmhouse. I noted in my diary, "People living in and about look nervous and strained." I was very happy to be back with the lads, though my real pals were at the Gun Lines where I would journey on the morrow.

After dinner in a small room, I was brought up to date with

Battery news by Bombardier Tibbles. He told me Gunner Rumble has been killed. Poor Rumble, killed twice apparently.

The ominous sound of Jerry bombers directly overhead.

"Making for Naples," said Tibbles.

"Are you sure?" I said from under the table.

We stood in the blackened courtyard of the farm and watched the spider's web of tracer shells etching the night sky, behind them the red tongue of Vesuvius. Inside the farm an Italian baby was crying, and the mother was trying to calm it in a hysterical high-pitched shriek, which eventually outdid the child, so it packed it in. Then we heard the husband come in and in a low voice try and soothe the wife, who answered in a high-pitched hysterical voice. Gradually his low voice raised itself to a high shout, reawakening the baby, who joined in again with an even higher voice.

"No wonder Mussolini turned it in," said Tibbles.

The row abated as we drank tea by the light of an oil lamp. The German bombers were returning and the Ack-Ack re-awoke the baby and the whole mad trio were soon yelling at each other again. It sounded like a vegetable shopping list.

"Too-ma-toeee! ... Poo-ta-toeee!" they shouted, "Minestrone!!"

I reflected, as I lay in bed, that I'd had a cushy few weeks behind the lines, but from the stories the war was not going to be a gentleman's one like we had in North Africa. Since those distant days I have actually met one of the German lads who was in the line opposite us in North Africa, Hans Teske. In fact, I organised a small reunion at the Medusa Restaurant in December '76 for those who had been involved in fighting in and around Steam Roller Farm, February 26, 1943. An officer present, Noel Burdett, hearing Teske and me stating that we must have actually fired at each other that day, said, "Your survival indicates you must both be bloody awful shots."

Later Hans Teske dispelled the belief that Germans had no sense of humour by inscribing my menu "Dear Spike, sorry I missed you on February 26, 1943."

As I lay dreaming, an unbelievable experience happened. In the dark a farm dog had got into our room. I heard him sniffing around. I made friendly noises and in the dark his cold nose touched my hand. I patted him and left it at that, the next thing the dirty little devil piddled on me. Was he Mussolini's Revenge?

MY DIARY: 0600 AM: DRIVEN FROM WAGON LINES TO GUN POSITION.

It was sunny, but everywhere wet, damp and muddy. Cancello is a small agricultural town on the great plain that lies on the North bank of the Volturno. I'm in a three-tonner with Driver Kit Masters. At seven we arrive at the gun position, the guns have gone, and all that is left are the M Truck Signallers who are to reel in the D5 lines.

"This is it," said Driver Masters, pulling up in a morass of mud.

I leap from the vehicle and land knee-deep in it.

"It's all yours," says Masters, and speeds away like a priest from a brothel.

Emerging from holes in the ground are mud-caked troglodytes. I recognise Edgington.

"Why lawks a mercy," he said in Southern Negro tones, "welcome home, massa Milligan, de young massa am home, praise de Laud and hide de Silver."

"Good God, Edgington, what are you wearing?"

"Mud, it am all de rage."

"I can't tell how good it is to be back, mate," I said.

"Oh what a pity – now we'll never know." I offered him a cigarette.

"You must be mad, why in God's name did you come back?"

"I ran out of illness."

"Get out! All you got to do is a pee against a Neapolitan karzi wall and you get crabs."

"Where's the guns?"

Edgington countenanced himself as a Red Indian. "White men gone, take heap big fire-stick and fuck off."

More mud-draped creatures are issuing from what had been the Command Post. I suddenly remembered!

"Where's all my kit?"

"We had to auction it off – it started to smell."

Jam-Jar Griffin alone and unafraid, his BO having driven the Germans from the Volturno plain.

"Don't bugger around, everything I treasure is in my big pack."

Harry shook his head. "Sorry mate, yer big pack has gone AWOL*, but yer kitbag's safe in G Truck with Alf Fildes."

"Where's Alf Fildes?"

"He's at the new gun position, last time I saw him he had the shits, anyhow your kit's in his truck."

My big pack, lost! It was a major disaster.

"You can report it missing killed in action," says Edgington.

All that I held dear was in there, things close to a soldier's heart, like socks, drawers cellular, worst of all my Nazi war loot, a dagger, an Iron Cross, an Afrika Korps hat, and a set of pornographic photographs taken lovingly from a dead Jerry on Long Stop. I was going to send them back to his home. Now never would his mother hold those photographs of three people screwing close to her heart and say, "Oh mein dear son". Bombardier Fuller is approaching.

"You're just in time, we've got to reel in the OP cable."

"Oh," I groaned, "I can't do that, I'm convalescing from sandfly fever, they've got all the sand out but there's still a lot of flies left."

He shoves me forward. "On that bleedin' truck."

There was no escape. The M Truck signallers start to reel

*Absent without leave

in the line. We travel North along a tree-lined road; ahead in the distance lie a range of mountains, some snow-capped: these are the ones we will have to cross to gain access to the Garigliano plain. Jerry has pulled back into them and is waiting.

"He knows a good thing when he sees it," says Fuller, looking at them through his war-loot binoculars.

OCTOBER 21, 1943

Reeling in a telephone line is very simple. A 15-cwt "Monkey" truck has a hand-operated cable drum on a mount, you walk along disentangling the line and the lucky Gunner stays on the truck and winds the drum. It was a fiercely contested position, bribes were offered, money and cigarettes exchanged hands. It never worked.

"I know just how a trained chimp feels," 'Ticker' Tume was moaning. He was in a ditch untying the line from a stake. "We're just trained bloody monkeys," he went on. "Once you're caught by a circus, that's it, they can do what they bloody like, make you ride bicycles, jump through hoops, it's all to humiliate. I never thought I'd see the day when *I* was a performing bloody monkey."

There were cries of encouragement from the lads.

"This isn't a war," he continued, "this is a bloody chimps' tea party."

There was a great cheer. The end of the line is up a water tower in the grounds of what had been an Iti Prisoner of War camp. Edgington looks at his watch.

"It's exactly 4.45," he informs us.

"Oh good," I said. "I must remember that."

The landscape was devoid of any signs of life. All the cattle and farmers had "scarpered".

"I feel we are the last humans left alive," Edgington said gloomily.

He frequently made such predictions. In post-war years, Harry's brother Doug told of an occasion in the thirties when Harry had predicted the exact date of the end of the world. When the appointed day came and naught happened, Doug felt cheated. He phones brother Harry and asks what went wrong, and Harry says, "Er – well, give it a couple of days."

Harry denies this story. Meanwhile, in Italy, Harry is sent up the tower to unhitch the telephone line. He starts to climb a dodgy ladder. I say dodgy, as the rungs came away as he grabbed them.

"Brew up," says Fuller.

We adjourn to one of the huts. It's the Camp Commander's office, now a mess of scattered papers, broken furniture, on the floor a picture of Mussolini, the glass smashed, footprints over the Duce's kisser. Graffiti on the wall.

"The Hamps were here."

"The Tebourba Tigers."

The latter refers to the name they conferred on themselves after a savage action at Tebourba in Tunisia. Where are those tigers now? Watching telly? Washing up? ... We make a fire of broken furniture, and put on the brew can. We add our graffiti to the walls. "Gunner Milligan was here, and will make sure he never returns." Someone wrote "Chelsea FC for ever." Such patriotism.

Jock Webster, our myopic driver, is i/c tea; he had a remarkable forehead, bulging like a balloon. Gunner Birch explained: "Before his bones 'ad 'ardened, someone put a pump up his arse and blew him up."

Why wasn't this man writing in *The Lancet*? "Myopic" Webster is now putting spoonfuls of compo mixture into the boiling water, well, not exactly *in*, just missing the tin. We reorient him with "Left hand down a bit, bit more ... right." How he became a driver is beyond logic. To keep him on the road his passengers had to shout endless instructions. "Look out, STOP," etc. However, he was such a nice bloke we hated to give him the push, but he broke down so often, we had to.

"Oo fort of 'ow ter make compo?" Tume asks.

"I fink," pontificated Fuller, "I fink they sweeps the floors of the tea factories, put it into tins and send it to us."

We are all squatting around the fire, some of us sit on broken furniture, Harry is balancing on a huge recoco three-legged chair, which gives him the appearance of a five-legged dwarf. We are all short of fags, but careful Milligan has a whole packet. I am persuaded to part with some: the method? manual strangulation.

With the sun setting we reel the last of the line in and set off for the Battery.

Bdr. Fuller, Tume and Edgington sit silently in the back of the Monkey truck.

"Monkey truck, that's just the bloody right name for this vehicle," says Gunner Tume, who is now desperately crouching forward trying, through the shaking, to light a dog-end that appears to have three shreds of tobacco in it. He goes on moaning.

"Monkeys, that's what we are," he said. "Trained khaki monkeys, and this is just one big bloody circus."

"If only we had an audience," I said. "We could go round with the hat."

No one was amused. No, we were all pissed off and bloody cold. We shout through the canvas of the driver's seat. "How much bleedin' further, Jock?"

"I've nae idea," came the Scot's burr. "I ha tae kip askin' the wee."

And true to his prophecy he kept stopping to "ask the wee". It was an experience to hear him asking "the wee" from a puzzled Moroccan Goumier.

"Hurry up for Christ's sake!" says Gunner Edgington. "The cook'ouse will be closed."

"Wonder what gaff this is?" Fuller says peering out of the back.

We are passing through stone-paved streets, with silent, locked buildings each side. I guess it must be Capua.

"Hannibal had got this far south with his Carthaginians."

"Very good, Milligan," says Edgington. "Go to the top of the class and jump off."

"Who were the Carthaginians?" said Bombardier Fuller.

"A Third Division team from Watford." Edgington is speaking heatedly, it's the only way to keep warm. "How do they expect ordinary London 'erberts like us to find our way around bloody Italy with a half-blind Scots driver askin' the way from A-rabs."

We are in a queue behind a column of Sherman tanks.

"'Ere – I remember this lot – they're the 7 Armoured," says Edgington.

"Tanks fer the memory," I said.

We are about to cross the Volturno, a slow process.

"Fancy having to queue for the war."

68

The Bailey Bridge over the Volturno

Infantry are marching silently past.

"They never speak," said Harry, "don't they ever chat to each other?"

"Oh yes," I said.

"What do they say?"

" 'Attention – Slope Arms – Chargeee'."

We start to move. "I'm getting bloody hungry," was a frequent statement, and it came most frequently from Edgington. He was a known hungry guts. Only one man out-did him, Driver Kidgell. Kidgell it was said, could smell a sausage at 300 yards – and hear a tin of duff being opened a mile away. What's this? The rattle, rattle, of boards???

"'Ere, we're on a Bailey bridge," says Trew, "We must be crossin' the Volturno."

"Ah! Guns! I hear guns," said Edgington. "We're getting near civilisation."

"Move over," an American voice is shouting. "The trucks have to get on the verge to let pass a dozen more Sherman tanks."

Our legs are starting to get cold, our bottoms numb, our stomachs empty, our tempers short. There is a gloomy silence. Milligan to the rescue!

"My favourite sauce is Worcester," I said.

"Worcester?" says Edgington.

"Yes."

"My favourite is HP" says Tume.

"I like OK sauce with bread and cheese," says Fuller.

The truck stops on a side road, we are lost. With our very battered map and a hand-covered match we finally get on the right road. We are looking for Map Square 132832; this was a tree-lined country road just south-west of Sparanise. The Battery are "housed" in a long irrigation ditch by the side of the road. Spaced about are a few derelict farm buildings. From that dark ditch come the sounds of wallops, groans and furious scratching, the place is alive with mosquitoes. Beating off the beasts we familiarise ourselves with our surroundings. The guns are adjacent and are already roaring out into the night. A red glow is seen. That is what we want: the cookhouse! Soon we are grovelling to the cooks.

"Where you bloody well bin then?" says Ronnie May, who had been laying in a bivvy dreaming of some grotty bird in Houndsditch. I had seen her photograph, and the best place to think of her was in a muddy field in Italy.

"We bin reeling in a line," said Bombardier Fuller.

"No one told us to keep any late dinners," said May, starting to wipe a diseased tin-opener across his apron. "Good job I kept the oven in," he said.

"You should always keep a few late dinners, Ronnie," says Edgington. "Theatregoers, you know."

We are all swiping left, right and centre to throw off the mozzies, "Let's all put on a fag and smoke 'em out."

Hurriedly we lit up and forming a circle facing outwards started to envelope ourselves in clouds of smoke. Soon we were all coughing like consumptives; it alleviated the situation but as soon as we stopped, the mozzies returned. To help them, Jerry starts lobbing over odd shells. Running and eating, we dive into the muddy ditch, there in the dank dark we squat and eat mouthfuls of lovely hot stew, mixed with dead mosquitoes.

"What a terrible position," grumbled Edgington. "I've eaten many meals," he went on, "but Mosquito Stew, never."

"Eat as many as you can," I said, "better still, bite 'em."

The rims of our ears were now a mass of red lumps.

Edgington continues, "You never know, in France these might be a delicacy like frogs' legs."

Whoosh! Plonk! Whoosh! Plonk! Jerry is lobbing over 155mm shells that we have been told to avoid.

"If you like tomato sauce, that tells me you're a carman's pull-up eater," I said.

"Wot's wrong with a carman's pull-up?" says Tume.

"I'll tell you," I said. "It's the tomato sauce . . . have you ever looked closely at the bottles? The tops are congealed with dirt and stale tomato sauce, they never wash the bottle out, they just squirt in fresh red crap."

"How do you know, clever Dick?"

"I know because I was on a tomato sauce round, we used to go around with a lorry, me and a bloke called Len Brockenbrow, we had great petrol tins full of this red crap, and a kerosene oil funnel. We'd stick all the bottles on the deck, I'd hold the funnel, Len would pour out the goo, and we never once see the bottles clean. I tell you there was stuff at the bottom of the bottle that was twenty years old; Len told me he once looked down the neck of a bottle and he saw an eye looking up at him."

"Was it the manager?" says Edgington.

"Anyways, there's only one good sauce to put on grub and that's Worcester," I said.

"Worcester? Burns the arse off you," said Fuller.

"Good," I said. "I always wanted to get rid of mine."

Jock Webster interrupts. "None of you ignorant swines has any idea of sauces."

"Have you?"

"No, I'm an ignorant swine too, but if there is a sauce that compliments a meal it's HP."

"Harry Prickers," said Harry.

"Wot?" said Wilson.

"HP stands for Harry Prickers," he repeated.

"I wouldn't stand for that," I said.

Wheeee, plop, wheee, plop. More shells, but they don't explode.

"Duds," says Trew.

"That or AP."

"AP?" says Edgington. "Wot's he want to fire Armour Piercing at us for?"

"It's the dinner they're after," I said.

"Gad, you're right," says Edgington, immediately seizing on the nonsense. "Once they can get a shell through the crust on a British Army Stew, the way is open to pour in reinforcements. In no time they would be behind the back of the cookhouse cutting off our supply of food, and bringing the Army Catering Corps to its knees."

"Imagine," I said. "Imagine what fixed-line Spandaus could do to a treacle duff. No, we'd have to surrender. We'd have to haul up the white pudding cloth, and hand over the entire plans of our Treasured Meat and Veg Stew.

71

For England the war would be over."

"Never," said Harry. "We could get to the colonies, Canada, Australia, and start making meat and veg stew with a new formula, and – "

He was cut short by a very close Whhhheeeee Splot. Another shell. There was a silence broken only by a chorus of mosquitoes.

"You alright, Harry?" I said.

"I'm just feeling meself to see if that was a direct hit . . . no, there's no holes in me so I'll continue in the service."

"Milligan? Bombardier Milligan?" the voice of our new AI Sgt. King: "It's no use keeping silent, I'll find you, the smell will give you away."

I give a weak "I'm here, Sarge", trying to throw my voice in another direction.

"Ah, I want you to make out a roster for the Command Post for twenty-four hours."

It's along midnight, I'm not wanted for any duties, so I must find a place to kip. Eyes now accustomed to the gloom, I see ahead of our trench a group of farm outbuildings. With blankets and kit I lumber across to them. Inside I find a manger. The roof is intact save a few slates that rattle when the guns go. A manger? Well, if it was good enough for *him*. . . . There are a few bales of straw around, soon I am lying snuggled down. I'm a bit worried about being above ground with Jerry lobbing over harassing fire, but I gradually fall asleep to the sound of 7.2s.

OCTOBER 22, 1943

I glanced at my watch, 0700 hours, the sun is shining like a spring morn. It had a cheering effect, so I gave three cheers. I arose from my straw bed and was soon at the cookhouse for breakfast. The mosquitoes return to the attack. We eat with gas capes draped over our heads.

"Where'd you kip?" said Edgington.

I pointed. "Over there."

"Jerry slung over a dozen in the night."

"I didn't hear them. Did they have silencers on?"

"Poor old Bill Trew, he was havin' a crap in the field, the first one landed behind him. He set off and ended up in the ditch, with his trousers still down."

"I heard that Captain Richards of 17 Battery has got the MC."

"What for?" I said.

"I dunno," said Edgington, "it arrived with the rations so he pinned it on, and our Johnnie Walker's been mentioned in despatches."

"Oh, what did he do?"

"Drinking a whole bottle of Scotch under heavy mortar fire, and never spilled a drop."

We all realised as we drank our tea that the guns were silent.

"Is it a strike?"

"No," says Bombardier Fuller. "There's Jerries in the area supposed to be massing for an attack, and so we don't give our position away, we been ordered to stay silent."

"Oh," I said, "are we talking too loud?"

"He's up there," said Bill Trew, emerging from under his gas cape long enough to point to a hill about 4,000 yards away.

"You mean he can see us?" I said.

"Yer," says Trew.

I gave a cheery wave at the hill. "Hello, lads," I called.

It was amazing, Jerry could see us but wasn't doing anything about it, a strange uneasy feeling; anticipating a Stonk* by Jerry, we set to and dug a funk hole into the side of the ditch. A plume of black smoke is ascending from the Jerry position.

"He's still got fags then," said Edgington.

We made a floor out of bits of wood that kept us off the mud. At the same time we were also involved in digging an alcove for the telephone exchange; also along the ditch was the Command Post, Cookhouse, Officers' Mess and Battery Office. It looked very much like a World War 1 trench. An incredible find by Edgington, a huge cupboard that we wedge into our funkhole – we sit inside with the door closed to avoid the mozzies.

At about 0930 the guns open up again and we could see our shells bursting on the hillside behind Sparanise. The siting of our guns was obviously good, behind a bank of trees that

*Concentration of Artillery fire.

73

hid them from view, but we gunners walked about the fields in full view like the silly sods we were.

I set about drawing up a Duty Roster for manning the Exchange. Normally, they would stick some poor sod on from six till midnight, then some poor sod from midnight till six, leaving signallers milling around scratching their balls and with nothing to do. So I drew up a schedule that spread the load more evenly.

OCTOBER 24, 1943

I invented this roster and it continued on for as long as I was with the Battery.

COMMAND POST SIGNALS ROSTER

24th Night			25th Night	26th Night	27th Night	28th Night
8.30.	11.30	Radford 8	Milligan 1	Sherwood 4	Hart 7	Birch 10
11.30.	2.30	Fildes 9	Wenham 2	Thornton 5	Radford 8	Milligan 1
2.30.	5.30	Birch 10	Pinchbeck 3	Gordon 6	Fildes 9	Wenham 2
5.30.	8.30	Milligan 1	Sherwood 4	Hart 7	Birch 10	Pinchbeck 3

	25th Day	26th Day	27th Day	28th Day	
8.30	Wenham 2	Thornton 5	Radford 8	Milligan 1	Sherwood 4
12.30	Pinchbeck 3	Gordon 6	Fildes 9	Wenham 2	Thornton 5
12.30	Sherwood 4	Hart 7	Birch 10	Pinchbeck 3	Gordon 6
4.30	Thornton 5	Radford 8	Milligan 1	Sherwood 4	Hart 7
4.30	Gordon 6	Fildes 9	Wenham 2	Thornton 5	Radford 8
8.30	Hart 7	Birch 10	Pinchbeck 3	Gordon 6	
	(Scotch up)	(Scotch up)	(Scotch up)		

25th Night		
	Scotch up	Hart
	Milligan	Scotch up
	Will Duty Sig. on at 0430 call Mr Wright	

Each signaller did three hours at night, thus giving him a good few hours' sleep.

A big attack is going in tonight. The Grenadiers and Scots Guards are the poor bastards. They've got to take the hill to our immediate right to deny Jerry observation and put our OP on it. The sirens have gone and an air raid starts on Naples. 0430: the Artillery opened up and fired non-stop until 0624, then a silence. From the distant hill we hear the dreadful sound of Spandaus and Schmeisers that are spraying the early morning with bullets, and I can't but wonder at the courage of these lads in the Guards Brigade going forward into it. What a terrible, unexplainable lunacy. There must have been a lot of casualties as there was talk of us having to send gravedigging parties. In the end they sent some Gunners from the Wagon Lines. When they came back they spoke of Italian civilians being shot out of hand by Germans. There must be a lot of needle between these two nations. I should hate to be a German prisoner thrown to an Italian mob. . . . The mosquito-bites and the scratching have turned our faces into what from a distance look like uncured bacon. In desperation I had rubbed Sloane's Liniment on my face, and lo! it kept them away!!

"I've done it, Harry," I said, rushing into the Command Post with bottle in my hand.

"What have you done?" said Edgington, turning from the Telephone Exchange, "and if you have done it in that bottle, don't empty it in here."

"I've stopped the mozzies biting me," I said.

"How?" said the great man.

"Sloane's Liniment," I said.

"How in God's name did you get 'em to drink it?"

Even as he spoke I regretted the new-found repellent, my face started to sting and then burn as though it was on fire. I had to plunge my head repeatedly into a bucket of cold water. It was hours before the stinging stopped, wasn't *anybody* on my side?

During the day there was a story that suddenly, on one of our wireless sets, a German had been heard asking for information. The Signaller recognised the accent and said, "Fuck off, Fritz." The answer was instant, "Alright, English bastards, Off."

OCTOBER 22, 1943

Thank God. Naafi today! A tin of *fifty* fags. With trembling hands we pounced on them and soon we are wreathed in smoke. I notice three brass hats with maps walking to a position behind our guns; one carried a shooting stick. He was a tall dignified man with lots of medal ribbons (or were they laundry marks?). I watched as he placed his shooting stick behind him and sat down. There was a pause, then the whole shaft of the stick disappeared slowly into the muddy ground, leaving the owner on his back. Guffaws from us all. The Colonel rose to his feet and shouted, "It's not funny." There was a great chorus back, "Oh yes it is."

Alf Fildes has been bed down, he's got the squitters and we keep our distance. Gunner Roberts and Gunner Ferrier sleep next to each other; now, Roberts *talks* in his sleep. Somewhere in the wee hours he says, "You're next, you're next." Ferrier, half asleep, says "Alright", gets up, gets dressed and goes on guard.

OCTOBER 23, 1943

Today non-stop firing. In the Command Post there's hardly time to light a fag in between Fire Orders. A party of our linesmen have nearly been driven mad; they have been reeling in what was an old telephone line. They went on reeling in for two miles only to discover that another battery was in fact reeling it out. Harry comes back on M truck and says, "We're all bloody mad, fancy two bloody miles of reeling in a line and another sloppy lot are laying it out. Good job we caught 'em up, otherwise we'd be the other side of the bloody Alps by now."

The mosquitoes are so bad that an official complaint has been made to the MO and now three engineers with spray guns are going round squirting the countryside and our dinners; it helped a little, but far too late. The mosquitoes had left, why?

"They couldn't find any space between the bites," says Fuller, whose face resembled a side of beef with scabs on.

Some of the lads' scratches went septic and they were daubed with some pink stuff that made them look like Indians in war paint. They came dancing from the MO's tent with war whoops.

OCTOBER 23, 1943, NIGHT

Command Post: I sat on a much-treasured wooden box, in front of me a telephone, a message pad, the panel control of the Tannoy; this last mentioned connected up a loudspeaker to each gun. Through this you relayed the orders. You would pass on the Command Post Officer's orders.

Me: Take post!

A Sub: A Sub answering.

B Sub: B Sub answering.

Me: Angle of sight 'something something' degrees, Range 15,000.

The subsections would then all answer back the orders to acknowledge.

The OP spotting fall of shot would come back. "More three degrees or add 500 (yds)" and so on till you hit whatever it was.

On this particular shoot, we were trying to silence Nebelwurfers. Six o'clock we get the BBC news. The Russians have broken through between Dneiperpertrovsk and Chemolk, large bridgehead created threatening Kiev. Goodski!

As we listen, the Naples sirens go, at once the Ack-Ack opens up. We duck through our canvas wall and see the sky alive with tracer. It was one of the entertainments of war, a sort of early television.

"See anything last night?"

"Smashin' air raid on Naples."

"Are they going to repeat it?"

We can hear the distant drone of Jerry planes approaching. We sit tight as they fly overhead, a short sharp burst of MG fire and a plane bursts into flames, immediately, a fiery coffin in the sky plunges a thousand yards south of us, hits the ground and explodes. The grapevine was soon through, a Jerry!! Great! It crashed near 18 Battery, a hundred yards from the Battery latrine, where the occupants had flung themselves to the ground, shattering their meditations. It was 8.30, my relief was Signaller Thornton. He saunters in.

"Evenin' all, see the fireworks?"

I bid Lt. Wright goodnight.

"Thanks for the help, Milligan, leave the pencil, it's the only one we've got."

I pushed into the dark, and stumbled towards where the Ten Line exchange was. Behind the canvas blackout flap I hear Edgington struggling with the calls.

"Just a minute – er – wot? – hold it, sorry sir – I oops! I gave you the wrong line – hello 19 Battery here, who? Just a minute – blast, what the – "

He sounded like the clues for the *Times* crossword.

"Having trouble?" I said from outside.

"Go away," he said. "Go a *long, long* way away."

"Did you hear the plane come down?"

"No, but they all have to come down some time."

"It was a German aeroplane . . . A E R O P – "

"Yes, yes. Hello 19 Battery, what? Hold it, I'll get a pencil, blast. Hello? 19 Battery – ?"

I left him struggling with the war effort, and went to our little two-man dug-out in the side of the ditch. God I was weary. I just slipped my boots and jacket off and fell into a dead sleep.

OCTOBER 24, 1943

MY DIARY: FEELING VERY NERVOUS. CAN'T EAT MY FOOD. AS DAY CAME TO AN END I FELT REALLY EXHAUSTED. WHAT'S WRONG WITH ME? ANOTHER JERRY RAID ON NAPLES.

OCTOBER 25, 1943

Morning. Medium day, cloudy, chilly, occasionally bursts of sun. Good breakfast. Drank three mugs of tea on the trot with three Passing Cloud. Most of us are fed up with the new Major, "Jumbo" Jenkins. "He is a pain in the arse all over," says Arthur Tume. He is finicky, difficult to contact. You can never get near him. He is the product of a spoiled or deprived childhood, and is playing at soldiers; every minute he is on fault-finding missions, you never see him smile. From his driver, Sherwood, we discover that he's a hypochondriac and carries a medical chest around with him. Driving along, he suddenly shouts "Stop." Sherwood jams the brakes on, out leaps Jenkins, lays on the bonnet and squirts drops up his nose, directly behind rolls up an American General bleeping his horn. Sherwood puts the car into gear and drives off the road, the American witnesses a British Major lying on his back putting drops up his hooter and wonders why we are Allies.

Bodies of the German aviators have been found. They are

BSM Griffin, seen here with a broken arm caused by over-saluting and drink.

buried by 18 Battery.

"See? 18 Battery again," says Chalky White. "They get all the fun."

Gunner Devine is passing with a bandage on his hand.

"There's a curse on 19 Battery," he says solemnly.

"A curse?" queries Edgington. "What is it?"

"Fuck 'em," said Devine, a great Liverpudlian grin on his unshaven face.

"That is indeed a terrible curse," says Bombardier Milligan. "I wonder who put it on us."

"It's 'Jumbo' Jenkins, 'ees the bleedin' curse on us," said White.

"Fuck him," said Devine.

"See? There goes that curse again," says Edgington.

Edgington borrows Fildes' guitar, and off duty, we have a little sing-song in our dug-out.

"Ahhhh! There you are," says a voice followed by the body of Sgt-Major Griffin. Our much-beloved Welshman has that half evil, half benign smile on his face. Before we can dive for cover, he says, "You, you, you, and you," all the

79

while pointing at me, "we're moving, lads."

A great groan rents the air.

"Oh, cheer up now," he says in a mock cheery voice, "the King is going to let you all have a nice shovel on loan for the day."

More terrible groans.

"We are going to make some nice little holes in the ground for our guns."

We are all packed off in a three-tonner. We drive through Sparanise, badly shelled and bombed, some buildings still smouldering. The inhabitants are in a state of shock, women and children are crying, men are searching among the ruins for their belongings or worse, their relatives. It was the little children that depressed me the most, that such innocence should be put to such suffering. The adult world should forever hang its head in shame at the terrible, unforgivable things done to the young . . . despite all this the lads strike up a song.

"Bang away Lulu, Bang away Lulu, Bang away good and strong, What you gonna do when you want a blow through and yer Lulu's dead an' gone" . . . a line of German prisoners go past, our wheels splatter them with mud, as usual we give them the full treatment of raspberries, two fingers and Heil Hitler salutes. They don't even bother to look back, they trudge on, all in step.

"Lucky sods, it's all over for them," says Gunner White.

The new position is a small flat area, about a couple of miles north of our last position, behind a railway bank, with rising wooded ground behind us. Again we are to use a dried-up stream bed to install ourselves. It's very much like the last position. My diary describes the day thus:

EVENING: ON FORWARD RECCY, NICE DEEP STREAM BED (DRY) FOR ALL PERSONNEL. MOST OF NIGHT SPENT DIGGING. CAN HEAR MORTARS PUTTING UP SOME HOT FIRE. SLEPT LIKE A DEAD MAN, AWOKE AT STAND-TO 4.30 AM. WE ARE STILL DIGGING. NO JERRY SHELLING TODAY (ONE OR TWO ODD ONES MAYBE). WROTE TO MUM AND DAD.

HEAVY ACK-ACK BATTERIES MOVING IN AROUND US.

OCTOBER 26, 1943

No sleep. Feeling tired. During the day the guns arrived and spread themselves about in their unexplainable pattern, two were ahead of us and two behind us with their backs to the wood. The Command Post was not to the liking of the Major.

"He doesn't like it," said Chalky White. "Nobody *likes* a Command Post, you don't see soldiers goin' around sayin' 'I like Command Posts'."

"He says it's not big enough."

All hell is let loose, Ack-Ack start blazing away, we all go head-first to the deck, a swarm of MEs roar over the position at nought feet. We hear the Major shouting, "Tommy Guns . . . Tommy Guns."

A laconic voice, "Tommy Guns is on leave, sir."

Edgington first to rise to his feet. "Any questions?" he says.

He knelt over me, made a sign of the cross and then started to feel my pockets for fags. I am notoriously ticklish, and using one hand to tickle and convulse me, the other had withdrawn my fags. There followed a friendly struggle during which Major Jenkins appears and says, "What is going on, this isn't a nursery, Bombardier, you ought to know better. Get these men on with the digging."

I jumped up and Yes-sirred him on his way. He's back before we stop giggling. "Did any of you men fire at those planes?" he said.

We admit we didn't. I explained. "It's not easy to shoot down planes with shovels, sir."

"You will keep your side arms within reach, next time I expect to hear a volley."

"Very good, sir."

In an hour the planes flew over, and we let fly. The Major is running up, waving his arms. "No, no, bloody fools, they're ours."

"Don't worry, sir, when they fly back again, we'll apologise," I said.

He didn't know how to take me, he stood there clenching his fists, his face a mask of frustration.

It was a mixed day of planes, one moment Jerry, then the

81

RAF, then Jerry. The Ack-Ack boys took no chances and fired at the lot. The Major was nearly out of his mind by day's end trying to co-ordinate all our efforts for maximum retaliation. Late that night, we hear him mournfully playing Schubert's *Serenade* on his clarionet. Smudger Smith on A Sub Gun answered it by howling like a dog. The Major sent Woods, his batman, to find out who the offender was. As fast as he silenced one howl, another one would start somewhere else; the pay-off was an actual farm dog behind us who took up the howling, and nobody could stop him.

Oh that night! Had we not learnt our lesson of not occupying empty stream beds, gullies etc.? No, we hadn't, so and lo! it raineth. By morning we had all learnt our lesson of not occupying etc. etc., and were mud covered and ankle deep in it. The Major, with memories of the Somme, orders a mile of duck boards. Meantime we attempt to scrape the mud off, we carve it off with a jack-knife like dough. Sgt. Donaldson dries the mud with a blow torch and breaks it off with a hammer, but not before setting his trousers alight! The duck boards arrived, in white pinewood, which stood out like a mark for all Jerry planes to bomb. Sure enough, the day after, there is a sudden roar of planes, Ack-Ack guns shooting everyone up the arse, Jerry machine-gunning for all his worth, all of us running in all directions, down holes, up trees, behind walls, under lorries, all in a split second, we looked like an early Keystone Cops movie. Major Jenkins had emptied his Webley pistol at the raiders and dropped it in the mud.

"Listen, all you lot." It's Sgt. King talking in his clipped nasal cockney voice. "These duckboards 'ave been adjudged as too 'conspicious', therefore we must go a-tramplin' on them until they match the rest of Italy."

The rest of the day we spend stamping in the mud and then stomping it on to the duckboards.

"If my mother knew I was doin' this, she'd go and shoot Churchill."

"How?" said Gunner White looking down at the brown sea, "how can we get out of this before we all go stark ravin' bloody mad?" He looked up to heaven and said, "God, save us from all this fucking around."

The position became known as the Wembley Exhibition.

82

"I've got a culinary surprise, lads," said Spike Deans.

He has just come off Command Post duty, the hour is 0600; none of us are pleased by the awakening.

"Why, in God's name, do we, the innocent of this parish, have to be aroused at this unearthly bloody hour?"

Deans taps the side of his nose with his finger, but nothing falls out, he gives a sly wink.

"It's to the lucky one's advantage tonight. In funkhole No. 3, I will be preparing a repast that I am willing to offer at five fags a go."

There is a general stirring at this announcement.

"What's the grub?" says bleary-eyed Edgington.

"Never mind what it is, it will be better than what the cookhouse give you; it will be served at 2000 hours, there's enough for five portions." So saying, he exited.

"Five fags is a lot to swop for a dinner," I said.

"Yer," says Birch, "supposing we don't like the grub, do we get the fags back?"

A guffaw from White follows, "You're joking, if I know Deans 'e's only doin' this because he's short of snouts."

"I've had enough of compo grub, I'll chance it," says Edgington, arising from his mud-encrusted blankets.

"Me too," said Bombardier Milligan. "I'm trying to cut down on fags, and build up on food."

"I'll help you cut down on fags," says Gunner White, who is pulling on a pair of underpants so ragged that they looked like lace, "I'll smoke yours fer you."

Through the day we got that which the farmers in the Sahara were dying for; it poured, it trickled through every aperture, the rim of my tin hat was a hanging ring of pear-shaped watery pearls. A merry game! Turn your head, see if you can make them run around the rim without letting any drop off.

A Catholic priest visited us this evening and asked if anyone wanted Confession and Holy Communion. I nearly went but since the war started, my belief in a God had suffered a reverse. I couldn't equate all the killing by two sides, both of whom claimed to be a Christian society. I was, as Gary Cooper would say "kinda mixed up inside".

Talking of mixed up inside brings us to the Deans evening *gastronomique*. He had cooked it in half a kerosene oil tin, which now sat over a fire of diesel. "It's got curry in," he warned.

Edgington, White, Birch, Bdr. Fuller and myself sat expectantly squeezed into the dug-out.

"Right," said Deans. From the tin of boiling water appears a giant suet roll which he has boiled in the sleeve of an old vest, he places it on a piece of wood. "First!" he said. We all hold out tins. He cut a slice of the roll, from it oozed a curry stain gravy with what looked like thin french beans and Dobies' Four Square tobacco. With the first mouthful I let out a scream. It was like eating raw chillies.

"Too hot is it?" enquired Deans.

I lay rolling on the ground begging for water.

"I'll break it down a bit," he said, and started mixing in hot water, turning the whole thing into a ghastly-looking death grey.

"What's this stringy stuff," said munching Edgington.

"That?" said Deans. "It's grass."

There was a shocked silence. Edgington, his mouth still open with shock. "Grass?" he said, "GRASS??"

"Now don't get angry," said Deans, "it's grass but specially selected."

"Yes," Edgington said, "specially selected for idiots like us! I'm not givin' you five fags for bloody grass. I mean, I can graze free with the bloody cows."

"Look! if you think you've been diddled, OK, but answer the question; until Trotsky 'ere – " he pointed to Edgington " – asked what it was, you were all enjoying it, weren't you? Believe me, in the Alps Maritime, this dish is considered a delicacy."

It did taste OK really, and by now the cookhouse would be closed, so basically we had no option.

"But," Birch added, "we should have been given warning."

"I wanted there to be an element of surprise in it."

"Oh, we were fucking surprised alright," said White, who then broke the bad news. "And I've got a surprise for you," he said. "I haven't got any fags."

"You sod," said Deans.

White grinned. "All life is six to four against," he said.

A head pokes in the dug-out, it's Ben Wenham.

Spike Deans waiting to steal a lorry.

"The news is on in the Command Post."

We all rush there to hear the BBC Announcer saying, "Heavy rain and conditions under foot, are slowing the Allied advance in Italy."

"Good heavens, it's raining here then," said Edgington, putting on an idiot grin. "It's strange – he never mentioned *it*."

"Mentioned what?"

"He never mentioned that in Italy we'd had curried grass for dinner."

I was on CP duty from eight-thirty. The weather had stopped the war. There was no firing save a few pre-planned harassing fire tasks. I wrote a letter home, then played Battleships with Lieutenant Wright, a slight, dark-eyed, gentle-faced young man, who looked as out of place in a war as Quasimodo in the Olympic high-jump finals. (Supposing he'd won?) We had the 22 Set beamed on to Allied Forces Network, now operating from Naples. I remember that night how nostalgic I got when just before midnight they started to play Duke Ellington – *Riverboat Shuffle*! Outside I went knee-deep in water and did my own Riverside

85

Shuffle back to my dug-out. My bed was raised on two large empty 8lb potato tins. Edgington was awake, writing a 10,000-page love letter to Peg.

"Still up?" I said.

"No," he said. "It went down an hour ago." He took the fag from his mouth. "I'm drawing on my last reserves of energy."

"Very quiet in the Command Post," I said as I slid my muddy boots off. "I beat Mr Wright three games to nil at Battleships."

"If that gets around he could be cashiered," said Edgington.

I pulled myself wearily under my blankets. (Hadn't I better rephrase that?) I fell asleep leaving sexually frustrated Edgington trying to work it out in writing. He certainly had a lot of lead in his pencil.

OCTOBER 27, 1943

REGIMENTAL DIARY: *Infantry pushing forward all day, we are bombarding and firing Y targets. Some slight enemy retaliation but not much.*

Good news! We are allowed to write home and actually tell our families that we are in Italy. Oh hooray.

Dear Mother,
  I am in Italy.
    Your loving son,
      Barmy Fred.

Rumours of yet another "big attack". The rain has stopped, a wind is blowing, so I will hang out my laundry that now lies reeking at the bottom of my big pack. Diving into those dark depths I pull out dreadful lumps of congealed mildewed clothing. Soon I am boiling a tin of water. Whhheeee Boom! an air-burst shell. It stops, I arise and see that the water is boiling, I drop in my clothes, then half a bar of soap and start stirring the lot with a stick. My idyll is shattered by another air burst; was Hitler trying to range on my laundry?

GERMAN OP OFFICER: Three rounds on to zer underpants Milligan. Fire! Ach Vonderschoen! a direct hit on zer soap! For you Gunner Milligan, the laundry is over.

Mail! father, mother, brother etc. And newspapers. It was a field day for me (every day I was in a field). I lay in bed and read a copy of the *Melody Maker*. Harry Parry and his Radio Rhythm Club were still going strong, and Benny Lee was voted England's greatest jazz vocalist. I often giggle about that when I hear him compering Old Tyme Dancing. I was reading "Last week, Mr Churchill entertained a Russian delegation to dinner in London. They were served venison that had been shot in the Scottish Highlands."

"Isn't it bloody marvellous. Russians eating Scots venison in London, and us eating curried Italian grass!"

"Winston is trying to impress the Russians, the Ruskies will go back to Stalin and report that the English are eating Royal Deerski, it's natural for Churchill to show the English still have an upper class."

"That's cobblers," says Edgington. "It's like this, Churchill likes his grub, but if he's caught eating venison on his tod, the *Daily Mirror* would be in an uproar. CHURCHILL EATS ROYAL DEER WHILE OUR LADS EAT CURRIED ITALIAN GRASS. So, as a cover he invites a load of hungry-guts Russians who are pissed off with black bread and onion soup, and they come at the double."

"Such are the vagaries of war, Edgington, I tell you, if Churchill asked me to come over for beans on toast I'd go like a shot, wouldn't you?"

"No, I've got my pride."

"Take it with you. You wouldn't turn down a trip to London, with that little darling Peg of yours waiting at the station."

At the mention of Peg his eyes went soft, and his trousers boiled. A terrible head with a dripping tin hat pokes its face in. We both scream. It was L/Bombardier Bill Trew, ex-London milkman. He curdled milk by looking at it.

"I 'eard you got some newspapers."

"Yes, but it's all cultured stuff. *The Times*, the *Manchester Guardian*."

"Doesn't make any difference," he said. "I only want to wipe me arse on 'em."

Trew is looking at my tea mug. "Gi's a sip," he says.

Trew sipped the tea and told us he'd heard that there was a rumour that we're – we joined in as he concluded – "GOING BACK TO ENGLAND".

That was the permanent rumour. They even said it when we *were* in England.

"We're *never* going back to England," Edgington said. "Never, never, never, the war was a life-saver for the Conservatives, it solved the unemployment problem, and American banks have agreed to prop up the economy, so? They are going to keep this bloody war going as long as they can, they're even trying to get Turkey to join in."

"Turkey for Christmas?"

It had always puzzled me as to how you got a neutral country to go to war. I mean, what did you say: "Come on in. The war's lovely."

"I know people, ordinary blokes, who *like* war," said Trew, sipping more of my tea.

"Who?" says Edgington, who is now unexplainably removing his trousers.

"Liddel, Gunner Liddel."

"What about him?"

"He told me he *likes* the war."

"Did he give a reason?"

"Yes, he said in peacetime he was so skint he had to wear his brother's left-off clothes. In fact his battle dress was the first bit of new clothing he'd had. Until he joined the Kate he'd never been put in charge of a job." The job being Shit House Orderly.

"Oh he's in charge of the job alright," said Edgington, who was now scrutinising the insides of his trousers. "He's in charge of every job that's done!"

Trew sipped some more of my tea.

"Wot *are* you doing, Edgington?" I said.

"I think I've got a flea in me trousers . . . or something that bites."

"Something that bites!" I said sitting up. "Could it be a dog?"

Trew sipped more of my tea. "Ta," he said and handed me an empty mug.

Now, whenever there's a reunion, I walk straight up to him and say "Gi's a sip", take his beer, drain it to the bottom, and say "Remember Italy." I don't think he does. Something strange. The dates October 28, 29 and 30 in my diary are blank save an oblique line drawn across them with the words "You've had it." What it was I had had I cannot recall. I've looked up letters, diaries, the only document that exists of those three days is this unfinished letter.

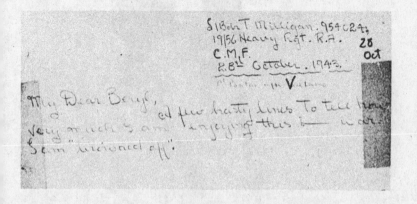

The girl Beryl is a mixture of singer/sweetheart/friend/resident of Norwood. She had sung with Carl Barriateau's band before and during the war. The only photo I have of her is the one overleaf on top of an oil tanker.

The letter seems to suggest that I was fed up. Well, I can't remember so I must have been fed up; of course, I might have been fed down, or I might have been fed-sideways, or fed intravenously, no one will ever know. Why I never finished the letter to Beryl is likewise a mystery; a bigger mystery, why did I keep it all these years? Did I intend to finish it? yes! of course, I'll write at the bottom, "That's all for now, love, Spike." *Another* wartime mystery solved folks! AGED GUNNER FINDS LOST LOVE LETTER IN OLD ARMY SOCK. "Thanks to that sock," says 159-year-old ex-Gunner Millington, "I have discovered my lost love, now we shall be married and I'll end happily ever after."

Miss Beryl Southby, sweetheart of my forces and singer with Carl Barriateau's band. Shown on the wagon, Norwood, 1941-2.

OCTOBER 31, 1943

MY DIARY: LOVELY DAY. PADRE HELD CHURCH SERVICE.
ALF FILDES' DIARY: *Lazy Day. Fry ups. Deans' coffee.*

NOVEMBER 1, 1943

REGIMENTAL DIARY: (I can't resist reporting this entry!)

Had orders to move from 083857 by 10.00 hrs as "X" Corps want to come into the area. The orders from 2 AGRA were vague and they were unable to indicate any hide area for us to go. They could not tell us where the enemy were, they could not tell us whether we were to go into action that day. So we aren't doing anything.

Any questions folks?

Ted Lawrence, our Don R, comes up and says, "Jerry's retreatin'." He ought to know, he's just stamped his bare

Ted Lawrence, with his pistol pointing in a direction that could ruin his marriage.

foot on a dog-end and comes hot-foot from HQ. We've all got to be ready to move at a moment's notice. A mad rush as we start hurling our crappy clobber into big pack, small pack kitbag, cardboard boxes, brown paper parcels all held together by miles of knotted string and bits of bent wire. It was really terrible to see what a once immaculate Battery looked like. No longer did we appear as Conquerors, no, we looked like families of impoverished Armenian refugees fleeing the Turkish slaughter. Bundles of canvas, tea-chests and waterproof sheeting were piled on the roof, obliterating the outline of the lorry which, in silhouette, appeared to be an extinct dinosaur. So, from our "Wembley Exhibition" site we all started to slither and slide to the main road. My God! What a mess! Vehicles were everywhere, all pointing the wrong way, the giant Scammell lorries with guns in tow had "jack-knifed", red-faced Sergeants were yelling abuse at the drivers, who in turn yelled abuse at the gunners, who pointed accusingly at the Sergeants. The signallers (us) are all OK. We are sitting in our trucks and have managed to get to the main road known as Route 6, facing the *right* way. We have brewed up. Great steaming mugs of tea are jamming the roadway. American trucks with coloured drivers are racing past shouting, "Out of the way, Limey white trash", and we shout back, "Fuck Joe Louis." We drank tea till our bladders were crippled and the tannic acid showed red through our skin, by which time the great guns had finally been extricated from the mud.

By eleven o'clock, we were in convoy, looking like Council Dustcarts on the move.

"Oh! *look* who's coming up the road! It's our leader, General Mark Clark! God bless 'ee zur!"

He is seated in a jeep, with four stars on the front. His driver I swear was W. C. Fields. As he passes down our line he grins at the good-natured shouting, "Got any spare dollars, Mate? Why aren't we getting ice cream like your men?"

He stopped at the head of our column, stood up, talked to his driver, turned round and came back again. He turned and gave a wave as he disappeared round a corner. Had he gone? No, a moment later he backs into view followed by a great Tank Recovery lorry. He waits patiently as the monster

Gunner Ben Wenham outside his country residence (Wembley Exhibition position)

manoeuvres round the bend and then he goes again. We're moving! Better still, we're moving forward! A desultory cheer is heard. Our destination is Map Ref. 018908, what will that be? "All these bloody *numbers*," says Edgington. "Everything's numbers, *I'm* a number, *you're* a number, the *truck's* a number, the World War is a number. Two. The pills they give us, what are they?" rages Edgington. "*Number* nine!"

"Yes, Kings of England from the right, number! George one! George two, George three, William the one, James the two."

I was babbling on like this when the beckoning face of Sergeant King appears. "Ahhhhh," he leers, " 'oo 'as been 'iding from 'is nice Sergeant?" He's looking at me. "You are to go with our dearly beloved Major Jenkins forward, in search of (a) the Enemy, and (b) an OP."

Soon I am in G truck with Spike Deans, Vic Nash and Lt. Wright. I am not actually with Major Jenkins, he's in H truck. Behind us is X truck; what had happened to all the numbers? In the back of the truck the ever-inventive Bom-

93

bardier Deans opens the pontoon school.

"I'll be banker," says Deans.

"Why?" I said.

"Because I thought of it."

"We should draw for it," I protested.

"Then you'll have to use your cards," said Deans.

"I haven't got any."

"Then I'm banker," he said, "because I have." He shuffled the cards with great dexterity and dropped them.

First hand I got pontoon! By the time we got to 018908 I accumulated a nice little kitty of about 300 lire.

"Well," I said, "I never thought I'd be 300 lire better off by the end of the day."

"You could be twice as rich," said Deans.

"How?"

"I'll toss you double or nothing."

He did. I lost the lot. 018908 was a small flat area with a small range of hills north of us, San Marco by name. In the base of them were numerous caves. We parked our vehicles adjacent to a line of trees, put up camouflage nets, and sat staring at each other.

"What now, gentlemen?" I said.

"Pontoon?" said Deans.

"Not on your bloody life."

"Alright, you suggest something," he said, folding his arms and grinning.

"I have suggested something," I said, folding my arms and grinning.

"What?" he said.

I said, "I have suggested that we don't play pontoon."

A voice is calling. "All personnel over here."

It's Lt. Wright, who is standing outside the mouth of a cave which looks like it's going to swallow him. With great urgency on our faces we amble across. Mr Wright waits patiently.

"Now," he says, looking at some orders pinned to his map. "We are now at San Marco, here," he taps the map, his papers fall in the mud. "Blast," he says.

I bend down to pick them up; he is now clutching a handful of muddy papers. "I was saying we are here, and we've temporarily lost touch with the Bosche – so we will carry out

94

maintenance of wireless sets, small arms and vehicles until further orders, that is all."

I clutch Bombardier Deans' arm dramatically, and whisper, "He's going to leave us. What are we going to do?"

A rattling sound reveals Sherwood's bren carrier loaded to the gills, with Lt. Walker, Gunner Ben Wenham, Gunner Pinchbeck and Lt. Budden followed by Don R. Lawrence – *they* are going forward to look for Jerry.

"Group looking for Jerry." Left to right are Don R. Ted Lawrence, Lt. Walker, Ben Wenham, Gunner Pinchbeck, Lt. Budden and Bdr. Brookes.

"My God go with 'eee," I said, striking a dramatic pose, one hand clutching my heart.

Ben Wenham grins and says, "Who's a silly bugger then!"

We wave them goodbye as they disappear over the brow of a hillock. Indeed the Germans had pulled back, quite a distance.

"They must be suffering withdrawal symptoms," I told

95

Mr Wright, "It's a sort of wartime coitus interruptus."

That night was wonderful. I remember it was crisp, cold, clear, starlit, that's if I remember: if not, it was raining.

NOVEMBER 2, 1943

ALF FILDES' DIARY: *Nothing doing. Enemy blowing up bridges, blocking and mining every L of C. Supposed to be flooding plains it took Italians 10 years to reclaim. We are now overlooking main Rome road, Germans are shelling it from their hills. Sitrep says we must now prepare for mountain war. BBC news still very good.*

"Major Jenkins' compliments, would Gunner Fildes and Lance-Bombardier Milligan please bring their instruments to the cave?" This from Gunner Woods.

"A Royal Summons," I cried.

"What's he want?" said Fildes suspiciously.

"I'll say it again," said Woods in an exasperated voice with a Cornish accent. " 'E wants you two to report to him with yourn instruments."

"We *know* that," I said. "But why? He doesn't like jazz, so what's he want us to bring our . . . ."

But Woods wasn't listening, he walked off waving his hand in the air saying, "I'm only a batman, not a bloody mind-reader."

Most certainly Woods couldn't tell the future, he couldn't even tell the present. In peacetime he had been a farmhand, and had known the pleasure of having two great shire horses pulling his plough.

I said, "What's it like?"

"Ploughing? 'Ow yew like to be eight hours a day looking at two great 'orses' harses."

Fildes and I entered the cave, which was very smoky from a fire in whose light sat Major Jenkins, still with his hat on. He was holding his clarionet, and playing his strangled version of Schubert's *Serenade*. When he saw us he stopped.

"Ah, you know why I've asked you to bring your instruments?"

"You want us to throw them on the fire," I said.

He didn't laugh. He patted the floor, inviting us to sit.

96

'No," he said. "You play all that nigger music don't you?
I'm going to teach you some *good* tunes, I want you both to
join in." Here he tootled the first bars of a tune. "Didn't you
recognise that?" he said.

"Yes," I replied. "It was Whistling Rufus, he was my
father."

Over his head it went and hit the wall with a loud plop.

"Yes, it's *Whistling Rufus*, a *fine* Military marching tune,
the Gurkhas marched to that during the Chitral Rebellion."

"It might have caused it," I said.

"I'll play the melody and when I point to you, Milligan,
play the descending obligato."

"What key?" asked Fildes, across the fiery divide.

"I play it in G major."

"G? Major? I knew it when it was only a captain, sir."

Over his head it went and plop against the cave wall. He
launched into a very fast version of *Whistling Rufus*, at the
given moment he pointed to me, and I played the obligato.
He seemed well pleased. When we finished he smiled, counted
two bars in and launched back into it all over again. We did
this several times, he enjoyed it to such an extent I realised
he'd never played with anyone before, it was all a new
experience for him, it was a new experience for me . . . a
bloody awful one. Woods brought him a cup of tea, Woods
didn't bring us a cup of tea.

"Now," said Jenkins, wiping his mouth with a handker-
chief, "shall we try some of your nigger music?"

"What about 'The Sheik of Araby' by Rudolph
Valentino?" I said.

"Jolly Good," he said and launched into a chorus. I
played the most awful corny obligatos and when I took a
chorus played with a terrible nanny-goat vibrato. Oh! had I
only a tape recorder that night! I'd have dropped it on him.

We were interrupted by a Despatch Rider from 2 AGRA
HQ.* A short dwarf, heavily wrapped up with knee-high
motor-cycling boots that came up to his neck, a crash
helmet that came down to his knees, and a khaki scarf wrapped
around the lower half of his face. Jenkins saw the word
URGENT on the envelope, hastily dropped his clarionet,

*Army Group Royal Artillery.

stood up to read the message. It would have read exactly the same sitting down but standing up gave him height. What it didn't give him was a view of his clarionet rolling slowly into the fire. . . . We let it burn a few moments and when it was too late said, "Oh, sir! Quick, your clarionet is on fire." (Rather like those French translations, i.e. The Clarionet of my cousin has been struck by lightning.) He rushed at the smouldering instrument, letting the top secret message fall.

"My God," he wailed, "my father gave me this."

He won't half give it to you when he sees it again, I thought. Meantime his TOP SECRET message was now burning merrily. We left him trying to read it.

I had put up my pup tent against a bank surrounding a field. I lay in bed and wondered if the helmsman's face was still showing white through the wheel house and where was that man Edgington? Sometimes known as Edge-Ying-Tong (the last two words were to become a song that came third in the Hit Parade of the late 1950s).

Edgington was even now speeding through the night in a traffic jam as the whole battery were homing in on our position, and they would be with us in dribs and drabs throughout the night. I listened and I could hear the first dribs arriving, followed by the drabs.

"Where's the cookhouse?" could be heard.

Food! This bloody army were food mad!

A posh voice: "The cwook house is over theaire and there'll be a hot meal in halwf an hour." Now I'd already had my dinner, my watch said 11.50, it was very late, I was tired, warm and comfortable and I wasn't hungry . . . nevertheless at 12.30 am I find myself in the queue. Ahead of me is another stomach on legs, Kidgell! The nearer he got to the serving table the more silent and tense he became. When there was only one man to go, Kidgell would go dead silent, sweat would appear on his brow, you could see him repeatedly swallowing the excess of saliva that was mounting in his mouth and nearly drowning him, then! . . . It was his turn! There was nothing twix him and the bubbling, steaming food containers, his trembling hands would hold out his dixies, he would crouch forward like a sprinter in the blocks, his eyes would extend from his head like organ stops. The moment the last drop of gravy from the cook's spoon had finally fallen into his tin, Kidgell would start eating immediately as he walked to a spot to sit down. By the time he got there he'd finished the main course and was into the duff. This gone he would gallop to the back of the queue hoping to get "seconds".

If he thought he was going to be recognised, he would put his tin hat on and keep his head well down to hide his face. What gave him away was his dribbling, drooling and shaking hand when he got near the grub; he earned his title, "the famine".

"I reckon," said our cook, "if he got to a field of wheat first, the locusts wouldn't stand a bloody chance."

Another Day at San Marco

"Gandhi's legs," Edgington reads aloud from a soggy *Daily Mirror* rapidly becoming an antique.

"What about Gandhi's legs," I said.

Out here in Italy there had been no news of Gandhi's legs since we landed.

"It says here," Edgington continues, "Gandhi's legs are the thinnest political legs in the world."

"Rubbish," I said. "My mother has the thinnest in the world. She has legs like old pipe-cleaners."

"Ah but she has *non-political* thin legs, we're talking about *political* thin legs."

"My mother voted Labour – she walked to the polling booth. Of course her legs are political."

Fuller sticks his head in our tent.

"We're moving."

"Moving?" I said, "I can't feel a thing."

"There's not enough mud here," chuckled Fuller. "The Major is reccying for a quagmire."

"When?" said Edgington mournfully.

"Tomorrow. 0600."

"Why do wars always have to be so bloody early – it's always 0400, 0500 – 0500!! What's wrong with 11.30? Eh? Who feels like fighting at bloody dawn? A man is much braver at 11.30!"

I left him raving in his damp tent as I went to man the No. 22 wireless set that kept us in contact with RHQ. It was 20.30. I went to relieve Ernie Hart, who was dutifully asleep on his set with headphones on. With true camaraderie I left him there and went back to bed. I am awakened at midnight, by an enraged Hart.

"Look at the time – you were supposed to relieve me at half-past eight!"

"I did but you was a-kip – wasn't you? I didn't have the heart to wake you."

The staccato rat-a-plan of rain drops on the canvas roof as the deluge started.

"Do I *have* to get up?"

"Yes, you bloody well do – it's 11.20 – you've got five minutes to do – "

Bugger. I sat at the set for five minutes. I called RHQ to test the signals.

"Hello, Dog Easy Fox – Dog Easy Fox – Able Baker Charley calling – over."

"Hello Able Baker Charley – Dog Easy Fox – answering. Hearing you strength nine-er, strength nine-er – over."

"OK, Dog Easy Fox – over and out."

I twiddle the dial till I get AFN Naples. It's Artie Shaw!! He's playing "The Blues". He is really a more elegant player than Goodman though Goodman was nearer to real Jazz. Birch – bleary-eyed, coughing, comes to relieve me.

"You're five minutes *late*," I said in Lance-Bombardier voice.

"Sorry, Bomb. I couldn't find me boots."

I climb out the truck, he puts on the headphones. He listens. "This isn't RHQ," he says.

"Yes it *is*," I said. "If you wait till the end of the tune you'll hear the Lt.-Colonel Scorsbie announce the next dance."

'Look, Bomb," he says patiently, "why not help shorten the war, hand in your stripe?"

"I can't, it covers a hole in my sleeve." As I walk back in drenching rain, I see a red glow in the Northern Sky – it gets brighter and brighter, then darkness followed by a low rumbling of a distant explosion. Some poor swine might have been killed in that, I thought, and then I thought, fuck 'im, and went to bed. My blankets are damp and cold. I don't know how we didn't all die of pulmonary ailments, perhaps I was dead – perhaps we were all dead, and this was hell. Of course! That's it! We're all dead! I shout into the night, "Good news, we're all dead."

I'd asked my father for Players – but no! I get Passing Clouds! Why? Because he's a *snob* – at his officers' mess he had made it clear that he would never drink inferior wine, smoke inferior tobacco – the reason was he was skint. Gunner White thought their flat Turkish shape was due to pressure in transit, and proceeded to roll them until they were round. I am smoking in the dark, the roar of the rain wonderful! It drowns out all sounds except a ghastly yawn from Edgington's tent.

"Harry – that you?"

"Just a minute, I'm putting my jaw back."

"You still awake?"

"Just."

"I wonder what it's like in London now."

"Don't make me homesick."

"I bet all the night clubs are open ... some of the big bands will be still playing. Ambrose, Lew Stone, all that lot, they go till three in the morning ... you ever been to a night club?"

There's no reply – he's unconscious, I must hurry and catch him up.

SATURDAY, NOVEMBER 6, 1943

Very cold. "We must be high up," Edgington is announcing.

"Why must we be high?" I enquire, because we were sitting down.

"The rations, *that's* why."

"What about the Russians?"

"*Rations!* You silly Gunner, *rations*. Haven't you noticed that in addition to our ration we now get little round vitamin pills?"

"I thought they were concentrated Plum Puddings to save shipping space."

For the millionth time we are in the back of a lorry

lumbering through a muddy cold landscape, winter black trees line our route like dying sentinels. I trace our position as we progress. The town we are passing through is Teano! I tell Edgington, "This is where Garibaldi invented spotted biscuits and reunited Italy for King Emanuel the umpteenth."

"I am thrilled," says Edgington.

"It was Garibaldi that caused the Bourbons to flee over the Rocky Alps."

"Ah, thereby hangs the phrase, a Bourbon on the Rocks."

Groans. We have halted. "Look what I've rescued." Vic Nash has come to the tailboard of our lorry. He holds a small wriggling black puppy; this was to be christened Teano, and was to become part of the Battery. We stroked him, petted him, gave him a bit of cheese and handed him back.

"Hide him from Driver Kidgell, won't you?" I said.

"Why?"

"Because he'll eat him."

Vic Nash giggled, the pup is furiously licking his face, so it can't have long to live.

"Get mounted," calls an important voice from up front.

"Get stuffed," comes the reply.

We move off in fits and starts, the lorry starts, we have fits. Climbing continuously on a secondary road between Teano and Rocamanfina about 1000 feet up. We sing a ditty oft sung in boring circumstances:

> "The good old Duke of York
> He had ten thousand men
> He marched them up to the top of the hill
> And he marched them down again.
> When they were up they were up
> And when they were down they were down
> And when they were only half way up
> They were Buggered!
> Good evening Friendssssss! Ching!"

We are on a mountain road with a gradient of one in four. We halt. "Dismount!" We climb out. On the right side of the road is a Church, semi-Gothic style. Just behind it is the Vicarage. The road opposite flanks a high bank with several

102

footpaths leading up to a cave set in a sort of browny-red sandstone.

"That's it," says Bombardier Fuller, riding up on his mo' bike. "That cave; get all the Command Post stuff in there."

We struggle and strain with all that bloody stuff we've carried so many times before. Edgington has developed the oriental carrying posture, balancing a battery on his head. We all copy and march Indian file up the slope chanting, "Sandy the wise, Sandy the strong".

"How long is this going to last?" he says.

"With time off for good conduct by the time you're eighty-three the future is yours."

Lieutenant Budden hoves to. "Has anyone seen Mr Wright?"

"Yes, sir," I said, "I saw him yesterday."

He looks at me in despair and says, "Can't you take anything for it, Milligan?"

Out of politeness I asked where the guns were.

"They're in the woods somewhere."

"Where are the woods, sir?"

"Ah! That's another question."

"Get the vehicles off the road and under cover."

We walk around muttering, "The woods are full of 'em!"

The lethal voice of Major Jenkins is penetrating the air. We drive up the slope and on to a small muddy plateau with numerous trees. We follow a small trail to the high bank. Under the trees we camouflage G truck.

"Jerry's been shelling the area, better dig in," says Bombardier Deans.

Dig? One thing I don't dig is digging. I'm not the first to spot the possibilities of sleeping in the church.

I move my kit in that evening. In the aisle is a catafalque mounted on a trestle. The catafalque is all black velvet with a great black cloth to cover the whole thing. What the hell! It looks great inside, so I make my bed in it. If I get killed in the night, I'm all ready. Great fun, I am asleep in my cata-falque, Bombardier Trew comes in to wake me up for my spell of duty. He is unaware of my macabre resting place. Gradually I arise from my box with the black velvet cover over my head. I let out a terrible howl and Bombardier Trew screams "Ghosts" and runs for his bloody life, and I find him gibbering in the Command Post to Lt. Budden.

An OP has been established on Monte Croce. Not again! Rain!!! Where does the stuff come from??? There's to be a big attack on Monte Camino, it's the 201 Guards Brigade to do the dirty work. I can't lie here, I must do something to help the war effort. I do. I go to the cookhouse for dinner. What's this I hear? That hungry bugger Kidgell, he's been having one dinner here, then running across to the American Battery next to us and scrounging another. He must have hollow legs.

"The attack goes in tomorrow night," so speaks Major Jenkins, who for once has deemed to tell us what's happening. I am on Command Post duty up till 11.30. Mr Wright is duty officer. In between firing he reads the *Daily Express*. At 1100 hours the thing called Edgington comes in, it carries a mug ahead of it.

"Good news," he says, he looks very merry, he should, there's been a rum ration and he's had his and a little more. "I've got yours here." He poured a measure into my mug.

"A Merry Christmas to you all," I said.

He empties a pocket full of chestnuts, soon they are roasting on our fire, and splitting open with a little bang. They taste delicious!!

"Alf Fildes is feeling groggy," he tells us. "He's got a sore throat so has gone to bed in the back of his truck."

There is nothing like a 15-cwt truck for a sore throat. Vic Nash is coming on duty. "Oh my poor guts," he says.

"He's got the shits! Keep away," we all say and cringe in the corner.

The guns report difficulty with the platforms, mud is making it increasingly difficult; each time they fire, the gun slithers in a circle. We can hear the swearing from the Command Post. But it's imperative they keep going as the attack is about to go in, they need help up there, so the back-breaking work of manhandling the guns back on target continues.

SUNDAY, NOVEMBER 7, 1943

ALF FILDES' DIARY: *Typical Sunday morning, people going to church opposite. Plenty of firing last night, and church has lost a few windows. After breakfast a dozen ME's came over and made trouble but left us alone, they made for the main road.*

Before the first mass we have to hide our beds – and make ourselves scarce.

I am walking to the cookhouse through a conglomerate of American foxholes and guns. The Yanks sound their air-raid alarm. It's noisier than the raid. Americans start running in all directions. I didn't. It was highly unlikely the planes could spot us in this heavily wooded position. They roar over the top of us, and later we heard machine-gunning and bombing somewhere down the Rocamanfina Road. Along with Edgington we explore the Church Annexe and find a piano in the vestry. Soon Italians in Church can hear distant Cole Porter tunes.

A Priest appears, he is not hostile, and stays to listen, I *think* his name was Father Alborghetti. He too took over the piano and then sang arias from *La Bohème*, *Tosca*, in a quivery ecclesiastical voice. We're all having fun! "Aren't you glad we've liberated you?" I said to the priest.

I do an all-night stint in the Command Post in promise of all day off. It's bloody cold, and in between Fire orders we all crouch over the brazier. The six o'clock news from the BBC is good. Kiev in Russian hands after a terrific advance. I'm so broke I could do with an advance myself. We are playing pontoon for matchsticks. Rumour that a Gunners' rest camp has been established somewhere on the Sorrento peninsula, is it true? Guns continue to fire through the night. The fight for Monte Camino continues, it's a bloody affair. I write some letters home.

Nov. 9, 1943

Dear Dad,

Nothing much to report except World War 2. Is it still going on where you are? It's winter here, lots of mud, and very cold especially in the mornings, so the balaclava and gloves you sent are very useful. Writing this in a cave, so we haven't come far from Neanderthal man, have we? There's always rumours of "going home", one look at this mob and you'd realise we're all going home. Thanks for the three Life *magazines, one reads and re-reads them over and over again and they are usually passed through every gunner in the Battery. I'm desperately trying to think of any news, and there isn't any. Read Beachcomber in the Express, he explains it all. I'm here and you're there, and every day is much the same as the previous. The conversations are food, sex, and after the war, sometimes its war, food and after the sex. I'll have to close as we're about to start sending deliveries of steel to the gentlemen of the Third Reich.*

Love to all
Your Loving Son
Terry

PS The Major tells us we must win the war because we're British.

Capt. Leo Milligan walking home to Orchard Way, Woodhatch, Reigate, Surrey, 1942-3, while second-in-charge of RAOC depot, Reigate. Now we all know.

TUESDAY, NOVEMBER 9, 1943

What's this? Edgington has made an incredible find. A free-range harmonium! It's in the Vicarage and the priest says we can use it, so the morning is spent playing jazz; as a mark of respect I play my trumpet muted, Alf plays guitar and the priest and his lady cleaner sit and listen a bit amazed, jazz under Mussolini had been banned as decadent; well, the music wasn't, but we certainly were. It was an unusual morning, the priest giving us an unexpected blessing

Sgt. J. Wilson, Bdr. Sainsbury and gun-crew filling in football coupons, Monte Santa Maria, apple orchard position, November 17 1943.

before we departed.

"What was he doing then?" said Edgington.

I explained. "It's a blessing."

"What good does it do?" he said.

"Well, it's supposed to be a solemn occasion on which he, as a minister, fortifies your soul by sprinkling holy water over you."

"It only made me bloody wet," said Edgington.

Grim news of the fighting on Monte Camino, the Guards are attacking but Jerry has reinforced his position with 1st/104 Panzer Grenadiers, and fighting is raging all over the peak.

NOVEMBER 10, 1943

MY DIARY: MUCH THE SAME. BAD WEATHER. WENT INTO THE VILLAGE OF TERRA CORPO, IT'S ALMOST IN RUINS. WE ARE TRYING TO GET A PHOTO TAKEN OF OURSELVES BY AN "ITI" PHOTOGRAPHER, HE SAYS "DOMANI" (TOMORROW). HE SAYS THAT EVERY DAY, TOMORROW TAKES A LONG TIME TO ARRIVE IN ITALY. WEATHER RAIN, SLEET, WINDY.

Just up the road before the village are a few houses, one is

107

occupied by RHQ. It is owned by a Doctor Fabrizzi, who was in the Abyssinian Campaign. We went there to play some music for the RHQ Signallers (who had invited us). It was a cosy large front room, nicely furnished, with a piano. We played some jazz, the Doctor, who looked like Cesar Romero, showed us photographs from the Abyssinian War, and a ghastly collection they were; they showed atrocities committed on Italian soldiers, which mostly meant emasculating them with a knife and letting them bleed to death. A Scandal! the wife of the Iti doctor fancies our MO, Dr Bentley (will he end up with his photo in the album?), and somehow they get down to Naples and spend a naughty weekend there. A touch of the Ernest Hemingways!

It has rained now continuously for five days. Sgt. Donaldson tells me that the guns are in a bad state. The carriages are starting to warp so badly that 15 and 18 Batteries are being pulled out of action.

"I wish to God my carriage would warp," I said.

"You know what they're going to do to reinforce them, weld railway lines round the front and the two sides."

"I suppose this means all the bloody trains will stop running." Sgt. Donaldson was up for some kind of vehicles' inspection.

"I don't know how the bloody things are still working." He was going on about the road conditions.

"They've organised a one-way system, half the day it's up traffic, the other half down traffic, if you come up early you have to wait half the bloody day before the down system comes in."

"Don't come up or down," I said, "come sideways, like the Chinese."

He stayed to have lunch with us, a lovely Stew, we sat under the altar of the church eating and telling dirty jokes. It was a bad day for God.

THURSDAY, NOVEMBER 11, 1943

Armistice Day. Ha ha ha.

Lt. "Johnny" Walker is at an OP on Monte Croce. He is suspicious that a white farmhouse is harbouring the enemy, so he drops a few 200 pounders around it; as they get closer a door bursts open and out rush a Jerry patrol who run like hell to a farmhouse a hundred yards away. Walker then shells that place, out runs Jerry back to farmhouse one, he does this till the Jerries are shagged out and finally double back to their own lines. "When I fight an enemy, I like to keep them fit," says Walker.

That night fairly quiet in the Command Post, Lt. Stewart Pride not feeling very well. "I must report sick in the morning," he says. "Any music on the wireless?"

I fiddle with the knobs. We are surrounded by hills and the reception is very bad. I get what sounds like someone singing in Yugoslavian.

"I don't understand, Milligan," says Stewart Pride, "you can't get our bloody OP, which is only half a mile away, yet you can get some idiot singing in Yugoslavia."

"That's because he's singing very loud, sir. If our signallers at the OP could be given training in opera, it would be easy."

It's two in the morning, bloody cold, Edgington has just come off Telephone Exchange duty, he comes into the Command Post for a warm. "Cor, it's taters," he says, making straight for the brazier. We all stand round it, the twigs crackling.

"What was the news tonight?" says Edgington.

"The Russians are advancing in all directions including upwards. The Allies are making steady progress, and Harry Roy is in hospital with appendicitis."

Edgington grins at Stewart Pride. "Do you like Harry Roy?" he says.

"I don't know, I've never met him," says Stewart Pride.

Buttoning up his overcoat Edgington bids us goodnight. "I will see 'ee in dawn's rosy light," and he slips under the canvas into the night.

We hear him fall in the dark and fade away swearing to himself. I shout through the canvas, "Don't forget, dawn's early light." Came the answer, "Balls." Oh what a lovely war. Not so lovely when we hear by the grapevine that our PBI are suffering 50 per cent casualties. Thank God I'm not in the Infantry. So ended Armistice Day, what a day to die.

FRIDAY, NOVEMBER 12, 1943

On this day my diary is blank. I think this is because I was too busy moving, as is borne out by Fildes' diary that says:

Move forward at 0500 hrs to new position. As usual the digging in the crackpot major loves so well. Beautiful country and orchard – mountains far away snow crested now. Lovely apples make place too much like England with green downs and autumn leaves. Xmas greetings mail being issued.

0500 hours! No wonder I didn't make any entry in the diary. However I have this excerpt from a letter I wrote home on the thirteenth and in it I say, ". . . today is like an English Summer's day, birds sing their repetitive little phrases, the village overlooking the field I'm in looks like a drawing from a Hans Andersen Fairy Story, excuse the writing but I'm laying down. . . ."

So where were we? The map reference was 999003 and that indicates a place called Monte Santa Maria. I never knew that Maria was Saint No. 999003.

OK. So what can I think up on the apple orchard position? . . . Well – like I said . . . it's a bit of a blur, except for the orchard itself which is very clear in memory – plus the view from the corner of it, of not-so-distant peaks,* snow-capped in the chilly Autumn morning, and rose-tinted, unmistakably, and spectacularly, in the early dawn light – the very first time I had ever seen, and I suspect a few other English city-dwellers like me, such a magnificent natural phenomenon.

If I can take a guess at the orientation in say the long axis of the raggedly-oval-shaped orchard, maybe sixty-eighty feet in length, was east-west, roughly, and those unearthly beautiful peaks were laying about south-east† as we peered southward over the thick hedge that completely surrounded the orchard. The altitude was accentuated by the fact the peaks seemed to be at about the same level as us across a deep valley** and to its east.

Of the apples in the orchard we identified at least six familiar types, though I'm sure there were considerably

*Abruzzi Mountains.
†Wrong. It was North. He's lost as usual.
**The Valley was the Garigliano Plain (Eh?).

110

more trees than that. Russets, Granny Smith's, Big
Canadian Reds, Cox's Orange Pippins were among those
I can still recall, while one tree had produced what Alf
and I concluded must have been a cross between an apple
and a pear, rather small, delicious to eat, and having a
quite marked perfume or scent into the bargain. I recall
that under each tree there was a veritable carpet of its
apples – windfalls – and the scene under the Big Canadian
Red tree was something to marvel at – the darkish-red,
highly-polished skins glistening with diamond-like drops
of moisture all catching the fitful shafts of sunlight just
breaking through the foliage. Only half an hour later or
maybe less we found ourselves being nearly suffocated by
the onset of a large patch of very dense mountain mist, the
minute droplets of water-vapour being concentrated as to
bring visibility down to almost nil and clog our breathing
alarmingly: it only lasted a few minutes but we got really
panicky in that time.

This coloured drawing – now that I've finished it – won't
mean much, if anything, to a stranger reading the book,
and the lads themselves – other than the Monkey 2 team –
may not recognise much of it, since the guns were virtually
out of sight from the road in the lower-level corner of the
next field, perhaps 200 yards or more from the road.

Edgington's crayon masterpiece, thirty years on

Certainly I've visualised it from a position nobody could possibly have occupied – twenty feet or so up in the air among the roadside trees of a fairly dense wood on the left hand side of the road as you came up it.

Edgington and I are off duty; to shelter from the unending rain we hole up in the back of someone's three-tonner. We chat about anything, we sing songs together, we like doing vocal arrangements. I play the trumpet part and Harry does the Bass accompaniment. We scrounge tea from Spike Deans. Lt. Joe Mostyn is passing by. I could see his Jewish soul burning with loathing of the war, not so much against the Germans, but the fact he was only on a Second Lieutenant's pay, when he really wanted to be in his schmutter shop in Whitechapel, doing mass-produced suits that all the Spivs would buy off the peg at five quid a go. I could see his gaze a long way from this muddy pit we were in, he was in the work-room, watching the girls on their machines, and fancying the one with the big boobs who was doing the padding in the shoulders. The times he had said to me, "Whoever designed the battle dress was a Schmock, the first thing to do when you dress a soldier is to make him look, or *think* he looks, attractive to the opposite sex, but look at this – " he would indicate my battle dress, " – no wonder the Yanks get all the women, what do you look like? A cripple! We *all* look like cripples! When we march past a saluting base, the natives think we're all going into a home for the deformed."

Yet, although he was never very good at Gunnery, or, as we used to call it, Goonery, he still was the man who kept the officers' mess topped up with little luxuries. I remember Lt. Walker coming to the Command Post, his eyes shining with orange sauce.

"Where in God's name did he get a duck in this wilderness?" At the Apple Orchard position, Mostyn detailed three Gunners who spent all day collecting sacks of apples, he gets the cookhouse to stew them, and for several weeks there was apple purée on the table. Mind you, he was suffering; his family were all Kosher, and he had started off following the Kosher diet, but as the war entered its second year he gradually became "christianised", the great temptation was upon him. At the rest camp at Amalfi, he was offered a plate of shellfish. Strained to breaking point, he said (according to

112

Lt. Walker), "Why should I go on being hated by Hitler for being Jewish? I'm going to take the pressure off." So saying, he plunged into the dish, beating his breast and shouting, "Mother! Forgive me, but *eat*, Joe, *EAT*."

Yes, Joe Mostyn was an unforgettable character. I last saw him in the foyer of the Cumberland Hotel at Marble Arch in 1952. He was a bit offish with me, and seemed loath to talk, but he did impart the info that he was "Teaching the Israeli Army Gunnery". If so, but for him the Six Day War would have been over in two.

The war is gradually having its effect on the officers. Bdr. Sherwood is at the foot of a hill on which our OP is sited. He is in his little bivvy by his bren carrier when the link phone buzzes. In Sherwood's own words this is what transpired.

SHERWOOD: OP. Link Answering.

LT. BUDDEN: Ah, Sherwood?

SHERWOOD: Yes, sir.

LT. BUDDEN: I'm bored.

SHERWOOD: What you want me to do, sir?

A PAUSE, SLIGHT BREATHING, THEN

LT. BUDDEN: Sing.

SHERWOOD: (*Singing*) Lay that Pistol down Babe,
Lay that Pistol Down, Pistol Packin'
Momma, lay that pistol down.

(He continues thus till the song is finished.)

LT. BUDDEN: Thank you.

SATURDAY, NOVEMBER 13, 1943

Because of the OP's field of view, and a thousand feet height added to the guns' range, the targets are never ending. Despite the cold the gunners are actually sweating. A casualty! my boots are leaking. I examine them seated in the back of G truck. White passes by sipping tea.

He stops. "What's on?"

"My boots are leaking."

"Oh? Outwards?"

"Outwards my arse, the bloody water's getting *in*, Jerry's

Above: *Lt. Cecil Budden, taken just before the asbestos roof behind nearly decapitated him. Today he is alive and well and living in Essex.*

got the right idea. Jack Boots, no lace holes. Great.''

"Have you tasted the apples here?''

"Not yet.''

"They're bloody marvellous, better than English ones, full of juice.''

Army conversations were unique, from leaking boots to apples in one line. I reported to the Quarter Master Courtney for new boots, he makes me take mine off and examines them. "Like a jeweller's glass,'' I said sarcastically.

"Well,'' he says, "we haven't got your size, see; you take an eight, we've only got twelves.''

"Twelves? TWELVES? Christ!''

"Take it or leave it.''

A choice! Size twelves or bare feet. It was like wearing landing barges. I used to haul myself around in the mud walking like Frankenstein's monster, my feet kept coming out of the bloody things, and I had to stand on one leg trying to tug the monster boot out of the mud. It was impossible, I told the Quarterbloke and he relented. "I'll send a truck to Base Depot and get you a pair of eights.''

The new size eights arrive and are like iron. They have been in store since World War 1. I have to attack them with a hammer to break them down. I cover them with great loads of dubbin, put them near the fire; I watched those boots absorb two pounds of dubbin, with a noise of Glug Glug. "The bloody things are alive,'' said Gunner White, watching fascinated as the boots devoured the dubbin. After half an hour's battering with a Tent Peg Mallet I tried them on. Great! they were as soft as buckskin.

We have news that 17 Battery has had a premature. No one killed but one gunner injured. This was strange as the gun had just come back from workshops, where it had been repaired for a previous premature.

SUNDAY, NOVEMBER 14, 1943

REGIMENTAL DIARY: *Weather once again wet windy and cold* (That sounded like most of us.).

ALF FILDES' DIARY: *Rain making things awkward.*

BDR. MILLIGAN'S DIARY: GAVE BOOTS ANOTHER GOOD
HAMMERING.

Lt. Budden is a greeny-yellow colour when he enters the
Command Post.

"You look off colour, sir – yellow to be precise," I said
sympathetically.

"No, I feel jolly rotten."

Jolly rotten?

"I've just come to collect my prismatic compass." He goes
to a little ledge, picks up a few belongings. He looks dreadful.
"I'm going into hospital, Milligan."

"Congratulations, sir."

He manages a wry smile and exits. I will miss him, he is a
splendid fellow; the only trouble was, he didn't understand
Jazz.

We are visited by Vic Nash, who has just come back from
the OP with Jam-Jar Griffin.

"What a bloody time," he says. "Fuckin' mud and fuckin'
shells, and fuckin' Jerry dead stinking away, now I've discovered I've got bloody Dhobi's Itch."

MONDAY, NOVEMBER 15, 1943

TORRENTIAL RAIN

I thought we'd had the heaviest rain possible, but now,
today, it is unbelievable! It's so damp that even under cover
you get wet. The only good thing is the rum ration. I can't
stand the taste of it, I keep it in my water bottle and put it
in my tea during the night shift. We bake apples and chestnuts by our Command Post fire. The path to the Command
Post is very slippery and poor old George Shipman slid off it
last night down a sixty-foot bank; he entered the Command
Post covered in slimy mud. "I just fell over the bank," he
said.

"I thought they were closed on Mondays."

There's a lot of illness in the Regiment, we are well below
full strength, especially me. It's come to something, our
Medical Officer, Captain Bentley, is in hospital with "Chinese Flu" (Jaundice). 15 and 18 Batteries have been pulled out
of the line for a rest, and their guns are at REME Workshops

in Naples. The Attack on Monte Camino was halted because of appalling weather. All that blood-letting for nothing. After the war a note in the 14th Panzer Corps (they were defending Camino) Diary for 13th states, "THE ENEMY HAS WON THE BATTLE FOR THE MIGNANO GAP!" . . . that was the day that General Mark Clark had told Alexander that we would have to suspend the offensive because our troops were exhausted. Kismet.

Our Gunners are so shagged, they have been falling asleep on the guns; Signallers, Specialists and Karzi attendants are all rounded up to do a spell on them. The Gunners sleep in their tents and don't even wake up for meals. The platforms of the guns are nothing more than pools of mud three feet deep. For the first time the entire Regiment is out of action. A strange silence settles on us.

"I can't sleep," says Signaller White. "It's too bloody quiet."

We all sit in our tents, watching the mountain of water falling.

"I've worked out that the rest of the world must be bone bloody dry!" says Edgington, putting a damp cigarette in his mouth.

"Cheer up," I said.

"Why?"

"I don't know why, give me time, I'll think of a reason."

TUESDAY, NOVEMBER 16, 1943

We have both run across to the cookhouse with our gas capes over our heads, it's early morning and what a treat! someone has got us a *fried egg* each for breakfast.

"Oh, magnificent egg," I intoned.

"Egg! oh Egg!" echoed Edgington like a Shakespearean actor. "I feel a powerful inspiration on the egg coming to me." He then launched into, "Oh long live the fried egg, even though for it we have to beg. The fact that these eggs are Italian, will have us bound up like a. . . ." I couldn't think of a rhyme, then Edgington says, "Like a stallion."

"Did you hear Jerry's long-range guns last night?" I said.

"Noo, I wasn't on duty, for once I had a good kip."

A period of eating and tea sipping.

"Here; last night I picked up some jazz from Naples AFN, they had a half-hour of Goodman with Charlie Christian on guitar, it was bloody marvellous, then about ten minutes of Jimmy Lunceford, they played that great sax arrangement of *Sleepy Time Gal*, it was great, I think Willy Smith was on first Alto, what a great lead he is."

"I wonder when we'll ever play again."

"Alf's guitar strings are all going rusty. He's going to try to get some new ones when he gets a trip into Naples."

Bombardier Fuller is calling for me. Despite my silence he finds me. "We're going to move soon."

"In this bloody weather?"

"In this weather . . . there's no rush, but start getting things ready, we can close down on Wireless, but we're keeping the OP Line open."

"Ours is but to do and die – and try and get bloody dry!" says Edgington.

It continues as a nothing day, we attempt to write letters. Some play cards, some sleep, some just sit and stare. New Disaster, the shit-pit has been flooded by the rain so it's all floating around the landscape; poor Sgt. Jock Wilson and his crew are all gently sleeping in their tent when the contents of the Shit-Pit float under the tent flaps. Chaos.

In anticipation of the moves the order goes out that all vehicles will have the tyre chains on. Drivers get into the most appalling state carrying out the order.

"Surely," says Edgington, "this rain must be longer than Queen Victoria's."

"Let's go to the Command Post," I said. "See what's on the wireless."

We double across, giving off our usual Red Indian War Whoops. In the Command Post, Vic Nash and Bombardier Edwards have folded up the Artillery Board and are packing the remaining bits and pieces.

The fire is glowing red, Edgington and I settle by it. We steam in the near heat. It was the only refuge in a grim world of mud and cold.

"I wonder what wondrous fairyland they are taking us to," says Deans. He takes a cigarette from his tin.

Little Vic Nash, "Give us one, I'm clean out."

Deans hands the tin across.

"Fucking Vs! These are personal fuckin' insults," says Nash, but still takes one. "It won't fukin' well light."

"You have to dry the bloody thing out first," advises Deans in sage-like voice.

"You know, I wrote to my MP in London about these bloody Vs, and said it was a disgrace that we had to smoke the bloody things."

"Did you get a reply?"

"Yes, he said there was nothing that could be done because these fags are made in India, and it's easier to ship fags from India to Italy than from England; he put a packet of twenty Players in a parcel and wished me good luck."

"Well, you don't appear to have had any," said Edgington.

"Have you see this," says Deans and hands us a page torn from the *Union Jack*, the Army newspaper . . . I was so smitten with what I read I copied it out.

Corridors of Power. MKI

General: Leaps tall buildings with a single bound. More powerful than a steam engine, faster than a speeding bullet. Gives policy to GOD.

Colonel: Leaps short buildings with a single bound. More powerful than a shunting engine. Is just as fast as a speeding bullet. Walks on water (if the sea is calm). Talks with GOD.

Lt.-Colonel: Leaps short buildings with a running start in favourable winds. Is almost as powerful as a speeding bullet. Walks on water in indoor swimming pools. Talks with GOD if special request is approved.

Major: Barely clears a Nissen hut. Loses tug-of-war with a steam engine. Can fire a speeding bullet and swims well. Is occasionally addressed by GOD.

Captain: Makes high marks when trying to leap tall buildings. Is run over by trains. Can sometimes handle a gun without inflicting self injury. Dog paddles, talks to animals.

Lieutenant: Runs into tall buildings. Recognises trains two out of three times. Is not issued with ammunition. Can stay afloat if properly instructed in the use of a lifejacket. Talks to walls.

118

2nd Lieutenant: Falls over doorsteps while trying to enter buildings. Says, "Look at Choo Choo." Is NEVER issued with a gun or ammunition. Plays in mud puddles. Mumbles to himself.

Sgt.-Major: Lifts tall buildings and walks under them. Kicks steam-engines off the track. Catches speeding bullets in his teeth and eats them. Freezes water with a single glance . . . HE IS GOD!

This occasion was at Santa Maria. The weather was bitter cold. The rain had stopped. For some reason, we had nowhere to sleep, so Edgington, Pedlar Palmer, Trew, Fuller and myself made a giant bed right out in the open. First we laid down a huge canvas Gun sheet. On that we all made our beds in a square, all feet towards the middle. That done, we laid over the top yet another giant canvas Gun sheet. I'm still desperate to remember *why* we did it, so I ring up Edgington in New Zealand, he recalls the occasion, but again the reason is unexplained.

ME: Harry?

H: Yes, is that you, mate?

ME: Yes, it's me, mate.

H: Cor strewth, what's the time there?

ME: It's ten past eleven here in the morning.

H: It's ten past ten at night here.

ME: Good night.

H: Good morning.

ME: Harry, I'm on Volume 4 of the war memoirs, now Rocamanfina . . . and Terra Corpo . . . do you remember the occasion of the great bed?

H: Cor yes, we did it right out in the open, we used gun canvas.

ME: Good! Can you remember why we did it?

H: Yes.

ME: Why?

H: We were all bloody balmy.

ME: I know that, but was there any other reason? Were we short of tents?

H: No, sanity.

So there we have it. In that bed we slept like babes. Alas

119

for Edgington, in the middle of the night someone from the Command Post tells us, "The line to the OP has broken." No one answered except the innocent Edgington. He gets up, and in his words, "I don't know why no one else heard the call. [I know.] I got up and for some reason didn't lace up my boots. I started to trace the line. I reached a stream that was so churned up by crossing motor traffic, the water was like porridge. I found the break, but had to cross the stream which was about three feet deep. On my return, I took my boots into the Command Post, which had the brazier burning. I was too tired, I just threw my boots in the fire and waiting for them to dry I fell asleep sitting up. Next morning I took my boots from the embers, they were snow white and as hard as iron. To soften them I had to soak them in water again." End of Edgington bit.

When the remaining Giant Bed sleepers awoke at dawn, the gun canvas was covered white with frost, yet I remember I had slept soundly and warm. End of Milligan bit.

I had been feeling a bit groggy all day. I could feel a cold coming on, so I dosed myself with hot tea and rum.

The 16th ended like it had started, with thunderous deluges of cold rain. It numbed the mind, the body and sapped the morale. My sleeping "Quarters"? I had found a small embankment. In it I noticed a crevice that was about the length of a man lying down. It was recessed back about five feet, and from this I made a small, very dry, little sleeping quarters. There was only room for the bed, my small pack and an oil lamp.

By astute placing of my gas cape and some "acquired" waterproof sheeting, I had made it rainproof. About ten that rain-swept evening, I lifted up the flap of my "den", climbed in, removed my soggy boots, trousers and jacket, and eased myself into the dank blankets. I left the oil lamp burning for a while to give a little cheer to the gloom. Thoughts tumbled through my head – home, jazz, women, leave, money.

I take another swig from the rum ration in my water bottle, ghastly, I take another swig from my rum ration, ghastly. . . . I take a swig from my rig ration. I take a rash from my swig.

WEDNESDAY, NOVEMBER 17, 1943

The BBC News: "Heavy rain in Italy is slowing the Allied advance." (Advance? What advance?) Today was a crisis day, the drivers tell us of chaos on the roads: flooding and cataclysmic subsidence has all but brought traffic to a halt. A Recce party return with the news that we have a new gun position at 966976.

"Come to romantic 966976 and take the waters, wallow in health-giving mud baths." I am saying all this from my den when Edgington's voice draws nigh.

"Hist! I hear a voice from yon catacomb." He pops his head under the gas cape. "Come on, I'm off to brekker."

The rain is running down the gas cape he holds over his head. I still feel groggy, but I don my clothes; together we slurp-slurp-slither towards the cookhouse. It's in a large tent among the apple trees. At the serving table stand Ronnie May and Charlie Booth. They've been up since six making the grub. Again! A fried *egg*! some spam stuff, bread, jam and tea.

Slip-slop-slur we go, sheltering the food under our capes. The Command Post fire is almost out. Wenham is inside, disconnecting the "Dags".

"I'm leavin' two new ones," he says in his Sussex burr.

Lt. Wright comes in behind us. "Oh dear, who's let the fire out?"

We quickly add more twigs. The twigs are very damp, but when they burn have a lovely applewood smell.

Still no firing, we call up the OP. Lt. Walker wants to speak to Lt. Wright, they pass pleasantries, he hands me back the phone. I speak to Bdr. Eddie Edwards.

"What's it like up there?"

"Bloody wet, Jerry is very quiet, it's live and let live at the moment, though he did a bit of mortaring around us last night."

"Don't come back here, you'll be killed by boredom. Is it dry up there?"

"Yes, we're in a building, what's left of it."

"I give up. What's left of it?" I laugh.

"You silly bugger."

"You know the guns are out of action."

121

"Yes, I know, but we've got to stay here for Observation, we've been flash-spotting Jerry guns at night."

"Well, I'm just going to finish me tea. See ya."

To emulate the events that happened the rest of the day, carry out the following exercise: pour three buckets of water over yourself, face a blank wall and chain smoke.

THURSDAY, NOVEMBER 18, 1943

Today was, as Sean O'Casey said, "A state of Chassis". Everything is now mud brown – men, machines, trees, mountains, apples. I hear Edgington singing "It's a Brown World without you" to the tune of "It's a Blue World without you". I try and match it with "When the Brown of the Night meets the Brown of the Day, someone waits for me". He tops that with "When you hear that serenade in Brown". I go on with "Brown Moon, I saw you standing alone". I sing "Am I Brown," he sings "St Louis Browns" then "In

Muddy conditions

122

my dear little Alice Brown Gown".

"Brown Skies".

"Brown Birds over the Brown Cliffs of Dover".

We have to be ready by mid-day. The only way to get the guns out of the mud is tractors. We are to try the Americans.

"Americans?" gasps our Major. "No, we must never sink that low."

"We *are* sunk that low, that's why we need them," we informed him. To our aid came three giant American tractors. They eventually help us on to the road facing northeast; Fuller revs up his motor bike.

"Follow me," he says, and goes straight into the ditch. It was all too much.

We leap out and pull the bike off him. What *did* he look like??? His face had disappeared; he is now convulsed with laughter.

I am now travelling with Ernie Hart, a thin cadaverous face, the rims of his eyes always looked red and sore. He was a nice lad with a quiet sense of humour, so quiet no one ever heard it. I tell him our destination.

"San Domenico?" he repeated, "lots of Sans in this country."

"Yes, sans fags, sans money, sans every bloody thing."

Behind us we can see Monkey 1 Truck, Webster's face showing occasionally through the windscreen wipers. Behind that a line of our vehicles at varying distances. A sign, "You are travelling over this bridge by courtesy of the USA 345 Bridge Building Co.".

We could do with more of this, "These shell-holes are by courtesy of the 74 Medium Regiment" or "This devastated landscape comes to you by courtesy of the 5th Army," or a sign pinned to oneself, "This crummy battle dress comes to you by courtesy of our mean bloody Quarterbloke".

Jerry has made a thorough job in blowing all the bridges, every one we cross has been laboriously replaced with a Bailey. Total weight of a gun plus the Scammell is nearly twenty-five tons; they have to slow up when crossing, and gradually the light trucks pull ahead of the gun convoy. The torrential rain forces us to pull down the back canvas of the truck.

We have stopped (big deal), we hear raised voices, a large

lorry has slidden off the road. The driver's face covered in blood, he is being hauled up from below; other mud-saturated figures are helping him into another truck; they all have to shout above the roar of the deluge. It's like a school for the deaf. We are off at a snail's pace. God knows how drivers can cope.

"Can you see where you're goin'?" calls Hart through to poor Driver Masters.

"No," comes the reply, "I'm driving in Braille."

It's about mid-day, or if you go by the light, midnight. We have been halted on a road; to our right, looming over us are Monte Santa Croce and Monte Mattone, both over 600 to 1,000 feet. They run east to west on a range that ends up near the coast with Monte Massico, 800 feet. "They ought to keep the draught out," says Hart. All that day we were truckbound by rain; if and when the bloody stuff stopped, we debussed and stretched our legs. There is no sign or word of the cookhouse.

"I think under the circumstances we should surrender," I said.

Somehow the cooks have managed to juggle up a hot meal, a temporary affair of two lorries about ten feet apart, with a canvas spread over to cover the area between. In it they have done the impossible. HOT DINNER! As I collected mine I told Ronnie May I was writing to Buckingham Palace to recommend him for an award.

"Never mind the bloody award," he says. "Ask them for some fucking matches that aren't damp. I have to sleep with mine in me pocket, otherwise this bloody mob wouldn't get any hot grub."

"Let me help," I said dramatically. "I would consider it an honour to sleep with your matches tonight."

Bombardier Fuller explains. "When this bloody rain stops, we got to dig the Command Post over there – " He points to a small land area about thirty feet below us in a valley. "We dig into that bank, the ten line exchange will go in that cave to the left – " he indicates a small cave " – and to the left of that, I think there's a cave big enough to take the Monkey Truck Mob." Poor Fuller, he's up to his eyebrows in mud; riding a motor bike in this weather is like going over the Niagara Falls in a gas stove.

The rain stops. I found a bank on the road, under the cover of a large tree; with my motley collection of boxes, tins, boards, etc., I rigged up a bed and got my tent into position. It was very damp, but at least I could kip in the "dead" position. The proximity of passing traffic to my bed was but a few feet, however, I had a "home". Before turning in, I listen to the BBC Overseas six o'clock broadcast:

"The Germans are pulling out to pre-prepared positions called the Gustav Line."

Mussolini is in Verona as head of the Provisional Fascist Government. The Russians continue their relentless advance even in midwinter. How *do* they do it? Here we were standing still: a German Propaganda Poster of the time reflects our predicament.

WEDNESDAY, NOVEMBER 19, 1943

Thank God today is SUNNY.

"Look," I shouted, kneeling and pointing a quivering finger aloft, "the sun, I tell 'ee it's the sun. People says ois darft, but I tell 'ee that's the sun. I 'eard people in England say if they sees the sun they report it to the police."

"Yes, yes," says Bombardier Fuller. "And that," he says, pointing, "is a shovel. Start fucking digging."

"I realise", says Vic Nash, "that with all the diggin' I've done out here I must have changed the shape of Italy"

Vic is short, about five foot five, looks Jewish but isn't. He was a pastry cook in the Old Kent Road before the war, but is now digging Command Posts.

"Why didn't they put me in the Army Catering Corps?"

"You should have asked," said Bombardier Trew.

"I did ask," said Nash, a note of exasperation. "I said look, I'm a pastry cook by trade, can I go in the catering Corps?"

Nash pauses, lights a cigarette. "The Sergeant said, 'Of course, you're lucky, they need cooks in the Royal Artillery.' So I thought I was safe, but now, fuck it! Look at this lot." He held up a shovel coagulated with mud.

We freeze as the sound of planes is heard. Whose are they, where are they? . . . they loom into view from the south.

"Bostons," says Trew.

Their engines are labouring under the weight of bombs, above them and to the right are a squadron of Kittyhawks. Americans!

"For Christ sakes don't move," warns Edgington, "or they'll 'ave us."

They move majestically towards the Abruzzi Mountains, Jerry flack peppering the air around them.

"It's astounding that so few planes get hit," said Deans, peering at the conflict with his right hand shading his eyes.

"Well," I said, "it's very difficult for the shell and the plane to be in the same place at the same time. By the law of averages it can't happen too often."

"Ooooooom, 'ark at bloody Einstein," says Nash, tapping his head with his finger. "I say this, the shell with yer number on will get you no matter where you're standin', for all we know there's one on the way to us now."

I cupped my hand to my ear and leaned forward. "List! I think I can hear it now . . . no . . . wait . . . no, it's not for you, it's for . . . for Mrs Ada Grolledes of Brockley."

Even as I spoke, a plume of smoke starts to trail from one of the Bostons.

"They've got one," shouted Ernie Hart enthusiastically.

The Boston turned in a slow circle and started to head back to base, we watched as it jettisoned its bombs. The smoke was still trailing from its port engine as it passed into the distance in the direction of what must have been Foggia aerodrome.

"I bet there's a few shitty underpants up there," said Edgington grimly.

"There's a lot of shitty underpants down 'ere," said Nash, who hadn't been able to get a bath for nearly ten days. The Boston gradually diminishes into the nothingness of distance.

"That made a nice little break," said Ernie Hart.

It sounded heartless, but things like planes on fire were all the real entertainment we had. If a lorry crashed in a ditch, men would come from all over to see it pulled out again, anything to break the boredom.

"There's a fortune awaiting the man who can invent portable holes. Edgington says this with a strained voice as he hurls a shovel of mud. There is a pause, then I sing:

> "Oles . . . Portable 'Oleeees
> They'd be useful to all the troops
> including the Poles.
> Yes we need 'oless, portable 'oles."

I'm stuck for words, so Edgington continues:

> "It would save us all for havin'
> to dig like bloody moles."

He's stuck, I continue:

> "Shovelling lumps of mud
> Is very bad for me.
> When I started I was six foot one
> But now I'm four foot three."

The flow of the muse is interrupted by the dreaded Major Evan Jenkins. He walks with his torso bent forward at a

" 'ere's me nose, me arse is following" angle. He looks at the hole.

"Why aren't you digging under a camouflage net?" he said, his little beady eyes boring into our souls. The answer came very simple:

"We 'aven't got one, sir."

"Send someone *at once* to Wagon Lines and draw one."

"Yes, sir," says Fuller, but the inflection sounded like "You bastard." "Bombardier Hart, take Monkey Truck and collect a scrim net."

Hart grins, he offs and soon we watch Monkey Truck pull away up the road. Jenkins is still trouble-hunting.

"Have you a track plan?"

"Yes, sir," I said.

"Where is it?"

Hurriedly I invented the track plan. "We keep to the edge of the drop and when we reach the road we turn right under the trees, sir."

"Mmmm," was all he said.

A track plan was this: so as not to leave new trails all over the landscape, we all kept to one path to draw less attention from Jerry observation planes. As the entire landscape was one great churned-up mud bath it didn't matter where you walked or drove, as the water in the mud washed away all traces of a track, but to keep the peace we pretended. We watched him as he dutifully walked along the edge of the drop keeping to the "track plan" that didn't exist. He did stop and pause once and look back as though he didn't believe me, then he walked on. Fuck him.

We continue combined digging and moaning. By evening we have a large dank Command Post ready. First thing, the fire!!! After the addition of twigs and a tin full of Derv, whoooosh, it ignites and settles down to give a friendly warmth. We hide inside for a while as Ben Wenham fixes up the lights.

"Lazy buggers," he says, seeing us all huddled around the fire.

"Lazy buggers," explodes Edgington. "Where were you when the shit hit the fan?"

Specialists are coming in with their gear. Signallers are setting up the No. 22 wireless set, connecting up the batteries. Mr Wright is duty officer, he ducks under our black-out curtain and surveys our efforts, "Very nice, ten out of ten." Ernie Hart has come in with extra firewood. "And what nice gunner is going to help bring in the Yule log?" He throws the firewood in a corner.

Yule log! My God! It would soon be December. . . . The first away from home.

"Out of the bloody way," says Shapiro, who backs in with a drum of Don 5 Cable. Behind him comes Pinchbeck, they've been laying a line from the OP and are well covered in muck.

"Where would you like it, me Lord?" says Shapiro.

I point to a spot by the wireless. Pinchbeck is baring the two wires with his pliers, and with professional deftness connects the telephone and buzzes the OP. Shapiro watches, a cigarette between his lips. Pinchbeck buzzes again, a look of anxiousness on his face. If the line isn't through, it means they have to traverse the whole bloody line again to find what's wrong. Pinchbeck smiles.

"Hello, OP? OK? . . . Yes, fine here . . . what? You'll be bloody lucky." He grins and hangs up. "Cheeky buggers, they want to know if tea will be served on the lawn."

"Who was it?" I said.

"Jam-Jar."

"Tea on the lawn," mocks Ernie Hart. "Where 'e lives he 'asn't got a bloody lawn."

"That is a truth," says Edgington pontifically, rubbing his hands together. "Let's face it, like us he is a common or garden citizen."

". . . and", I added, "as we haven't got a garden or a common, that's why we're in this bloody hole in the ground."

"Grub up," a voice from outside speaks and enters by pushing a dixie of hot stew, followed by a hand then a body belonging to Bombardier Edwards. There is a mass exodus, but I am clutched by the arm.

"You stay and make like you're on duty," says Bombardier Fuller.

Bugger! I seek solace in a fag. Opposite me, Lt. Wright sits on a wooden box reading a book. It made little difference if he was sitting on a book reading a wooden box. It's all very cushy, with the fire going, with headphones on I'm wrapped up with the music. A tap on the shoulder, turning I see Ernie Hart.

"I come to release you from your bondage."

"What's for dinner?"

"It's M & V again."

"They *must* run out of it *one* day!"

The batmen and slave labour have built a very fine officers' mess cum billet, they have laboured the long day to achieve it, "Woody" (Jenkins' Batman) tells us.

"Next we's goin' to build a bloody 'otel with hot worter."

NOVEMBER 20, 1943

The morning of November 20 burst cheerily on us with an exciting cold downpour. Gad! It was good to be alive, the question was, were we? We are concluding the finishing touches on the Command Post, a sandbagged blast wall on the open side of the dug-out. There are many brilliant minds at work in the war, Radar, Infra-Red Telescopes, Mulberry Harbours, but no bugger has invented how to get wet mud into a sandbag. We are almost pouring it in. When we seal the sandbag the mixture starts to squeeze through the hessian like thin spaghetti! We fill them to bursting, yet when we lay another bag on top, it flattens like a wafer.

"This isn't a job," moans one miserable Gunner. "This is a bloody sentence!"

17 Battery tell us they have managed to fire twenty rounds in the afternoon.

"The bloody fools," says Alf Fildes, "if we all kept quiet Jerry would pack up and go home."

Gunner Birch is amusing his little mind by standing on the sandbag and giggling as it sprouts myriad growths of mud spaghetti.

"'Ere," he says in a surprised voice, "it's sexy."

"Sexy," says Bombardier Fuller. "You must be bloody hard up for it if you get the Colin' watchin' that."

Across the road a Battery of 3.7s let off a salvo of gunfire. The noise is such that all conversation is silent, we start miming, and it gets out of hand; Edgington is caught in the middle of an involved mime standing on one leg and

130

licking the back of his right hand.

"I give up, what was it?" I said. "A one-legged man eating a toffee apple?"

We are silenced again by the 3.7s. While we cavorted in the mud, in the bright sunlit days on the Dodecanese the British are losing the Greek Islands to the Germans. It's all on the News, in slanted terms. "British troops are fighting a 'skilful' retreat on the Isle of Leros. HQ Middle East Command say 'The more we delay them, the better it is for us.'" As we listen to this statement the faces of the Gunners break into wry disbelieving smiles, who are they kidding?

"It must be for home consumption," says Trew. "My mother would listen to that and think we were winnin'."

It was strange coming from him because it was a fact that when Trew had sent his first photo of himself in Italy to his family, they wrote back and asked if we were losing. Birch had sent his photo (taken by a street photographer) back to his sweetheart, and she wrote back asking who it was. The worst was Gunner Collins, his family sent his photo back marked "Not known at this address'. My mother, father and brother had sent me a photo intended to boost my morale, taken by a neighbour in Brentwood. When I saw it I thought they were all convalescing from rabies. They were all white-faced, with fixed false-teeth smiles and staring eyes. The explanation was it was taken by magnesium flash, badly printed, and the photographer, Mr Wheel had asked them to "Open your eyes wide" to get a good expression. The result, dead people standing up.

Deans, Nash and Fildes have done a great job on their bivvy. It now has a fireplace, and so in the evenings Harry and I go in for a warm. It was one evening with the rain running in rivers that we cooked up a tune, "The Rocaman-fina Rhumba". From somewhere I had obtained an ocarina, and with Edgington banging on a box of matches we gradually bring the tune to life. The lyrics were:

The Rhumba	Caramba!
Roca-manfina Rhumba	All the natives say
It's a snappy little number	Caramba.
Roca-mana-fina way.	Rocamanfina Rhumba
	Rocamanfina way.

It was in the charts for about three weeks, but it never became a hit. Jam-Jar Griffin comes in, he's heard the music.

"Is this where all the action is?" he says, his bulk blocking the entrance. What a waistline! just under his armpits. It seemed wider than his shoulders, when he "jitterbugged" he appeared to be wearing a lifebelt under his jacket.

"Bloody Jerry officer at the OP! said the war would last another two years!"

"I think he's right," I said.

"Oh," says Griffin, "he's *right*, but . . . it was the *arrogant way he said it*, as though *he* was personally making it last two years. I told him where to bloody well get off, I said *we* could finish the war tomorrow, we just keep it going so we could kill off as many of you bastards as we can."

"That's no way to talk to an officer," I said. "Under the Geneva Convention he could report you for swearing at a prisoner of war and you'd be fined 10/- and a week to pay."

Jam-Jar puffed up in anger. *"Swearing* at him? He's lucky I didn't fuck him."

I understood his feelings, being at the OP is no holiday, being mortared and shelled along with infantry attacks starts to build up a "hate". Whenever I was at the OP and saw any of our dead or wounded I really felt burned up with rage. Having lost many friends in the fighting it's very hard to take a passive view. . . . Gunner Forest had just come in

Jam-Jar Griffin about to be run over by a jeep.

our tent and asked if anybody could "read a letter to him". Edgington volunteered; the letter readdressed from his parents' home.

"Prepare yourself for a slight shock," said Edgington. "From the Borough of Ealing. Rates overdue up to the month of July 1940. Three pounds eighteen shillings. If not paid within twenty days proceedings will be taken."

Forest rose, took the letter! "Fookin' 'ell. A fookin' rates demand."

At six o'clock it's as black as a nigger's bum at midnight; still no news of any firing. Rain. Deans is in his cooking mood and about to hurl on to us a giant long flour-and-water pudding with curried cabbage inside. It's christened the Mongoid Monster.

"I think we're bloody lucky, all this grub, steaming hot, tea, marmalade duff to follow, high-altitude chocolate ration. . . ." Edgington stops to poke some grub between his dinner manglers. "Those poor bloody Infantry lads, up in the front. . . ."

"You're telling me," says Jam-Jar. "The last OP we could only get grub up by mules and they were lucky not to be eaten. . . . Oh yer, it's cushy back here, this – " he looked around the humble interior. "This is fucking luxury."

"I am going to stagger you," I said. "Luxury? You don't know what it means."

I was feeling in my pockets for a tin of Manikin Cheroots that my father had sent in advance of Christmas. With a great gesture I took the brown tin, opened it and let their eyes feast on it.

"Corrrr. Cigars!!!" Edgington shouted, then putting on his cross-eyed Ritz Brothers look, he took one with old world flourish and with a new world flourish stuck it behind his ear. The aroma after dinner was that of a London Club after the Port, we all felt relaxed, so we continued with our Ocarina, Guitar and Matchbox concert, this time with others joining in on empty mugs and tins. We sang and yarned until eleven o'clock, mad midnight fools that we were! Harry Edgington is singing a song he wrote to his unborn child:

> "Your mum and I
> We spent a lifetime apart

133

And through the war years
We knew our heartaches
But that's over now
And you've made your bow
To your mum and I."

We are all very moved, but not the 3.7 Gunners behind us, who let fly a shattering barrage. That wound up the concert. Good nights. In my damp roadside bed, with traffic a few feet from my head, I fall asleep to the tyre marks on my head.

NOVEMBER 21, 1943

MY DIARY: SUNNY EARLY MORNING. RUSH TO HANG BLANKETS OUT TO DRY.

ALF FILDES' DIARY: *Began sunny but developed into the usual rain.*

REGIMENTAL DIARY: *At mid-day 19 battery reported 2 guns ready for action. Bombard fired. Little improvement in weather.*

MRS GRONKS' DIARY: *Cat died. Cancelled milk.*

My watch points the hour of ...???? My watch has stopped. Bombardier Syd "Butcher" Price, he knows about watches.

Bombardier Syd "Butcher" Price wearing whitewashed boots for locating in the dark.

134

"You have to wind it up, you see," he said.

How silly of me. Down in our little valley there is a small stream where women of the village do laundry. I approach one who is only too glad to accept my chocolate ration to do it, her name is Maria. *Everybody* in Italy is called Maria, the men, the dogs, the trees.

With two guns nearly ready for firing, we're all back on duty. Monkey 2 truck takes a party up the line to see if it's still there. I have a good look around the area, there must be a hundred artillery pieces packed into a half mile square, ah!! Bombardier Marsden is up with the rations! A mob are assembled around the tailboard of the 15-cwt truck. Marsden and Dai Poole used to run the Naafi issue, Dai was stone deaf. If you gave him a hundred lire note with twenty lire change to come, he would put it into the cash box and ignore you. Repeated requests for change were met with deaf indifference. He must have made a fortune. After the war I saw him once, at a Symphony Concert. A strange disease has shown itself: Diesel Dermatitis, it's mostly among the drivers. Doug Kidgell has his face covered in a purple dye.

"What is it?" I said.

"It's called Gentian Violet."

"You look like a leper."

"Yes. I've got a beggin' bowl in me cab," he giggled. He was up from the Wagon Lines to help winch some of the guns into position. "We're behind that village over there," he pointed towards San Domenica. This was Coletti, where RHQ were now ensconced in comfort; the dream of every Gunner was to get a job at RHQ, usually in a house, and thus home from home. At this moment that skinny bugger Evan Jenkins was in charge at RHQ in the absence of Colonel Scorsbie, who had left to visit the Regimental training area and visit ''the sick in Naples Hospital''.

"Visit the *sick*?" said Kidgell. "Who does he think he is, Florence Nightingale?"

"No," I said, "he's more like Florence Nightingoon, the Lady with the Lump."

Mick Ryan is calling: "Kidgell . . . never mind orl dat chattin', come and help get dis bluddy gun on der platform."

"Comin', Sarge," says Kidgell, and waddles (yes waddles, the short arse) away.

"Quack, quack," I shout after him; he doesn't turn, but raises two fingers behind his back. I'm laughing when a lorry passes and speckles me with mud. What's this? I'm on duty starting at 11.30 through till 2.30 along with Birch. Loaded with my writing pad, old *Life* magazines and two Mars bars from my Naafi purchases, I set myself up in the Command Post. Lt. Pride is there, he has his boot off, trying to hammer down a nail with a stone.

"We start firing at 0100, Bombardier," he said.

"On one leg apparently."

"If needs be, Milligan, yes."

"I will not stand in the way of a one-legged order, sir," I said.

Bombardier Deans is doing various computations on the Artillery board with a pencil that I swear is half an inch long.

"Who's at the OP?" I asked.

"Lt. Walker, Nash, Griffin and Bombardier Edwards. I don't know which signallers." He cringes and says, "You won't report me for that, will 'ee young master?"

Trouble with wireless communication; surrounded by mountains, reception is down to strength 3, I put up the extension aerial, no go. We have to transmit by talking in little dots and dashes, a test of one's ability to remember morse code. I had a Charlie on the other end from RHQ who sent this message, ". . . Reviset Sit Reps enrot via Don Her," translation "Sit-Reps enroute via Don R".

The rest of the day was a plague of these 'messages". One I just could not understand: "Cptlevinact for Cptbentlymo" . . . days later it came through in part two orders, "Captain Levine to act for Captain Bentley, MO" – by which time it was too late for Captain Levine to act for Captain Bentley because he had fallen and fractured his bloody ankle. So! we had *two* MOs ill!! At last the biter bitten. Bentley has diagnosed his own illness as Malaria, only to have another doctor diagnose it correctly as Jaundice. Not to lose face Bentley insists that the Medical Report states he has Malaria *and* Jaundice.

We have a brief spell of gunfire from A and D Sub, a total of ten rounds apiece, then "Stand Down." Bombardier Begent from the Gun speaks on the intercom.

"Hello, Command Post, we haven't had any Overseas News today, could we hear it this evening?"

"The reception's bad, mate," I said, "but the war's still on. How are the lads?"

"Pissed off. If it weren't for Naafi up today we'd have deserted."

"Never mind, it'll soon be Christmas."

"Christmas? What's that?"

2.30. Pinchbeck has arrived, "Right, off you go."

Pinchbeck and I had both lived in India, and often conversed in Urdu.

"*Kitna Budgi hai.*"

"*Sara dho,*" says Pinchbeck.

"*Shabash.*"

Lt. Price looks up. "I think we have a couple of wog deserters here," he says to Deans.

"Shall I search them for Curry Powder, sir?"

Where is that Edgington? That Edgington is in a cave. A strange affair, the entrance hole is but the size of a man but within we see the entire Monkey crew spread around the commodious interior. He is of course clutched in his writing fever, he holds up his hand, a signal that I am to remain silent, he scribes on. I imitate a violin playing hearts and flowers, he is unamused, he is apparently in a self-hypnotic trance where he can almost feel the presence of his beloved Peg. At the start of my music he looks up with a strained sexual look, part Lochinvar, part Svengali and part-time soldier. His lovely head again bends to the letter as he finalises it with myriad kisses.

"You mustn't get yourself into these states, Gunner Edgington, it's not good for you, you'll get lumps in yer groins that can only be reduced by the cool hand of the temple maiden with a pot of starters." Question: What is "starters"? Well, dear reader, it is a naval term for a pot of Vaseline. It should be self-explanatory. If you can't explain it to yourself a call to the Admiralty PR Department should clarify the situation, as 70 per cent of the officers are Gay up there. He licks the edge of the Airmail and sticks it together.

"Well," he finally deigns to speak, "that's that."

"That *is* that," I agreed, "and *this* – " I pointed to my ear

137

" – is this, also." I pointed at the fingers on my left hand. "Those are those."

He could not stay grim for long. He smiled. "Ahhhhh, *there's* a good boy," I said, "diddums is smiling."

"Diddums will give Mummy a nice little kick in the cobblers in a minute . . . *ahhh*!" He has a complete change of mood. "I've got a new tune, mate!" We were on common ground.

He hums the first chord to give me the key, then sings the melody, occasionally dropping in a few harmonic notes. Like all his tunes it's beautifully melodic.

"The words", he mused, "will be something like – " He sang, "Remember, how we kissed in the Autumn, September turning green things into auburn."

I was never to hear the completed tune until the year 1956 at his home in Wood Green. I am standing in the half-light of the cave, listening to Edgington singing this tune, when there enters one unromantic Pedlar Palmer from Devon's shores, a true "Urzlom-Burzlom".

"Ahhh," he says.

Why a man wants to say "Ahhh" is beyond me.

"Where has the great Swede basher who says "Ahhhh" been hiding?" I said.

"The great Swede basher", he replies, "has been getting his Naafi." He starts to empty his pockets. Toothpaste. A new toothbrush, three bars of chocolate, a packet of Wrigley's chewing gum, a packet of Beecham Powders, pot of vaseline, and powers that be!! a dozen pairs of bootlaces. "Well," he explains, "after the war there'll be a shortage of them, you see, and I'm not going to be caught walking round Devon with no laces in me boots."

As there was no bootlace drought after the War, I can only imagine that Pedlar Palmer now lives in a home crammed with World War 2 Naafi bootlaces. He could have started a panic. I mean, a man rushes into the tent and says, "There's going to be a post-war shortage of denture fixative." Men run out and start buying it to open post-war Denture Fixative Shops and making a fortune. They would rupture themselves carrying kitbags and big packs bursting with tins of denture fixatives across Italy. Imagine the Germans! they take prisoners who appear to own nothing but sacks of dental fixatives, to live on.

HITLER: Dental Fixative, hein?
ROMMEL: Ya, mein Fuhrer.
HITLER: It is a trap.
ROMMEL: Trap?
HITLER: Ya, einer dental fixative trap!
ROMMEL: How does it work?
HITLER: Ve don't know yet, but ve vill soon. I haff arranged for zer 14th Panzer Regiment to haff all zeir teeth taken out, and make mit zer false choppers using zer captured British Dental Fix Mix ... soon ve vill know what zer secret is!

NOVEMBER 22, 1943

MY DIARY: RAIN! TALK OF SPECIAL PITS FOR GUNS SO THAT THEY CAN FIRE AT MAXIMUM ELEVATION.

FILDES' DIARY: *Terrible guts due to this prolonged tinned food.*

Strange? I didn't know our tinned food was prolonged! When did I last hear a gunner asking for a tin of "Prolonged Meat Stew"? We now have a serious problem with Wireless Communication, that is, we haven't any. Talk of putting out a half-way wireless relay station.

Gunner Edgington's Public Appearance

"Crabs! They've got crabs!" the cry runs through the serried ranks.

The "Theys" were the crew of Monkey 2, it was the first mass outbreak of crabs in the Battery, how proud we were of them, at last the label dirty bastards could be added to the Battery honours. The only other mass outbreak of crabs was Gunner Neat in Bexhill. He told the MO he got them off a girl in Blackpool. "I brought them south for the sun, sir," he said.

Among the crab-ridden is Gunner Edgington. Let him recount the grisly details.

We hadn't had our clothes off for some considerable time, much less our underwear, such as it might have been, and as I've said, a bath was something we only vaguely remembered from long ago. My hair was a matted lump. The whole world we knew at that time was to get phone lines out and keep them going – all else was sleep and food and a good deal of the latter was often scrounged from strange outfits we encountered while out on the line.

Nor surprisingly we began to smell strongly and then to scratch: the irritation became incessant and something obviously had to be done: I don't think Bentley came to us . . . it was just arranged by phone calls, that we go over to RHQ.

I think there *must*'ve been more than the M.2 team, for the "crab-ridden" were taken in a three-tonner to where some showers had been erected in the corner of a field. The showers were a Heath Robinson contraption mounted under a tin roof on angle-iron supports, but they were thoroughly efficient.

Capt. Bentley, keeping a distance, called down instructions from the safety of his room on an upper floor of an adjacent building.

"Strip off!" he called to us, and this was just the Monkey 2 gang at this point. "Have a thorough wash-down all over as hot as you can possibly stand it."

In the middle of this field, in full view of civilians and soldiers alike, we disported ourselves joyously under four very efficient jets of steam and near-boiling water to the accompaniment of screams, yells and cackles.

"Blimey, you can see the bloody things! See 'em moving under the skin? Those little bastards."

Sure enough, I could see my collection in the skin of my belly just above the "short-and-curlies".

Some five minutes, and Bentley calls:

"OK, that's enough – get up here like lightning!"

Away we went in a tight bunch for the steps which led up the side of the building; these being only wide enough to permit one at a time, it meant some of us had to ease back to create a single-file rush up the stairs, all naked and freezing. Into a small bare room we thundered, its only furniture a bare table, on which stood in a row seven

The terrible crab-ridden M.2 team

empty cigarette tins, and a large dob of cotton wool alongside – no sign of Bentley though.

Looking round puzzled, we see his grinning face peering round a distant door at the far end of the room – he had no wish to get near us. The legend "crabs can jump six feet" still lingered on.

"Right! Each man grab a tin and a blob of cotton wool. Dip the cotton wool into the tin and dab it generously all over the affected parts . . . quickly now, quickly!" He slammed the door, in case any escaped.

Looking in my tin I saw a clear mauve liquid. The lads were all still chortling and crying in mock agony – "Unclean! Unclean!", the war-cry we had been bellicosely hollering from the lorry that brought us – and ringing imaginary handbells.

The fluid was liberally applied – backs, balls and bellies as well – not one of us having guessed what it was, it took about ten to fifteen seconds to act. Then everyone's balls caught fire. It was raw alcohol.

The first "Cor-mate!" was rapidly echoed all round, followed by a growled "Awww! Gawd blimey!!" Faces were transfixed with pain and cross-eyed agony, they yelled, they screamed, they fell and rolled, they jumped, they ran back and forth, they twisted, cannoned into walls – each other – they fell over the table. At the height of the chaotic fandango I was sat on the floor, knees drawn up, left arm wedging my trunk half upright, right hand fanning my "wedding-tackle", when through the melée of flailing arms, legs and prancing bodies I saw the inner door open again slightly and Bentley's face appear in the narrow gap. "Merry Christmas," he said and was gone!

For Edgington to remember that occasion in such detail thirty-five years after the event is quite a feat of memory. Mind you, one doesn't get crabs every day, not even at the fishmongers.

NOVEMBER 23, 1943

"Milligan? Fildes?" a voice of authority calls. It tells us we are to take twenty-four hours' rations, drive to the top of Monte Croce and set up the wireless relay station.

"They say the reason for the bad reception is adverse metals," said Fildes.

Adverse metals? I thought. "What are adverse metals?"

"Fuck knows," he said.

"Do you think it's the metal rings on the laceholes in our boots?" Fildes shrugged.

"Adverse Metals," I intoned repeatedly. It was a lovely phrase. I buzzed up the now crab-free Edgington.

"Hello," replied an angry voice, obviously suffering from burning balls.

"Is Edgington there?"

"Yes, I'm here, what you want?"

"How is the old Scorched Scrotum?"

"Ohhh Christ," he groaned, "you should see 'em, they're goin' up and down like yoyos'!"

"Have you any Adverse Metals?"

There is a small pause. "What?"

I repeat the query.

"Adverse Metals?" he chuckles, "I cannot tell a lie, I have no adverse metals but I have a pair of bright red cobblers."

"Do you have any effect on wireless communications?"

"No," he chuckled, "they aren't picking up any signals."

"Then you can't have any adverse metal inside them."

"That's very comforting, it's bad enough having them skinned raw without lumps of metal inside."

Fildes has put chains on the wheels of the truck. Does he think they're going to escape? We wave goodbye, and take the road that travels round the rear of our position skirting the foot of Monte Croce, we get on to a rough mountain road slippery as grease. The road finally disappears. "It's come to something when the road can't get up the hill," I said. By steady driving Fildes gradually makes it to the top; we pull up just below the crest. The slopes are slightly wooded, with a scrubby grass floor. We look down into the valley at our gun positions; so skilful is the camouflage that we can see everything as though under a magnifying glass. Cautiously we peer over the crest into enemy territory. The view is obscured by drizzle and mist. Comfort! *that's* the thing. Brew up! Hot water boiled for dinner. Make up beds in the back of truck. We stow our spare gear in the driving cab. Attempts are made to contact the OP, no luck, we report this to the Command Post, they say stay up there on listening watch, we put the set to "receive" and put the earphones in a mess-tin, to amplify the sound.

"What was that place with the church?" said Fildes. He's writing an airmail home.

"Terra Corpo," I tell him, "freely translated it means Land Body."

"Land Body?" he echoed.

"Yes, we're somewhere round about the legs, the foothills you might say, ha, ha, ha."

It's night, we have our dinner, in beds. The back flap is buttoned down, a light run from the battery. I am smoking and listening to AFN Naples. "French Moroccan Troop reinforcements have arrived in Italy." Japs resisting like fury on Bourganville. Tito's Yugoslav Partisans are holding down over twenty German and Bulgarian divisions.

"It's starting to go our way," I remember saying to Fildes. Laconically he sang, "It doesn't seem to matter which way it's going, we're still all in the shit out here."

It's remarkably peaceful on our mountain, the night has no sounds save the gunfire from the valleys below, the rushing sound of twenty-five pounder and five-five shells can be heard travelling overhead. We can hear mules and men.

They are bringing up rations for the infantry, I *think* they were the Berkshires. I wonder who they thought we were. *I* thought I was Lance-Bombardier Milligan, but I'd been wrong before, once back in Tunis I had been pulled up by the Military Police who asked who I was. I said, "Napoleon," and they said, "This way to the Police Station." I fell asleep leaving Alf Fildes scribing away. In the dark night the war went on, being able to sleep peacefully, dry, snug and warm was I suppose, Luxury.

Alf Fildes writing cheques for his wife Lily.

NOVEMBER 24, 1943

MY DIARY: UP VERY EARLY TO CONTACT OUR GUN POSITION. RECEPTION STRENGTH 9, BUT THE OP STRENGTH 1. WILL TRY AND PUT UP VERY LONG AERIAL.

FILDES' DIARY: *Officer from 17 battery arrives to pass on shoot for "Jenks" (Major Jenkins), nice chap, we had an affable day.*

The aerial! This was a metal interslotting series of metal poles with a cross-shaped antennae at the top. Its maximum height was twenty feet.

We contacted Ernie Hart at the Command Post.

"Any mail up, Ernie – over."

"Yes – over."

"Any for me or Fildes? – over."

"Hold on."

We wait, during which time he makes enquiries. "Yes, there's some for both of you – over."

"Great. Any news about leave? Over."

"Nooo. Nothing. There's a rumour about forty-eight hours in Naples – ."

"Can you tell Edgington that the mist is on the Swonickles? Over."

"The what? Over."

"The mist is on the Swonickles – over."

"What's it mean? Over."

"He'll understand – over and out."

The pattern of the day is only broken by rushes to do a slash and cook the lunch. We keep our bit of fire area dry by laying a gas cape over it. We make tea about every two hours. Doing a "pony" is difficult and entails getting a rain-ridden bum. Of course, our leader, Winston, he's not kipping in the back of a truck, no, he and his crony Roosevelt are in sunny Cairo, and as it's Thanksgiving Day, he's got Roosevelt carving great lumps of turkey at his villa,and so stoned does the old man get that after the scoff, they put the gramophone on and the Prime Minister of England dances with a Mr Wilson. What's happening to the war you say? So! Churchill is foxtrotting in Cairo; Milligan is kipping in the mud of Italy; game, set and match to Churchill.

145

On the 8th Army front, the 78 Div. and the Indian 8th Div. have attacked and got across the Sangro. God knows how they did it in this weather. Perhaps they had umbrellas.

The evening comes in dark and gloomy, Alf boils up a couple of tins of stew, sitting up in bed we eat it and small talk. He tells me his missus has sent him a Conway Stewart pen. I clutch the bedclothes with excitement. He shows me the latest photo of his wife Lily and their two kids. I clutch the bed clothes with excitement. On the morrow we would try and extend the aerial.

MEANTIME, NEXT DAY

"I'll try and put it up this tree, Alf," I said, with good intentions.

"You should look good in a tree. I always thought, in your paybook where it says place of birth it should say Tree."

"Hold this aerial, Alf," I said, "and I will climb up and insult you from a great height."

The words rang clear on the morning air, also clear in the morning air was my lone scream as I fell ten feet.

"You alright?" said Fildes with a whimsical smile.

"Of course, don't you know falling ten feet from a tree is always alright?"

Clutching and swearing, twigs snapping around me, I managed to get up to the lower branches and let out a Tarzan call.

"Pass me up the aerial, Alf," says Milligan.

It would appear I have climbed too high for him to reach me.

"You'll have to come down a bit," he says.

The tree is winter-green and slippery; in various contortions that are only done by a man with strychnine poisoning, I get to a lower level and give a Tarzan cry.

"Here, grab 'old," says Fildes, holding up the aerial. I firmly grab one of the Windmill antennae, it snaps off.

"Never mind, there's still three more."

I try and haul the thing through a complex of branches and boughs; now, a twenty-foot-long pole is no manoeuvrable item. It was like trying to thread a giant darning needle and I wasn't trained for that. I gave another Tarzan call, it got to the stage where I was trapped between the branches and the aerial.

146

"Shall I chop the tree down?" said Fildes, giggling.

"It's the antennae that's in the way," I said. "I'll unscrew them."

I soon have three loose antennae in one hand, and I find the other hand insufficient to climb *and* hold the aerial.

"Catch," I said, and dropped the antennae. Looking up, Fildes loses his balance, and starts to slide back down the muddy slope. So smooth is his progress that he doesn't realise he's moving; gently the back of his nut collides with a tree. I gave the Tarzan call, and a lot of bloody good it did. The antennae are now slopped in the mud. I, in contrast, am covered in the green moss of the tree trunk and covered in scratches. This is called modern wireless communications.

"Shall I come up and help?" said Fildes.

No, I need no help, I am the complete wireless technician. I give another Tarzan call to verify it.

A wet officer from 17 Battery appears at the bottom of the tree. He explains to Fildes that he is to pass on a shoot for Major Jenkins. Fildes explains that this is not possible until the aerial is up. The officer can hear swearing issuing from the tree behind him because Milligan has ripped the knee of his battle dress. It's letting in the cold mountain air, something his London-bred knees are not accustomed to. The officer is Lieutenant Pascoe, young, slim, very refined. He could hear a very unrefined voice from behind a tree saying, "Fuck all this, if it doesn't work this bloody time, I'm packing it in."

I have managed to tie the aerial to the top of the tree. "Throw the antennae up, Alf."

Using Olympic-style javelin throws, Alf manages to hit me on the chest.

"Can you tell the man up the tree that the shoot has to go through at 1430 hours?" says Lt. Pascoe.

Fildes shouts up the message. Milligan is unaware of the officer's presence, and replies thus:

"They'll be fucking lucky."

I give one more Tarzan call. On descending I was confronted by a smiling Lt. Pascoe.

"Did you leave Jane up there?" he said.

"Oh hello, sir," I said. "We're having trouble with the aerial."

"Yes, I heard you having trouble."

We immediately tried the strength of the new aerial; it's no better. As it is a prearranged shoot with no adjustment of ranges, it goes through on morse. The target lay on the rear crest of Limata Grande.

"What's so important about that?" I asked Lt. Pascoe.

"Nothing. It's a registration shoot for future reference." With that he demands tea.

"Yes, sir," I said and demanded cigarettes.

He gave us one each. Tea concluded, he took his leave, wandering off left towards where his transport was hidden. We hear a "Heloooooo" from further down the slope. Was this the spirit of Arcadia? There, amid the greenery we see a clutch of muddy gunners in various stages of climbing. They are Bombardier Syd Price and his merry ration carriers.

"Come down here," he calls.

"Why?"

"Because *we* can't get up *there*."

"If *we* come down *there* where you can't get up from, *we'll* be down *there* as well not being able to get back up *here* where we are *now*."

"It's yer bloody rations, take 'em or we'll eat 'em here."

A desperate situation. Alf and I slither down the hillside. Rations are rations and we'll do anything to get them. Along with them we find "Two bloody great batteries for the wireless." We manage to get the rations up, but the weight of

Drill instructor at the low port.

the batteries is too much, so we leave the things on the mountain. Syd Price puffs his pipe as he and his "porters" slither backwards down the mountain.

"When are we going to be relieved?" I asked as a parting question.

"Use a tree," he calls.

We are alone again in our little heaven in the clouds. A small group of silent Infantry men are leaving their position. They pass us in silence. We've had a belly full of wireless.

"Let's pack it in," I said, "I feel a bit feverish." I bed down and Fildes prepares an evening meal. I had fallen asleep before he served it.

THURSDAY, NOVEMBER 25, 1943

ALF FILDES' DIARY: *Still up here on the hill but rather enjoying it.*

MY DIARY: FEEL BETTER THIS MORNING. COLOSSAL DOWN-POUR OF RAIN. EVERYTHING DAMP AND SOGGY, ESPECIALLY ME.

I awoke to the roar of rain on the canvas roof. Six o'clock! What's the matter with me? It's this Army habit of "early", it was catching and now *I* had been affected. It will take years of post-war training to get back to normal. I make the morning tea and wake Fildes, who is lying on his back sucking air in through his open mouth.

He opens his bloodshot eyes, for ten seconds the brain doesn't register; I hold up his chipped brown mug with the steaming tea, a soppy grin spreads across his face and a clutching hand takes the tea.

"Oh, good luck," he says, sips it, and screams as he burns his tongue.

"So what'll we do today?" he said.

"Nothing."

"That's all we've bloody well done since we've been here."

"Yes, it's a serial."

We roll up the back flap of the truck and sit looking out at the rain-drenched mountainside, which gradually disappears into the mist of the downpour.

"I haven't heard a sound this morning," said Fildes. He

149

peers round the back of the truck. He is checking his patent water catchment. This is a hole with a piece of canvas placed in it.

"It's full," he said.

It seemed lunatic to be catching water in weather like this but we need it to wash in, saving our Jerry can of clean water for drinking. Silently, a dripping soldier appears.

"17 Battery," he announced. "We've come to relieve you." He pointed down the mountainside to his truck on its side. "We can't get it up any further," he said.

"Did you put chains on?"

"No, its bad enough wearing battle dress."

"The *truck*."

"We had everything on, it's took us two hours to get that far."

He pointed to the truck on its side.

"Look, it's impossible for us to get our truck down, and you can't get up, so it's pointless you staying here." He nods agreement.

Poor bugger collects his belongings from his truck and disappears down the hill with the driver.

That night, out of sheer boredom I read my Army paybook.

"Interesting?" says Fildes.

"Incredible, says I was born in a tree."

We off with the light, and lie back smoking in the dark. The rain continues; fancy, right now Churchill will be sipping brandy and smoking a cigar.

NOVEMBER 26, 1943

It was like a spring morning. "I don't believe it," said Fildes. "The sun." It changed everything, colours once brown were now green, green, green. Today I would shave. Today I would organise my life anew. No more slobbed in bed all day, today I would do things. What those things were I didn't yet know, but it would be "things", the first "thing" would be breakfast. I build a fire and soon make the bacon sizzle. The smell is wafting through the morning air. A string of mules accompanied by Cypriot attendants come from the left and pass slowly by. They are a little amused seeing us in nothing but socks, boots and shirts. Fildes is shaving.

"Marvellous what the sun will do," he says.

He whistles in between strokes of the blade. I will do the shave "thing" after the breakfast "thing".

"After this I'm going to have a look over the hill "thing" at Jerry's positions," I declared.

"I'm beginning to wonder how long we'll be up here," said Fildes. "It's been four days now, we were only supposed to be here for twenty-four hours."

Someone in the valley below is trying to attract our attention with a mirror.

"I wonder what they want."

"We better switch on the set," said Fildes.

We get through and the message is "Come in. Position being closed down." We take our time. I stroll to the top of the mountain ridge for a last look, a marvellous view meets the eye, 1,000 feet below us is the great Garigliano plain, with the snow-mottled Aurunci Mountains on the far side of the river. To the left is the Gulf of Gaeta. In the distance at the curling point of the bay is Gaeta itself. Even as I watch, a great plume from an explosion starts skywards, Jerry carrying out demolitions. Why can't I get a fun job like that? The last of the infantry are leaving their foxholes, and wearily making their way back down the mountain.

"The line's moved forward," says a tired-looking Corporal in answer to my question.

"You never see many of 'em smiling or laughing," reflected Fildes.

"They've got bugger all to laugh at. I mean what do you say, 'Cheer up, Charlie, we're being mortared', or 'Cor, talk about a laugh, we were shelled all night and ten of us was killed.'"

Boooommmmm. Another explosion in Gaeta.

"There won't be much of the bloody place left," said Fildes.

Boooommmm!

"Christ, they've got it in for that place."

"Wish we had some binoculars," said Fildes.

"Can't you hear without them?"

Oh what a lovely sight! Spitfires with *American* markings, so there was *something* of ours that they were using, usually it was us borrowing from them; they fly in threes, at about

151

10,000 feet, then suddenly go into a dive towards the foothills across the Garigliano; soon they are shrouded in flack. We hear the Spits' cannons going, then they shoot straight up from the dive, alternately turning left and right from their target, then coming in for a second run. They repeat this three times then turn away and race back for our line, climbing as they do. We just sit and watch it as though we were at the Palladium, "Encoreeeee, bravoooooo."

Fildes starts back for the truck. "Come on, Milligan, we don't want to get stuck in the dark."

While we are up here on this hill, there had been excitement in the valley. The officers' mess had caught fire! We couldn't stop laughing. Officers off duty were in bed when the conflagration started. They were seen in their pyjamas hurling buckets of water (filled by their batmen, of course), and Major "Looney" Jenkins was seen to rush in and from the smoke and flame hurl his possessions to safety, where Gunner Pills (who hated him) was seen to throw them all back in again. What remained of Jenkins' kit was a sorry incinerated mess, his appearance on parade next morning was a joy to behold; in a charred hat, smoke-blackened battle dress, and his right arm in a sling from burns, he had the gall to enter in Part 2 Orders "Injured in Action". I remember I penned an "Ode" to the occasion in the style of McGonagall, I didn't preserve it but it went something like this:

> Ohhhh 'Twas in the month of November
> In Nineteen Forty Three
> That the officers' mess caught fire,
> Oh dearie dearie me.
> And into that terrible fire
> Major Jenkins did rush in
> To save his precious possessions,
> His wig, his teeth, his gin.
> But as he threw his treasures out
> Gunner Pills committed a sin,
> For as fast as the Major threw them out
> He threw them all back in.
> On parade next morning,
> Our names on the roll to check,
> Major Evan Jenkins appeared

A charred and tattered wreck.
If only he had stayed inside
And been burnt to a cinder,
He'd have given us all a laugh
Much bigger than Tommy Trinder.

Whistling merrily, we pack all our gear and prepare the descent. The ground was like grease, Fildes drives down at one mile an hour, engaging four-wheel drive. I have to walk ahead and scout out the least dangerous bits, gradually the gradient became more acute. The truck starts to slide down with a gathering momentum. All I could think of saying was "Goodbye, Alf, I'll tell the missus." Alf doesn't want to die. He remembers an old bus-driver's trick. He puts the truck into reverse, and the counteraction of the wheels slows the vehicle up and it gradually comes to a halt. He looks out the cab and grins.

"Cor bloody hell, I want more money for this job."

"That was brilliant! *Brilliant*, do you hear me, Fildes! I won't let this go unnoticed . . . you see, by tomorrow morning you'll be on the honours list and an extra egg for breakfast, a present from a grateful nation, god bless you, young Alf, you and your see-through underwear. England isn't finished yet . . . it'll be finished tomorrow."

Together we gradually slither down the hill, and with perfect timing arrive back as Bombardier Deans is making coffee.

"It's the men from the hills," announces Nash.

"Yes, we bring good tidings, Jerry is blowing up Gaeta."

Fildes has raced to the battery office and returned with mail.

"You always get more than anyone else, Milligan."

"Well, you unimaginative buggers only write to one bird, I wrote to ten; you're paying the penalty for monogamy."

I am drinking Deans' coffee and luxuriating in my letters. Ah! Romance! Darling I love you, Dearest, my Darling, Darling Terry, Darling, darling, darling, good luck to them all I say! Alf is depressed, one of his kids is ill with scarlet fever. Fancy being a child in this war, shortages, fathers away, might get killed, bombs, and scarlet fever on top.

"They're only going to give forty-eight hours' leave in

153

Naples," Jam-Jar comes in with the news. There is a stunned silence. "Didn't you hear?" repeats Jam-Jar, removing his tin hat, leaving the lining on his head. "*Leave* . . ." he starts to spell it out. "L-e-a – "

"Alright, alright, we heard," I said. "Me and my friends are in a temporary state of shock. We're not used to such announcements."

"Naples," says Deans looking up ecstatically.

Fildes isn't enthusiastic. "Forty-eight hours? That's no bloody good, it'll take us half a day there and back, all we'll get is an afternoon and a morning, what can you do in that time?"

"I should imagine, if you have the right addresses and you're quick, you could get in ten shags, three Litres of Vino and a ton of spaghetti," says Nash.

"Shags!" Jam-Jar has a look of horror on his face. "Don't you know Naples is the most Syphilitic city in Italy?"

"That's nothing, *we'll* make it the most syphilitic in the *world*!" says Nash with a sweep of his hand.

"Perfidious Albion," says Jam-Jar.

"Vitreous China," I reply.

"We're going to look a bloody scruffy lot, we need a clean change of clothing."

"Clothing," I mocked, "we need a complete change of body, I smell like the inside of a Guardsman's sock."

So that I will be nice and fresh for the journey I've been put on Command Post from 2.30 in the morning till 5.30! Lt. Stewart Pride is on duty. No! he's got malaria; I peer into the officers' billet.

"Hope you feel better soon, sir."

He looks up from his camp bed. "Thank you, Milligan," and so saying downs half a bottle of whisky. He looks terrible and is sweating like a pig. Whisky. They all admitted that it was this fiery Scots anaesthetic that made them try for a commission. I get my head down early. At the dreaded hour of two twenty-five and three quarters, Alf Fildes wakes me. "Spike!"

"Ahhhhharggh – Arggh!"

"Your turn."

"Arrrggg – Arrrggg Argg-er"

He stands over me, pulls the blankets off. "You'll go blind," he says.

154

In the Command Post Lt. Budden is talking to Bombardier Edwards. The night is a quiet one. Thirty-six rounds fired of harassing fire. I doze with my back against the wall. Towards dawn I fall off the box I'm on. The phone buzzes. "Command Post," I say.

It's the 8th Survey Regiment, or rather one of them. They give me a message that is all gibberish, I write down the string of figures and hand them to Lt. Budden.

"This must mean something to someone," I said.

Budden takes the message, screws his eyes up, they appear to have a left-hand thread.

"Ahhh, at last, Deans," he handed the message to him.

Deans takes it. "Ahhh yes," he said.

From it they start doing sums, and drawing lines with protractors and set squares. I return to the dozing, and I fall off the box a second time. This way I pass the long hours till dawn.

It's now Saturday, November 27.

I have to alert the cooks, so I take my mug. Gently I wake May, for he is a cook, and therefore God. I help him find his boots and assist him to his feet, all the while saying, "Ronnie May is a prince among men, for his is the truth and the light and walks in the ways of wisdom."

"You want some fucking tea, don't you?" he said.

"Ahhh, the master can even read the human mind."

I stick around as he starts up the field oven by throwing a lighted match into the dripfeed tunnel. Whooooosh. It ignites.

"Food, bloody food, that's all this lot think of, all I am is a total slave to the intestines of this lot, how can a public schoolboy like me, with a future in the jewellery business, end up stirring porridge in a world war?" he moaned merrily as he placed dixies of water and food over the fire. He unrolls the bacon from their gold-tinted compo tins, and slops them into the dixie.

I get the first breakfast of the day. "G" truck is silent with the sleeping Fildes, Nash and Deans. The camp is stirring, odd guns bark around the area.

Naples! I try to make myself look respectable, I have a good shave in hot water, and wash my hair; the removal of

155

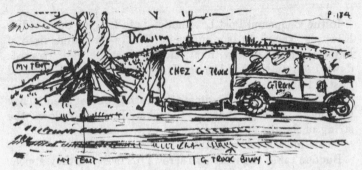

"G" truck with its "tented" attachment and Milligan's terrible tent.

all that dirt leaves me light-headed and I have to sit down. God knows what will happen when I have a bath, it could mean a wheelchair.

Basenji. Did it really mean non-barking dogs?

The three-tonners are warming up, we are all getting aboard, it's eighty miles to Naples, on these roads it would appear to be two hundred. By nine o'clock we are all packed in the back, by 9.30 we are still all packed in the back. Impatient swearing is emerging from the passengers, it gradually swells into a roar and then the chorus of "Why are we waiting, waiting fucking waiting, why oh why are weee waiting." The *ting* was always, under my musical direction, hit loud and hard, "*TINGGGGGGG*"! the word reverberated around the gun position, cries from those left behind of "Take the bastards away."

The lorry suddenly lurches forward, a great jeering cheer comes from the passengers and it continues as we jerk and slither down the secondary road.

"Our King is sending us to Naples to get Syph," cries Smudger Smith.

"Hoorayyyy," comes the mob's reply.

It was a dreary nightmare journey, along worn muddy secondary roads in transport that was also secondary, in turn we looked like secondary troops, it all fitted.

SATURDAY, NOVEMBER 27, 1943

At mid-day we pulled into the Piazza Dante, clogged with

vehicles and people. Italians are screaming at each other – some are screaming at walls some are screaming at themselves. The city pulsated with life, some drunks were pulsating with death, the pavements were crammed with pedestrians who overflowed on to the street, Allied soldiers, civilians, all jostled together. There was that peculiar smell of Italian cigarettes permeating the air. As we jump from the truck, several pretty girls are touting for restaurants, "Nica-a-food-anda-wine" says one ravishing little beauty; as bait she handed us a plate of fishcakes; delicious! "*Molto buono,*" I said. We followed her to a side street into a Trattoria.

"This bloody menu's in Italian," moaned Wenham. We put away a mountain of spaghetti, some set about with a knife and fork. "This isn't a meal, it's a bloody puzzle," said Wenham.

"You're supposed to swallow it *long*," I said.

"And lassoo me guts?"

"How do the Ities manage to eat this day after day?" said Griffin.

"Like I told you, with a *fork*."

Alf Fildes has his head back at forty-five degrees, it was something to do with the wineglass he was draining. "Ahhhh, lovely stuff."

"Be forewarned, all you Lochinvars," said Deans, "there's pox galore out here, one good screw and yer prick will swell up like a marrow and yer balls drops off."

"Now, why doesn't Thomas Cook put *that* in his brochures? All that 'See Lovely Naples and Sorrento, cities of Love and Music' crap!! He *should* be saying Round Trip to Naples and back to an old English Syphilitic Ward, £67 return."

We window shopped. Such luxury goods! Silk shirts, stockings, watches, suits, shoes.

"How come back 'ome we got bleeding cardboard boots and suits made out of Gunny sacks in our shops and the Ities got all this?" said Fildes.

"Ah! but *we* have better tanks, aeroplanes and guns," I said with a cheerful inane grin.

Fildes is looking at a magnificent ladies' kimono. "What's Seta Pura mean?"

"It means Pure Seta," I said.

It was stockings and knickers that seemed to be the main purchases, thousands of parcels were in transit to wives, girlfriends (and some boyfriends), the basic reason was the sexual thrill the squaddie had in buying them and waiting for that inevitable letter back saying, "When you come home you can put them on for me." Alas, by the time they got home some bloody American had already taken them off. I bought a leather cigarette case for my leather cigarettes, it was real hide and I bore in mind that if boiled, Kidgell would eat it. Fildes buys a silk bedspread, hair-pins, and guess what? Silk stockings. We repair to the new Mecca of the British Army, the Army and Navy Club! This one time Universal Store, now adapted as a Naafi, staffed by pretty girls.

FILDES' DIARY: *Lounge, music room with Iti Trio, cakes, sandwiches, hot dinners, tea and silk stockings, all at reasonable prices, everywhere an air of elite comfort.*

So, if blokes in crumpled battle dresses with their boots up on the table, cheeks bulging with doughnuts and jam dribbling down was élite comfort! Then luxury would be a Gunner eating a bully beef sandwich in evening dress, seated in a workman's hut.

There are some ugly girls serving, a red-faced Infantryman is looking at one and saying ecstatically, "Corrrrr, just look at 'er." There is a time for ugly women, and World War 2 was it. I have seen desperate soldiers as handsome as Greek Gods escorting women who looked like Arthur Mullard in drag.

We ensconced ourselves in the Lounge and listened to the Iti trio. The violin-leader was a thin, febrile male, circa seventy-two, deepest eyes, they appeared like two holes drilled in his head with someone from behind looking through. Another old man with bald head and a curly white moustache (or was it a curly head and a bald moustache?) played piano, a huge stomach forced him away from the keyboard, he had to play arms stretched. One more big dinner and he'd never make it. On drums, a Gorgeous Italian Girl with shoulder-length raven black hair. They were grinding their

158

Waitress at the Army and Navy Club, Naples, fanning flies off soldier's soup.

British troops being driven insane at the Army and Navy Club, Naples, 1943. The soldier slumped at the end is almost ready.

159

way through a selection of "Touristic" melodies, "Pistol Packing Mamma", "In the Mood", it was totally unbearable.

"I suppose he thinks 'e's Glen Miller," I said.

"He sounds more like bloody Max Miller," said Fildes.

Jam-Jar Griffin and Spike Deans are approaching, they are excited, they've been buying silk stockings. It's late afternoon, we've had tea, we go and visit the Duomo; this was an interesting vaulted shopping Arcade, high enough for pigeons to fly within it. It's cruciform in shape; after four hours' walking around, so were we. In a moment of petroleum-induced madness we all piled into a dying Fiat taxi, the driver could barely see over the bonnet, we thought he was standing in a hole in the floor and propelling the vehicle on foot.

A quick drive around town, then he dumped us back at the Piazza Dante; there was a terrible argument over the fare. Who was going to pay it? Inside every Christian there is a Jew shouting to get out.

"We better get to the billet before it gets dark," said Deans, who was being mother.

The billet was on the dock front, we knew when we got to it, it was the only building standing. "Fifth Army (British Contingent) Transit Camp. All intakes report to the Guard Commander." We hawked our stuff off the truck and presented ourselves at the Guard Room.

"Yes! What is it?" said an officious, chubby, red-faced, totally idiot RE Sergeant.

"If he was in Germany Hitler would make 'im a Gauleiter," said Wenham.

"A Gauleiter? He couldn't make a cigarette lighter," said Jam-Jar.

Words didn't count here. We each produced our 48-hour passes. The sweaty Sergeant took them all, walked to the window and squinted at them, he took three minutes to digest each one.

"They're all the same, Sarge," I said kindly.

"No, they're not!" he snapped. "Numbers and names are all different."

The shit. He then proceeded to laboriously enter our names in a book. He wheezed as he almost etched our details on the paper. "'Oo's senior here?" he said.

"You are," I replied.

"I'm senior NCO with this party," interjected Deans.

"You'll be responsible then," said the shit.

"Responsible for what, Sarge?"

"Never mind what, you're responsible, understand?"

"Yes, Sergeant," said Deans crisply. "Partyyyy shunnnn."

We all did nothing.

"From the right Number."

"6 – 12 – 1091 – $2\frac{1}{3}$," we said.

"Partyyy Quickkkkkk March!"

We all hibbled-hobbled out of step from the room, before the startled gaze of the shit.

A large warehouse with beds.

"Aye," said a dopey room orderly. "We not bin open long, you first lot we 'ad today."

"What time's dinner?" we chorused.

"Ooo, seven o'clock till eight."

We tried the dinner from seven to eight. It was bloody terrible.

"You going out after this?" said Jam-Jar.

"I don't think so," said Fildes. "I'm shagged out walking."

"I'm shagged out eating that bloody food," said Griffin. "I think I'll have an early night."

"Yes," I said, "why don't you all try your silk stockings on?"

The dopey room orderly is putting black-outs up at the windows. One miserable yellow bulb cast a depressing gloom around the room. We are all in bed when the air-raid warning goes. We all sit up.

"What are we supposed to do?" said Wenham.

"We're supposed to be frightened," I said, "quick, put your silk stockings on!"

There was no sound of planes, and I fell asleep not knowing or caring. Tomorrow I *must* buy some silk stockings.

SUNRISE, NOVEMBER 28, 1943

MY DIARY: DID THE SAME TODAY AS WE DID YESTERDAY.

VERY COLD, BUT SUNNY. MUST BUY SOME SILK STOCKINGS.

FILDES' DIARY: *Leave today at two o'clock*.

We all lay in bed long after breakfast, anything to avoid it. We drive back into Naples, and after half an hour in the Army and Navy Club, we are off. Driver Kit Masters says we should be back by about "I don't know when."

"Forty-eight hours! we spent *fourteen* of them at the Transit Camp," estimates Griffin, "and how long did we spend in Naples? *Four bloody hours*, it's all balls, we had absolutely no time for perversions."

"We'll do some on the way back," I said kindly.

On that cold bumpy muddy ride back there were no perversions other than a "Jimmy Riddle" over the tailboard. We arrived at Teano, there's a God Almighty hold up, long lines of trucks are ahead of us, the drivers outside banging their hands on their sides to keep warm.

FILDES' DIARY: *We got out and picked oranges and looked at the appalling damage to the town. An old man even excreted in the street with no comment.*

I don't understand! *ORANGES* in midwinter? What had Fildes been drinking? and, crapping in the street with "no comment"? I mean, what was the old man supposed to say? Olé!

We are off again, soon the sound of the guns comes wafting. It's pitch-black outside, it's pitch-black inside, there's no choice.

"So that was Naples," said Fildes, "I can't believe it, all this switching from civilisation to war, it's hard to get it together."

The luminous ends of the cigarette are dancing in the dark. One flies out the back as its usefulness ends. We arrive back "home" at eight o'clock, shagged. We make for the cookhouse; after a mess-tin of steaming M & V,* we turn in; it's very cold tonight, I sleep in my battle dress. Outside the rata-clack-squeak of tanks going north.

*M & V. Meat and Veg.

"Wakey, wakey."

My watch says 0500 hours.

"Wakey, wakey my arsey, why don't you fuckey wuckey offey?" is my clear language reply.

Oh dear, it's no use, it's Sergeant King, he says, "You are goin' hup the Ho-Pee – it's only for twenty-four hours."

"That's long enough to get killed," I said.

In Sherwood's bren carrier I travel a fifteen-mile road to Sipichiano. At times we are in full view of Jerry. He doesn't shell us. But you have that feeling that any minute he will and that's like being shelled.

"How come they picked you?" said Sherwood.

"I wasn't quick enough."

Whee-crashhh!

"He's spotted us!" shouts Sherwood.

He drives off the road behind a deserted farmhouse. Whee Crash. Whee Crash. 88s! Is he going to drop one behind the farm? No, he just goes along the road. Five more rounds and then stop. Is he waiting for us to come out? Only one way to find out. Sherwood revs up and then rushes out on to the road. I cringe . . . nothing, soon we're safe behind covering ground. The OP was manned by Bombardier Eddy Edwards, Signaller "My brain hurts" Birch and a Lieutenant from 18 Battery whose name I can't remember and a face that's left an indelible blank on my mind. The trench was in low scrub on a forward slope, indispersed among the Infantry and to our right an OP from 74 Mediums which I, muggins, had to crawl to, linking them up to us by phone. At the bottom of their trench grinning upwards is L/Bombardier Ken Carter. Little did I know I was looking at the man who would one day produce *Crossroads*. Had I known I would have killed him there and then. During the night I spoke to him on the phone. I'd heard he was putting together a new show. "Yes, it's a pantomime . . . *Ali Baba*."

"Same cast as *Stand Easy*?"

"Bigger, much bigger . . . about a hundred."

"Hundred? Christ, who's left to fire the guns?"

"I want it to be really big, West End stuff, the lads must be fed up with all those skinny bloody six-handed ENSA shows."

163

"Think you'll be allowed to do it?"

"Yes, I've already spoken to Brigadier Rogers."

"Did he speak to *you*, though?"

"Yes."

"Another class barrier has fallen! Headline! Bombardier addresses Brigadier and lives."

Our hushed conversation was terminated by Jerry artillery.

"I suppose it's to keep us awake," said Bombardier Edwards.

Squatting in a trench for hours is hell. The pain at the back of the knees is exquisite. After dark we stand up to stretch ourselves.

"What we need are detachable legs Mark One," I said. "A heater in the seat of the trousers, a lubrication-point at the back of each knee, hollow rubber feet that can be filled with hot water, an electrified nose-muff, and a collapsible Po."

"I agree with all that, Bombardier," said the Lieutenant, "save for the last mentioned. I think a Po would make a man lose that wild sense of freedom that he has as he sprays the foliage of Italy with a deft hand and a flick of the wrist."

The shelling is big stuff, Jerry 155mm, it's falling about 200 yards to our right where the Infantry have some Vickers machine guns. The phone emits a faint buzz. I snatch up the hand set.

"OP," I whisper.

"Command Post here." It's Pedlar Palmer, God's gift to ugly women. "Line OK?" he says.

"Yes . . . clear."

"Anything happening?"

"A bit of Jerry shelling, that's OK, it's Edwards' breath that's killing us."

"You bastard," said Edwards. Palmer continues,

"It's all quiet back here, anything up your end?"

"No, there's nothing up my end."

"Dirty little bugger you." He goes.

The shelling stops.

"The poor darlings must be tired," says the Lieutenant.

A burst of heavy German machine-gun fire. A bren-gun starts to answer back with its laboured chug, chug, chug. Why did the idiot want to fire back? It was only upsetting

Jerry! Christmas was coming, we should be making paper chains and funny hats to hang on the officers. We open our vacuum tea tube. It's now very tannic and burns the tongue but it's hot. The front goes quiet, a gossamer-thin quilt of light starts to furnish the sky to our east, it grows almost imperceptibly; a lone, very strong crowing cockerel shrills the air.

"Silly cunt," said Birch.

A soft lush pink mounts the heavens and I watched over-awed as it turns almost crimson, then pales into the lucidity of daylight. Hello, who's this approaching on his stomach?

"Sorry I'm late," it says, as it slithers into the trench.

Ah, I recognise those brown teeth, it's Thornton, my relief. What a relief!

"Sherwood's waiting behind the hill to take you back in his little Noddy car."

I collected my small pack and crawled back, always conscious that a bloody German might spot me and riddle my arse with metal, but no! I'm safe and riding back in the bren carrier.

"It's dodgy along here," says Sherwood.

"It's your own bloody fault for coming in daylight."

"Couldn't help it," he said. "Thornton was late seeing the MO."

"Excuses, bloody excuses, this bloody army is made up of them."

"Keep moaning," said Sherwood. "It's the only way to promotion."

Heeemmm Bammmmm! Wheeem Bamm! It's the same bloody 88mm from yesterday! Lucky he has only spotted us as we go round a hairpin bend out of view.

"We're not safe yet," said Sherwood. "Those bloody things can fire round corners."

They couldn't. What they *could* do was wait for you to reappear, and when we did, he was waiting. Wheeeem Bammm! Wheeem Bammm! He was getting too close, we'd have to take evasive action. Sherwood pulls the carrier off the road down a very steep gradient, it takes us out of view but puts us at a perilous angle. We wait, listening intently. We know what to do, it's a terrible trick, you wait for a vehicle going in the opposite direction, and while Jerry is

165

following him, you scoot out the other way. This we did, some poor bastard in a recce car came by and got the lot, and Whoosh! the khaki cowards were gone!

Back safe and sound, I collected my breakfast, and join the G Truck bivvy. The fire was being rekindled by Vic Nash, fresh from his bed and looking like the spirit of dawn in his shirt, boots, half a fag, and coughing his lungs up.

"They didn't get you then?" was his cheery greeting.

"No, but you'll be glad to know they nearly did."

"You could go back again."

"No, they've stopped piece work."

"Ahhhhhggggg."

Enter Edgington, a dixie in one hand, a tea mug in the other. His unlaced boots reveal a late dash from bed to cookhouse.

"My God, you got to be quick," he said.

Now Fildes enters eating and walking. "Ahhh Milligan . . . you just been up the OP, what's it like?"

"Darkness is the best time to go."

"Oh fuck! we're going up in an hour's time. I'm taking Mr Walker and the relief party. How far is it?"

"About fifteen miles."

A spark from the fire has shot out into Edgington's tea.

"Ah well," he says philosophically, "it can only improve it."

"I am now going to kip, as is my just due," I said.

What had started as a clear day now became overcast, and I hurried to sleep to avoid it. During that sleep the big push for Monte Camino was moving to its starting lines. Three Divisions. But what's this on my bed? A piece of Army form blank with a St Andrew's cross on it. Was this an invitation to a game of noughts and crosses? No, there in a clear hand was the warning: "The Phantom Arsole strikes again." What had started as a promising day now grew black with clouds. I slept the clock round; that is, I went to sleep in November and woke up in December.

DECEMBER 1, 1943

REGIMENTAL DIARY: *Supported fire continued through the night.*

FILDES' DIARY: *The "do" begins tonight.*

MY DIARY: RAIN, BLOODY RAIN.

"And, on the fifth day, he divideth the land from the waters." Not any more he didn't, for "On yer umpteenth day, he mixeth the land and the water and lo! he maketh mud, and he putteth his beloved son, Gunner Milligan, up to

Christmas greetings card showing conditions in the Italian theatre of wàr.

his neck in it.'' Command Post very busy all day, preparations for fire plan for attack at 2200 hours.

Ammunition is being dumped by the guns, through the day the pile of mustard-coloured shells mounts up. Mud is everywhere. Are they going to attack in this weather? Up a mountain? At two in the morning? I couldn't help but recall Siegfried Sassoon's World War 1 poem:

> He's not a bad bloke
> Said Harry to Jack
> As they humped their way forward
> With rifle and pack
> But he did for them with his plan of attack.

(I *think* that's right.) Did that thing still happen? To add to our emotional confusion we are issued with Christmas Air Letter Cards. They have no particular artistic merit, done by a run-of-the-mill artist. Most certainly I wouldn't let him run my mill.

Christmas? It didn't seem possible. Yet, somehow, the ancient message was still relevant (a bit of a white relevant), and the echo of Childhood Christmasses held strong in the memory. That distant happy time had strength, the call of family and close feelings remained indestructible. Hearts and flowers, please!

The truck from Wagon Lines has arrived with Christmas Mail. Smiles all round. A parcel from my dear mother. It's sewn up in a cloth wrapping, giving it the appearance of a mummified cat. With jack-knife, Army for the uses of, I, stitches parcels for the undoing of did. Fruit cake! Mars bars! Holy medals, holy pictures, cigarettes, holy smoke!

We have to double up on Command Post duties, one signaller on the wireless set, one on the telephone and the Tannoys to the guns.

"Christ, no sleep for us tonight," said Ernie Hart.

Ben Wenham is testing the dags, and topping them up with distilled water.

"Give 'em a little drinkypoos," he said, talking to himself.

The OP party have left, Lt. Walker, Bombardier Trew, Jam-Jar Griffin, Pinchbeck, they've gone in our newly acquired jeep, with a "cheese cutter" on the bonnet. This was an upright metal bar that was introduced when Jerry patrols started putting taut thin wire across a road after dark, which resulted in decapitating the passengers. Long lines of supply mules are heading up the line, kicking, braying, biting, their Cypriot handlers forever leaping out of the way with shouts of "Oushi! Oushi!" The weather has grounded all flying (it's even grounded walking) though we do hear one lone plane that sounds like a Jerry, it is, he drops some splinter bombs in a graveyard!

"I think he's losing his nerve," said Lt. Stewart Pride.

All is ready for the big do, codename "KONKER".

A sub gun lets off occasional harassing fire so the pre-barrage silence is not too obvious. Edgington is out with the line maintenance signallers. Every half-hour a check call comes through from them.

"Hello, Line Maintenance here, line OK?"

"Yes, OK."

"Thank fuck."

Yes, we were all fully employed.

0200. Barrage Starts

After preliminary fire orders are given to the guns, the fire plan takes over and we just sit and wait for targets from the OP. There are nearly a thousand guns savaging the night.

0400. The Attack Goes In

Like a miracle the rain stopped just before zero hour. Is God on our side?

A Tale of Gunner Edgington

'Twas a dark and stormy night and the Monkey Truck signallers lay dead asleep. At the soul-shattering hour of 0100 hours, with a gale blowing and rain squalling the tempest-black night, a cry is hurled among the dormant bodies.

"The OP line is 'dis'."

Reacting like a Pavlov dog, Edgington rises, dons his boots, and plunges into the night. He follows the wire, falls into a three-foot muddy stream, mends the break. At dawn, while we were taking the first tea of the day, a spectre appears at the Command Post entrance, it is the same height as Edgington . . . it *is* Edgington, from head to foot it drips with water and mud overlaid with a fine layer of frost. Two eyes look out from the mud. It groans.

"Edgington!" said Vic Nash, "you naughty, naughty boy, I've told you never to play with those boys next door! You just wait until your father comes home." Nash is lucky to be alive.

DECEMBER 2, 1943

MY DIARY: MISSED BREAKFAST.

"Sorry I'm late, Ronnie," I said in a grovelling voice, "I didn't get to sleep till late."

"I'm sorry, matey, it's all gone, there's some tea left, and some bread."

"Tea and bread? Oh yum yum, can you make the tea as cold as possible, and the bread nice and stale, I don't want to get used to luxuries."

Ronnie May grinned. I always wondered why a man with such a refined Etonian accent ended up cooking. Apparently he came from a very upper class family in the jewellery business. He went to Harrow and but for the war would have gone to Oxford. He had fallen in love with a working class girl, and the family frowned on the prospect of marriage. The war had come along and to prove that he wasn't a snob he had turned down a commission and become a cook. This was all to impress the girl, who then went off with an officer. I reheated the tea on Spike Deans' primus, and toasted the bread on the G truck fire. Seeing my foodless plight Deans says, "Would you like something to spread on that?"

"Oh Christ, yes," I said.

"There's some boot polish in my pack."

The utter swine. Revenge! I contacted Bombardier Sloggit at RHQ. He worked in the Q stores. He in turn phoned

Deans and said,

"Report here at once, there's something for you to collect."

Deans reported and was given the empty boot-polish tin and told, "If ever you get some butter, you can keep it in here."

Checkmate. Ten o'clock, my turn for Command Post duty. Taking a writing pad and some old newspapers, I walked down the incline across the small depression, up the slope. I passed Maria doing a mountain of military laundry.

"*Buon giorno*, Maria."

She smiled and blushed, the innocence of Italian country girls was something to see. Something else to see was the top of her stocking tops as she bent over.

"You're ten minutes late," said Ernie Hart.

"I'll give you a receipt for it," I said, "and if that's not

Command Post, Fontana Fredda, December 1943

171

enough, tonight I'll wear a hair shirt studded with hob-nails, OK? Now, if you hurry up you'll see the back of Maria's bum.''

We were very busy all morning, a total of 587 rounds were fired in support of the Camino Battle. On the Infantry network I hear a new map reference: ''Bare Arse Ridge''. How it got its name is hard to conceive. Lt. Walker said it was during a previous attack, the Guards had come upon several Jerries squatting down having a ''Pony''. One would be hard put to it to find a memorial that said ''To the Fallen of Bare Arse Ridge'', and yet that was the case.

We came to a slack period. I start writing seasonal letters, and some poetry which was crap. I read it to Lt. Wright. ''What do you think of it, sir?''

''I'm afraid, Milligan, I shall never think of it,'' he said.

The rain had let up, a weak silver sun strained to make itself felt. Suddenly, from what seems directly above me, comes the roar of aero engines, oh God! are we for it?, a long burst of machine-gun fire. We all rush out, there are shouts of alarm, men are running and looking up. There, at about 500 feet, are a squadron of American Kittyhawks; the leading plane appears to be coming straight for me. I don't understand, I hadn't ordered one. His machine guns are blazing away, a figure hurtles from the cockpit, a parachute mushrooms, the fighter flashes past and hits the ground a hundred yards to our left. There is no explosion, so! Hollywood had been lying to us. The pilot is floating down on to an adjacent field. Our idiot Major appears.

''Follow me,'' he says as though we're the Light Brigade. He leads, holding out his pistol, he doesn't run straight for the pilot, no: we follow the track plan, we skirt the edge of the field in Indian file, the pilot is extricating himself from his chute and wondering why we are circling him, the Major bounds up, he points his pistol at a man chewing gum, wearing a red flying jacket with the words HANK, THE KID FROM IDAHO on the front, and a yellow bird on the back inscribed FLYING EAGLES, he is taking a cigarette from a packet of Camels.

''Hands up! English or German,'' says the looney Major.

The American went purple. ''You're fucking lucky I'm anything, it's your trigger-happy fucking Ack-Ack, why don't

172

they make up their minds whose fucking side they are on."

The Major was a little taken aback, steadied himself and said, "Consider it a gesture in return for the number of bloody times you've bombed us."

This was great fun – Christmas, not only fighting Germans but each other. After being entertained at the officers' mess with a cup of tea, he was whisked away by a USAAF jeep driven by a coloured private wearing a white bowler hat. Don't ask me why. We waved them goodbye.

"Come and crash on us again some time," we called.

Edgington is stumbling from his cave. "What happened?" he said. "I was writing to Peg."

I grabbed his arm dramatically. "Writing to Peg?" I echoed. "You missed the crash? Wait, I'll see if I can get him back."

They all go across to see the remains of the Kittyhawk. The thieving bastards make towards the wreck with chisels, hacksaws, screw drivers, I call, "Leave a bit for me."

Circling the wreck Edgington had said, "I wonder if there's anyone underneath."

White bends down and shouts: "Anybody underneath?"

FRIDAY, DECEMBER 3, 1943

MY DIARY: POURING RAIN. DUG A DEEP DRAINAGE PIT AROUND MY BIVVY TO DIVERT FLOW OF WATER. G TRUCK NOW HAVE LOGS ON THEIR FIRE. VERY COSY. UNENDING BREW-UPS OF TEA AND COFFEE. BACK ON COMMAND POST DUTIES. MUST ANSWER LETTERS.

A letter from my mother and father had said that my brother was to go into the RAF (as he ended up a private in the Ulster Rifles, I began to feel uneasy about my parents' sanity). My father's letters were getting to be a pain in the arse. He seemed obsessed with the idea that I "didn't answer your mother's letters". Now at that time I thought he might be right, but on checking with my Correspondence log I note that I answered each and every letter. Since then and down the years to his death, he continued to insist with his accusations, so much so that I registered all my letters (over the years it cost a bloody fortune) and stuck all the receipts in a book that I presented to him on his seventieth birthday

173

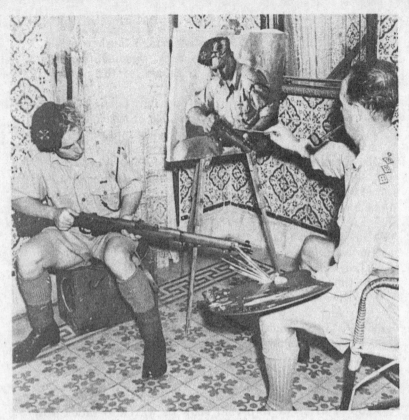

British soldier forcing officer to paint his portrait at gunpoint.

with the message "To dear Dad, a small token to prove that I always answer all Mum's letters." He looked at it and said, "This is a fake, my memory is the real proof of your laxity in letter-writing to your poor mother." He even wrote to all our relatives asking them to write to me and pressurise me to "answer his poor mother's letters". It was a true case of mania. He died saying, "Promise you'll write to your mother today." She was standing beside me at the time.

My mother's letters were equally a mass of instructions, "Pray to Saint Patrick and Saint Theresa *every night*. Go to Confession and Communion every Sunday! Say prayers morning, noon and night, always wear your scapular medals, don't swear, keep your holy pictures in your pockets" . . .

How do you go into action? On your knees?

OP OFFICER:	Target tanks.
ME:	Yes sir, *Et in secular*, target tanks, Amen.
OFFICER:	HE 119 Charge four.
ME:	Yes sir, HE 119 Charge four. God forgive me for attempting to kill Germans.
OFFICER:	Angle of sight 03 degrees.
ME:	03 degrees. Holy Virgin, bless these fire orders.
OFFICER:	Right ranging.
ME:	Right ranging *mea culpa, mea culpa, mea maxima culpa*. Amen. Fire!

I know now that Evelyn Waugh was a Catholic, and in Yugoslavia, pissed out of his mind, went all out for medals by standing up during bombing raids and shouting to poor Randolph Churchill under a table, "Come out, you yellow swine." Well, I wasn't *that* good a Catholic.

DECEMBER 5, 1943

MY DIARY: RAIN. GUNFIRE. BOREDOM, HOMESICK, LOVESICK.

These early December cold, rain-soaked days were hanging heavy on us all. The boredom was only alleviated by sheer effort. Off duty we would foregather at "Chez G Truck" bivvy. The consumption of tea was enormous, we had more of it than ammo; for men to return from mud, shells, rain and cold to enter our little den and see a woodfire was great. Edgington was a linesman, whereas *I* was a wireless operator – the ratio was that of navvy and bank clerk. Edgington's intelligence warranted more than linesman – but his performance on a wireless set during hectic fire orders would have ground the war to a halt. He couldn't do things at anyone else's pace, it had to be his *own* – he was his own total master, he gets it right, but all in *his* own time and you can't do that in a war. He squats near the fire, his mug to his lips.

"Ahhh!" he gasps, "Heaven."

"Heaven?" said cryptic-voiced Nash, "call this bloody heaven?"

"It was a momentary lapse," said Edgington, "it's passed

off. I no longer think this is heaven – I'll rephrase it – it's Fucking Hell."

Edgington has just returned from OP line maintenance, he tells us there's very little Christmas spirit up there. The season of goodwill is stone dead, and so are our young men. We outstare the fire in silence, Nash throws his stub into the flames. The saltpetre flares blue. Fildes is uncasing his guitar.

"Gonna burn it?" said Deans.

Fildes ignores him; attentively he tunes the strings.

"Play 'The Nearness of You'," I said. Alf nods. "E-flat," he says.

We all sing it. Enter Jam-Jar Griffin.

"Oops sorry, vicar – is there a service on," he said reverently, taking his hat off.

"Yes," says Nash, "active-fucking-service."

"Can I join in?" guffaws Jam-Jar, taking off his overcoat. "Let me partake of this seasonal red tannic-acid tea – and wish my guts the compliments of the season. A real Dickensian Christmas to you all."

Guffaws. Alf Fildes laughs long at Jam-Jar's old world posturing.

"'Ark," says Nash, cupping his hand to his ear in fairy-like gesture, "isn't that an old Dickensian 7,2 gun goin' off? – 'pon my word I didn't know Christmas was so near – I must to the workhouse to put my Christmas Puddins in place."

Alf starts to play "I'm Dreaming of a White Christmas", we all join in. All evening Deans had been in a state of agitation, finally, "It's no good," he said, "I'll have to open it."

Open what? He has a bottle of Marsala! he has been waiting all night for us to depart, but couldn't wait any longer, now he *had* to share it! He consoled himself with a mug-full before letting us into it. It tasted like vinegar.

"It's corked," I said.

"Corked? it's fucked."

"Let's think of something nice," said Deans. "Are you going anywhere for Christmas?"

"Yes," I said, "I'm going to spend a few days in my tent in Italy."

"I think I'll take a stroll round my truck – never know who you might meet," said Fildes.

176

Buzz-buzz. Our private phone is going. Deans raises it.

"Hello – Chez G Truck . . ." he hands me the hand-set. "It's fer you."

Gunner Hart in the Command Post is asking me, " 'Ave you taken the pencil?"

"No, I haven't, I've only got my own." Can he borrow it, otherwise the Battery will be "out of the war".

In a few minutes he appears covered in mud.

"I fell over," he said.

I handed him the pencil.

"Cup of tea?" said Deans.

"Just a sip," said Hart. "They're waiting for me to start the war." He took a hasty mouthful. "Ta," he grinned.

"Fire one for us," we called after him.

"Any special colour?" we heard him say.

The drumming of rain starts on the canvas ceiling, I throw a log on the fire, it reflames, a shower of needle-sparks fly up the chimney.

DECEMBER 8, 1943

This day the battle was won. Jerry pulled out and Monte Camino was ours. I don't think a battle could have been fought under worse conditions. The pace now slackens, I manage a wayside bath in a tin. It's so cold you keep the top half fully dressed while you do the legs, then on with the trousers, strip the top half and do that.

We are all fed up with being in the same position, and rumours are flying. We're going home, etc., and the best one of all – the war is going to finish in eight days!

DECEMBER 9, 1943

I can't take much more of this bloody rain. It's time we had a rest. I must have been depressed because on this day my diary is empty.

FILDES' DIARY: *I'm getting fed up with myself here and will be glad when we move or go for a rest.*

REGIMENTAL DIARY: *Body of soldier reported lying dead in passage in RHQ.*

It wasn't mine. It turned out to be an engineer who had committed suicide. "Lucky bastard," said Nash. I think we were all feeling like that. At 1530 hours came orders that might have saved his life. "17 and 19 Batteries will move to rear position for refitting and rest." The news fell like a bombshell, it galvanised smiles back on to our faces. We were walking around and saying like Mr Barrett to Elizabeth, "You must *restttt*, my dear."

I give the order from the Command Post to all Guns, "Cease fire – prepare to move." We could hear the cheers come back over the headphones. The tempo changed as though we'd all been given a shot of adrenalin. I got radio AFN and plugged it through to all the gun-pit Tannoys.

We danced with each other all day.

DECEMBER 10, 1943

Today we go back! Griffin enters G Truck bivvy, a garland of withered flowers on his unshaven head, a blanket, toga-fashion, around his ungainly body. "Beware the Ides of March."

"Beware the Clap of Naples," was the reply.

"I come to bury Caesar, not to praise him."

"The shovel's in the lorry."

"The evil that men do live after them."

"We must fill in the shit-pit before we leave."

"We got ter clean up the battlefield." Bombardier Fuller, known back home as "Stop thief", is passing on the commands of our Major. Soon, carol-singing gunners are roaming muddy fields gathering fag ends, packets, bottles, dead mules, tins, and place them on a funeral pyre. As the flames roar up, a cry, "Anyone for suttee?" Other guns are firing, not us! Wasn't it lovely? We stand and watch the sweating gunners on the 3.7s; when they loose off a round we all cheer and they tell us to piss off or they'll turn the guns on us. Nasty men.

In the Command Post, Lt. Walker, MID, has liberated the souls of the duty signaller and specialist with excerpts from a whisky bottle. We start rolling in the telephone lines, and dismantling the equipment.

"I could do this with my eyes closed," said Ernie Hart.

"Try it then," said Shapiro. He did, and dropped it in the mud.

"Stand by to move!" What we are supposed to stand by they do not say. I choose a tree. You never know when you might need it. I have Kung Fu'ed my kit into my big pack and kitbag. I have wrestled my tent to the ground, got a half-Nelson on the tentpole and heaved it from the earth, then with a great javelin throw I have hurled the lot into the back of G Truck.

"Owwwww fuckkkkk," so the truck is not empty. Through his burnt binoculars, Jenkins has spotted some rubbish in yon field, and he sends yon Gunner Hall, and we can hear yon swearing from him.

Yes. We're all ready to move. All the rubbish has been picked up. The pits filled in.

"Yes," Edgington reflects, "we've done everything save strew fresh grass-seed."

We were ready to move. We stand by our vehicles, all smiling, and as I say, ready to move. We warmed the engines up, ready to move, cleaned the windscreens, ready to move. Oh yes, we were ready to move. I said so. "I'm ready to move, aren't you?" I said to Edgington and he said, "Oh yes, I'm with you on that, as sure as I'm 954022, I'm ready to move."

For three hours we were ready to move, then four, five and six hours. We were all falling silent. On the seventh hour Bombardier Deans said, "I think somebody's fucked it."

Lt. Walker is passing with a bemused smile on his blond face, he turns and says, "What are you waiting for?"

"Anything," I said.

He paused then walked on towards his truck, where he turned and shouted, "If it's any consolation, I'm as pissed off as you are."

"There's a big hold-up on the Teano Road," said BSM Griffin, trying to help.

"There's a bigger fucking hold-up here," said Jam-Jar. "I'm going to see a lawyer!"

"Give him my love," said Griffin.

All night we sat and froze with only tea and bread scrounged from the cookhouse truck as relief. In painful positions we tried to sleep out the rain-filled night. It was like being tied up in sacks and thrown in the Bosporus. The growling of empty stomachs rings round the valley. At the sound of a snore a sleepless voice says, "Lucky bastard." I have had my legs in every position except behind my neck, and I'm saving that for an emergency. I am just dozing off with my legs behind my neck when the truck jolts.

"Mummy, mummy." I shake Deans gently by the throat. "Get the bucket and spades, we're off."

Along the dawn-haunted roads we slush along. By now, life has so little interest, an announcement that the world was coming to an end could only have cheered us up. I am dozing, dozing, smoking, dozing. . . .

"Wake up! We're 'ere."

BSM L. Griffin as he appeared in Volume 3

180

Deans is clambering out the truck, sleepily I follow, and where are we? It's a farm. We are in a large courtyard flanked by a large four-storeyed redbrick Victorian Gothic building with a circular Camelot-type tower, along with numerous other utility buildings. The courtyard was knee-deep in crap. We donned our "Wellies". We are all assigned a building, the Specialists and Signallers are given what is a shed being used as a coal-bunker.

"You'll have to clear it up if you want to get comfortable," said Sergeant King. I dumped my kit on the coaldust-laden floor.

"Can't we burn it and start again?" I said.

There was the "sorting-out-where-to-kip" time-lag, and then at 10.30, BREAKFAST! By which time most of us had forgotten how to eat. Hard on that we parade for Captain Sullivan.

Captain Sullivan, who personally supervised the chicken-shit clean-up.

"As you can see, this yard has been crapped in for the last hundred years by chickens, cows, sheep . . .".

Was he going to say, "now it's our turn"?

"If we've got to spend Christmas here, we don't want to spend it up to our neck in shit, so we've got to set-to and clear it up, the sooner the better."

He then left us to clear up the shit, while he went away not

181

to. The lads set-to with shovels, but I could see that it was going to take days. I put the great Milligan brain to work and I came up with the answer. Some large squared-off timbers lay around, the thickness of a tree trunk; they were about twelve feet long by about four feet square. To these we attached dragging ropes and by pulling them along the yard up a slope, we deposited the crap into an adjacent canal. Any chicken that tried to crap here now got a brick on the back of the nut. Clouds of black coaldust swirled in the air as we set about our shed. We got so black that soon the strains of "Swannee Ribber" were heard, and what appeared to be negro gunners doing the cakewalk.

"I don't think this was always a coal-bunker," said a blackened Deans. "It's been used as a garage at times."

"Oh what a relief," I said. "These little bits of unsolicited information do wonders for us."

It was a weary bunch of gunners that bedded down that sooty night.

With the usual ingenuity, each man had concocted a bed of sorts, the most painful was Gunner Devine's. He slept on a sheet of corrugated iron, it made the most devastating clanging noise every time he moved.

DECEMBER 12, 1943

MY DIARY: COLD AND RAIN. CONTINUED TO SHOVEL SHIT AND COALDUST.

Much the same as yesterday. After the overnight rain the courtyard has refilled with crap, and we start all over again. The Signallers and Specialists attacked their billet. They enlisted Ted Wright, who drove the water cart in and turned the taps on. There is nothing to report for the days that followed, save the horses. (Save the Horses. A new appeal.) The fallow fields and meadows housed a collection of horses and a few donkeys. A ride wouldn't be a bad thing. With this in mind the Gunners Devine, Nash, White and Milligan strode manfully over the canal bridge, and closed in on three shaggy looking equines. At our approach, they looked up, ears forward; with lots of outstretched hands and utterances, "Good boy, here boy, woah boy", and "Come here, you bastard", we managed to get one to stand still while Vic Nash prepared to mount. Had he ridden before? He thought so. Up he goes. He sat there for a few moments savouring the height; being a short-arse, this was all new to him. He lights a cigarette.

"Never mind the bloody fag, get the thing going."

Devine was anxious to see the display. White was somewhere chasing a brown filly that had almost taken him out of sight. We had heard him shouting implorations, but he was now down to slinging lumps of turf after the reluctant creature. Here, however, Nash was preparing. He threw his cigarette away, then said to the animal, "Come on . . . off we go." She didn't go off. He tried several more "off we goes", but she went on grazing.

"Get 'er head up, will you," he instructed us.

This done he tried a sudden use of the heels and in doing so fell off.

"I thought you said you could ride," said Devine.

"I thought so too," insisted Nash.

Devine helps him up again but they still argue.

"It hasn't moved yet and you've fallen off."

"It takes time to get back into the swing of it . . . when I say ready, give her a smack on the arse. . . . right?"

Right. Nash settles, takes a firm hold of the rope and the mane.

"Right," he yells.

Devine connects his palm with her rump. SMACK! loud and clear. We helped Nash up again.

"I don't think I'm going to be able to remember," he said.

Devine pats the horse. "I can do better than that: I've never ridden, but it should be easy. I seen tons of cowboy pictures . . . they never fall off." Milligan and Nash hold hands as a step. Devine is on!!! He smiles in triumph. Devine is off. White has come running back, he has chased the brown horse out of the province. He settles for a donkey. Great, he's on, he stays on, and manages to get the animal to run around.

"Anyone got a camera before it's too late?" he shouts.

After the trials of "Cowboy" Devine I got on and rode the

horse at a canter around rather muddy fields. I hadn't ridden since I was a boy in India. I had forgotten how wonderful it was, and that smell peculiar to horses; we messed around like this until we hear a terrible yell and a splash. Nash is in the canal. Devine had challenged him to leap across and he had failed. Devine is laughingly helpless as Nash thrashes the shit-strewn waters and swears his way to the bank where Devine hauls him up, only to find himself on the same side he'd jumped from. There is a shivering run by Nash along the canal to where the bridge is, some quarter of a mile away. He divests himself of his now reeking battle dress, and hangs it outside to dry. It's past redemption. The smell is appalling. He tries to exchange it at the Q stores; he had only been in there two minutes when everyone ran out. When he ran out after them, they all ran in again. They told him to get it washed and it would be alright. The farmer's wife fainted when he showed it to her. Finally, he boiled it. It killed the smell but the suit shrank twelve inches. In a fit of despera-tion, he put it on; his appearance in the Q stores sufficed to point the need for a new one. Alas, the new one was two feet longer than him. The moral is, don't go riding. But many persisted; every evening, the meadows were full of galloping horses with gunners hanging round their necks. The Italian farmer wondered why every morning his horses were too shagged out to pull his wagons. He reported this to the Major and Part 2 Orders read, "The practice of riding farm horses in off-duty hours will cease forthwith, as the animals are only for agricultural use." "Thank Christ its all over," said Nash from somewhere inside a battle dress.

Ahhhh! The Army Kinematographic Corps have visited us! they set up their cinema in our billets! There's to be three shows starting at three . . . second house six . . . last house nine.

"Signallers and Specialists in the last batch," said Sgt. King.

Bloody nerve, it was in *our* billet, we had to move all our beds, and we had to wait outside until nine at night. We all strolled over to the Tower house, where Edgington and mob are in a frenzy of pontoon. Lire notes are piled in the middle, and like true punters and sportsmen their faces are masks of utter misery. Smudger Smith is Banker. They have been

playing nigh four hours, and the total winnings are somewhere in the neighbourhood of twelve shillings, there could
be suicides before the night is over.

"Stand behind me, Milligan, you're Irish, bring me luck,"
says Money-Mad Edgington.

Strangely enough, his luck did change, he lost the lot.

Some of the lads had seen the three and six o'clock show
and knew it by heart. The film was *Casablanca*, dubbed
Case-of-Blanco, with "Humphrey Gocart".

Every entry by Bogart was greeted with "Now listen, Blue
Eyes." Ingrid Bergman got " 'Ave you had it yet darlin'?"
Bogart in Casablanca town was repeatedly warned "The
invasion's cummin', piss orf before you're conscripted."

At one stage as Bogart nonchalantly put his hands in his
pockets, a warning to Bergman, "Look out, darlin', he's
going to show you the white-eared elephant."

Claude Rains was greeted with "Here comes the weather
report." When Bogart's victim fell to the ground there
was "Stretcher bearer!", kissing was greeted by 200 gunners
making suction noises. I can never ever watch that film
again. I report in full Alf Fildes' diary, it gives an interesting
insight as to what an ordinary soldier was thinking on that
day thirty-five years ago.

*Cinema Show in our garage, so we're out all day till it's
our turn. Good film* Casablanca, *lots of barracking. Humphrey Bogart, Ingrid Bergman and Claude Rains, but made
me rather lovesick and homesick, nevertheless very entertain-
ing. Most of the lads sweeping up muddy courtyard along
with parades. Maintenance with Milligan leading mad moments of his latest invention called "Drooling", a new game
with effects on victims, who are pounced upon with verbal
hoots and groans like gorillas. How mad we all are when
there's a war on and no artificial pleasures. Jerry still holding
his winter line cleverly with MG's and Mortars but 5th Army
gaining yard by yard.*

CAMINO MONASTERY *piled with dead of both sides and
therefore unoccupiable since rock surface affords no graves for
bodies, it must have been horrible to clamber up that sheer-
razor rock with mortars dropping with lethal accuracy but,
after changing hands a number of times, it is now definitely
ours and the 46 Division are advancing with the Yanks.*

TUESDAY, DECEMBER 14, 1943

Mobile Shower Unit have arrived, naked gunners all over the place, steam, soap, whistling, songs, pranks. A Quartet of naked men are standing in barber-shop formation – Edgington, Milligan, Devine and White. The water cascades down them, patent-leathering their hair to their heads, water jets run off their noses, elbows and willies.

"We're poor little sheep who have lost our way, baaa, baaa, baaa." This is all done with a fine feeling for dramatic gestures, arms shoot up in all directions, occasionally the steam would obscure them completely. We sang for nearly an hour; when we came out all of us were bright red.

"I feel giddy," said Edgington.

"It's the loss of dirt," I said. "It leaves you dizzy."

Having given us a shower we are now told to don our denims and "Clean the underside of all the signal vehicles." An hour later we were all shit-black again. As luck would have it, the showers unit was still working; soon from the steam came "We're poor little sheep . . ."

The Bath Corporal said, " 'Ere, weren't you lot in this mornin'?"

"Yes."

"You're only supposed to 'ave *one* go."

"This *is* only one go," I said.

"This is the second time you been in. I recognised the singin'." Fame at last!

He forthwith switched off the water. We were left naked, covered in soap and shivering.

"I'm not 'avin' this," said Devine, who runs after the Corporal. Soon the water flowed again, but then it went off again, and on again, and off again . . . we could hear a scuffle out back somewhere, then the thud of a body falling to the floor. Devine reappeared with a turncock, he had blood coming from his mouth. "The bastard! I told him."

What had happened? Simple. The Bath Corporal now lay unconscious by his control valve.

"Hurry up, then," said Devine. "I didn't hit him very hard."

THURSDAY, DECEMBER 16, 1943

REGIMENTAL DIARY: *RA Band visited 10 Corps area and gave performance in the Teatro Garibaldi at Santa Maria, and Capua Vetere.*

MY DIARY: ONLY EIGHT SHOPPING DAYS LEFT TO CHRISTMAS. OH DEAR, I MUST HURRY.

FILDES' DIARY: *Still no Naples or rest but plenty of graft.*

Graft yes. We are cleaning and recleaning our Signal equipment.

"I can't clean this wireless set any more, Sarge."

"Why not?"

"It's starting to scream."

Afternoon. All ranks other than those on guard and regimental duties will proceed to Santa Maria for the RA Band Concert.

The Garibaldi Theatre fronted a muddy street. The interior was a wonderland of plaster work, gilt, marble columns and red velvet. Built 1840, in classical style, it would be a show-piece anywhere. Right now the RA Band are pumping out "Colonel Bogey". We listen to a few Sousa Marches and off out. American Red Cross Cinema! That was for us. It's full. Round the back, Milligan. Open door. On to the rear of the stage. Fildes, White and I lay on our backs on the reverse side of the screen and watched George Brent and Mary Astor in a film I think called *Black Victory*

When the titles came up, White said, "This must be the Joe Louis versus Max Schmeling fight."

I wish it had been. The film bored me to death, it was a series of doors opening and people coming into rooms, talking about an inheritance, then leaving; after door number fifty opened I fell asleep. I'm woken by Fildes to "stop bleedin' snorin' ''', I can't imagine what people on the other side of the screen thought as this inexplicable snoring was heard in a scene where the Will was being read.

Home to dinner and we lay awake a long time yarning about Christmasses from yesteryear. Deans asks what the film was like.

"It was a film where suddenly! nothing happened all the time."

FRIDAY, DECEMBER 17, 1943

Today was like Tuesday the fourteenth without the baths.

We have a new MO, a Captain Duggan from the RAMC; he was a pink-looking Irishman with freckles, about six foot, and tall with it, thin, and a hat that seemed to be loose on his head. He walked about a bit like Jacques Tati. At the sick parade all the men felt worse after seeing him. He had come from Kerry, and been a smalltown doctor, mostly farmers.

Gunner Bailey went sick with a twisted and swollen ankle; he was given aspirins. Gunner Musclewhite went in with Dermatitis and got Castor Oil, "Jock" Wilson went in with a boil on his nose, and was told to "Run it under a cold tap."

"It stands to reason," said Bailey, "if you went in with appendicitis, he'd give you a holy picture and tell you to pray."

A stickler for fresh air, Captain Duggan slept with the windows open. A week later he was taken from us with Bronchitis. As his stretcher was slid into the ambulance a Scots voice was heard to cry, "Don't forget, run him under the cold tap."

It's mid morning, there's lots of work everywhere, but nobody doing it. Where are we? A small shed among some trees behind the big Tower block. From it come low voices and palls of cigarette smoke. This is the hideaway, the inside reeks with gunners making tea and smoking; they are ignoring distant voices of sergeants calling, "Where are you, you bastards?"!

The game is to make occasional appearances. We always left a skeleton staff on maintenance while the bulk of the layabouts hid. It was Crown and Anchor with Dai Pool, he brought the board up with the rations, he doled out our cigarette allowance, one hour later he had won them all back. I think today he has a villa on Malta and lung cancer.

SATURDAY, DECEMBER 18, 1943

Zounds! Great Grundles of Gerzolikon. It's happened. I feared this day for many a month. There, in black and white in clear language on Part Two Orders. "Guard Commander: L/Bombardier Milligan. S. 954024." So Milligan was trapped. There was one privilege; you got the afternoon off to prepare your kit. One could never place a brush to a boot without the remark, "After another bloody stripe, are we?" I blancoed my webbing, polished all my brass, then wrote a letter home.

Major Evan Jenkins is driving his batman insane.

"He wants 'ees battle dress 'ung up to attention, 'eees boots angled out at forty-five degrees, mustn't put 'is 'at upside down, it's an insult to the gun on the cap badge."

As retribution, he used to swig Jenkins' whisky then top it up with water, and Jenkins used to wonder why he could never get pissed on it.

"Very good turn-out, Bombardier," said Captain Sullivan of the guard mounting.

"Yes, sir," I said, "I wonder what's gone wrong."

I saluted him. He saluted me. We saluted.

"Dismiss the men, Bombardier." I saluted, he saluted.

I saluted him. He saluted me. We saluted. They saluted. I turned smartly.

"Old Guardddd, officer on paradeeee – dissss missss . . . New Guard . . . to the Guard Room . . . Dissss . . . misss."

Boots thumped on the cobbles and the men trooped into the guardroom, leaving Driver Alf Fildes on first stag picking his nose. Like a good guard commander I slept smartly to attention that night. I awoke once when Gunner Jock Hall knocked the tea bucket over. I leapt to my feet and saluted it.

SUNDAY, DECEMBER 19, 1943

Next morning I wrote in the Guard Report, "0545 Hrs, Tea, buckets for the use of, knocked over, spilling contents. Took immediate action and returned bucket to upright position. Signed L/Bdr Milligan. S."

The dawn was clear, and stars were still lingering in the morning sky, underfoot a hard white frost. The Billet was still and quiet, sleeping forms locked in their dreams. What better than to cheer them up, CRASH, CLANG, I dropped all my webbing and sang "God rest ye merry gentlemen, may nothing ye dismay." Why then were they so dismayed?

Here I was awakening them, so that they would not be late on parade, and what do I get? But wait, what is Gunner White saying to me, his hands round my throat, "You cunt! . . . today's SUNDAY . . . SUNDAY!"

The more religious had gone to mass at RHQ. I didn't. I was a bad Catholic and I didn't want to spoil my fine record. I wanted to be like my father. All his life he totally ignored his religion, but when he's told he's dying, suddenly! it's Good Catholic Time! "Call a Priest," he says. "No, wait, call a Bishop."

In those moments before death he was re-baptised seven times, went to confession a dozen, and took communion six times. He used to say, "What's the use of being a good Catholic for seventy years? All you need is one confession before you die and it makes up for all of it, and look at the time and money you've saved!"

The Sunday was all letter-writing, yarning, darning holes in clothes, reading, and fishing in the canal. I spent an hour feeding worms to the fish and gave it up. Gunner Miller of 18 Battery has a real line, and is catching Roach, Dab, etc . . . He gave me two. Ronnie May grilled them and I gave one to Edgington (who doesn't remember the occasion), he complained bitterly, "It's full of bloody bones."

"Of course it is, everybody is, you'd fall down without 'em."

DECEMBER 20, 1943

"Looking forward to Christmas, Harry?"

Edgington looks up from his mess-tin. "I'm not sure, mate, in one way yes, in another no, the no part is spending it away from home. You can't help feeling homesick, and it's worse at Christmas."

There is no place to be at Christmas except home. I thought of the Christmasses I remembered from boyhood days in Poona. I remember the little room I slept in at the back of the house in 5 Climo Road, the indescribable excitement of waking at four in the morning, with the world of adults all silent, finding the pillow-case full of boxes and toys, and the magic as you unwrapped each one. . . . I remember waking up at the very moment my mother and grandmother were putting the pillow-case at the bottom of my bed, explaining how "Father Christmas had just gone", and when I asked which way he went, they pointed at the window; as it was covered with chicken wire, I worked out that he was magic, had got through the holes and was now a jig-saw puzzle. All that and more was moving in the memory bank of my past, and I too knew that Christmas on a farm in Italy could never be the real thing. Ted Lawrence, the Don R, brings news of Kidgell; he's in Naples at the REME Depot.

Driver Kidgell

191

"Lucky buggers, billeted in the middle of Naples for *three* bloody weeks."

Edgington is reading a shirt. "Remember that girl in Bexhill with the hairy legs who played Chopin?"

"Yes," I said, "that's all I ever think of, she and her hairy legs playing Chopin."

"I wonder what happened to her?"

"I suppose she's shaved her legs and they now play Rachmaninov."

"I remember the time we were pulling out of Bexhill——"

"You pulled out in Bexhill? What was the poor girl's name?"

He ignored me. ". . . we were pulling out, and we were detailed to clean up the officers' billets——"

"Trevissick?"*

"Very! . . . we were just finishing off, when you spotted a crate of booze in the back of the garage. I remember one bottle was rum, and you and I started to sip it, remember?"

"Yes, if I remember, I sipped half the bottle and you the other, we carried the bottle through Mill Wood, getting more and more pissed, we finally got out the other side on the Ninfield Road, and you remembered this bird because you'd tried to have it away with her, but she wouldn't have it because she was getting married."

"I know, I told her I was trying to warm her up for the honeymoon. . . ."

"Helpful old you. Anyways, we arrived at her place, it was about mid-day, she let us in and you insisted that she play some Chopin."

"Yes, I remember. She didn't half play me up, she took me home one night, straight into the bedroom and, laugh, she was a mass of Women's Mag clichés. When I pulled her skirt up she said, 'There was a flash of pink thigh, and a rustle of silk petticoat', then when I kissed her, she turned her head away and said, 'She turned her head away and felt his warm breath on her neck.' I began to think she was a dummy being worked by Barbara Cartland. When I gave up trying I got up to leave, and as I combed my hair, she said, 'He stood, nostrils twitching, combing his plum-black hair.' I never saw her after that, though she did leave a message

*Name of officers' billet in Bexhill.

with the Battery office for me to contact her. 'Tell him I've changed my mind', was the exact communication; what it was she changed her mind about I'll never know."

Gunner White is sitting on an oscillating petrol tin, and reads from an old *Bexhill Observer*. "Listen! German raiders attacked several points along the SE Coast, a bomb was dropped on a farm, the explosion blew the door off the bull pen, the bull made his way to the cow pasture and the farmer had great difficulty in getting the bull back. He himself was attacked."

Gunner Birch, shrouded in cigarette smoke, tells us that in a letter from home his father told him there was a theory that Hitler was insane as the result of piles.

"Hitler has piles?" chuckled Edgington.

"*I* don't know,' said White, "it's my father, he says – " here he picked up the letter and read, "Ron Lester, the publican, said that Hitler went mad through piles, he was operated on by a doctor, and the operation went wrong, and he still has them."

"It was a Jewish doctor," I said. "That's why he had it in for the front-wheels."*

"Don't tell me," said Edgington sitting up, "don't tell me World War 2 is due to piles."

"What a sobering thought," I said. "To think, a case of Anusol Suppositories could have stopped it."

"It's not too late," said Edgington. "We should load a Lancaster and drop three tons of pile ointment on his Reichstag."

"You see? Nothing's sacred these days, even a man's Reichstag."

Birch blinked and listened at the conversation he had started. "What's a Reichstag?" he said.

"Grub up," is all someone had to say to empty the hut.

Drooling

Fildes has already mentioned this, let me amplify.

The Oxford Dictionary says it's "To drivel, to slaver". I give you the lie, in our battery Drooling had an entirely

*Front-wheel skid = Yid.

different meaning. It started on the farm and, in our case, the cause of drooling was sexual frustration. If you saw a lone gunner for no perceptible reason suddenly make a low groaning sound that sounded like OOOOLEEEEDOO- LEYYYYYY, at the same time appearing to grab an erect invisible phallus with both hands that by their position suggested a "chopper" about five feet in length, which he then proceeds to thud against the nearest wall with a cry of OLLEEEDOOLEE, THWAKKKKK!! OLLEEEDOOLEEEE THWACK!!, this was the new Drooling craze. It was not abnormal to come into pre-parade gatherings of bored gunners all apparently holding mighty invisible choppers, thudding them against walls, trees and the ground. When Major Jenkins first witnessed this from a distance, he asked Sgt. Jock Wilson, "What are they doing, Sergeant?"

And Wilson said, "It's something to do with the shortage, sir."

Jenkins parried, "The shortage of what?"

Wilson replied, "We don't know, sir."

Travelling on the back of a lorry, the sight of a pretty girl immediately erupted into mass drooling until she was out of sight. Of late, the song "Drooling" had come to light; it was sung to the Flanagan and Allen tune, "Dreaming".

> Droooooooolingggg
> Droooooooolingggg
> Each night you'll find the lads all Droooo-lingg
> A little Drool don't hurt no body
> And if it does then we don't give a Sod-dee
> Droooo-ling
> Droooo-ling
> It's so much better than Tom Foolingggg
> A little drool can ease your heavy load
> So keep Drooling till your balls explode.

The author is unknown, he wants it that way.

The farmyard square (now that it had been cleared of three hundred years of dung) displayed a fine cobbled courtyard; the farmer, who had lived on the farm since he was born, said he didn't know it existed. The lovely tall tower of the main farm block afforded a good all-round view from its oval windows that was repeated all up the staircase at- ten-feet intervals. The tower had nothing at all to do with farming, nor had the building. It was obviously some landed gentry's country manor that had been vacated or sold cheaply to a farmer. The farmer kept horses and a few cattle and grew crops, along with a few fruit orchards.

Devine has returned from a fruitless fishing trip, "Are they sure there's fish in this canal?"

"Where else, you silly sod?"

"Then why didn't the fuckers bite? All I caught was this."

"That's a . . . er . . . it's not a salmon," said Liddell; not a bad guess, the creature was three inches long and black.

"It's a nigger's dick," said White.

"Oh, great," grinned Devine, "I'll smuggle it back to Liverpool and hire it out to old ladies."

"Oh dear," said Deans in a female voice, "and I've cooked all these chips." He stamped his foot on the floor, from which arose a cloud of coal-dust.

Bombardier Fuller has arrived, "There's a little line-laying to be done – no panic it's only a short one, about a quarter of a mile." As we clamber aboard M2 truck, we witness the spectacle of a Driver Ron Sherwood of Reading, riding a bicycle backwards. Ask him to do a job and he's gone in a flash, but ride a bicycle backwards, oh yes, he'll do that all day. Sherwood was a lovely footballer on the wing with a slight tendency not to pass to anybody, and he wasn't a bad pianist, no, he was terrible. He could get the right-hand melody going, but with his left hand he would hit *any* note, but he did it with such panache, a smile and a wink, that cloth-eared gunners would say, "Corrrrr, you can't half play the piano", and they were right, he could only half play that piano.

Very quickly we laid the line to RHQ. I opened the door to see a gaggle of our top officers all swigging whisky; among them was dear Major Chater Jack, now a Lt.-Colonel. It had not changed him, he was still knocking it back.

"Hello, Bombardier Milligan," he said warmly.

"Nice to see you again, sir – can you see me?" He laughed.

With a few pleasantries exchanged, I connected up the D 5 telephone.

"There's some of the lads outside, sir."

"I'll come out and see them. . . ."

From the top he waved down to the lads on the truck, we

all wished he'd never left us. It was the last time I would ever see him. The date was December 16, 1943.

I remembered the first time I'd seen him in Bexhill, a smallish, very dapper man, a weathered face, always ready to smile. I had noticed he was wearing a very fine brand-new pair of brogues.

"Very nice shoes, sir."

"My batman doesn't like them."

"That's because he has to clean them, sir."

This Christmas Concert is bothering me, I tell BSM Griffin, "If we don't get a piano we can't do the concert."

"Oh, we can't have that," he said, his Welsh accent thick as the Brecon peaks. "It's going to be alright, Spike. Lt. Walker's going with you in a truck tomorrow to look for a piano."

Great. I tell Harry. "Oh good," he said, "pick a good one."

"Pick one? They don't grow on bloody trees."

"A twenty-foot Beckstein, otherwise I refuse to play it."

He and others were on "shit scraping" duties. This was the general title given to any cleaning jobs, and as the farm and the buildings seemed never to have been cleaned since the Renaissance, the crap was everywhere.

MONDAY, DECEMBER 20, 1943

MY DIARY: 0830. OFF WITH LT. WALKER LOOKING FOR A PIANO. SPARANISE FIRST. PLACE HAS BEEN HAMMERED TO BITS BY ARTILLERY BUT PEOPLE STILL LIVE IN IT. NO PIANO. ON TO CAPUA, NO PIANO. ON TO SANTA MARIA LA FOSSE, NO PIANO.

We weren't having much luck. I went into the Teatro Garibaldi hoping we might knock off the piano. As I entered I hear someone playing a splendid rendering of the Liszt Concerto No. 2 in B Minor. The pianist was a young American sergeant. Outside again, I walked around a street market and (so my diary says) for some unknown reason I bought an aluminium washing basin. On the off chance I asked the old vendor if he knew where I could get a piano. Immediately he said, "*Si, vengo qui domani alla mezzo giorno.*" I tell Lt.

196

Walker but he had already had a success, he too was to go to an address at two o'clock. We repaired to a restaurant.

Strange, the memories that exist for me from those days. The cities of the Campagnia seemed grey, dank, the streets permanently wet or muddy, the Italians looked drab. A sort of melancholia lay over the land. It didn't affect me, as I was by nature hyperthyroid and mindlessly happy, but I remember those atmospheres as though it were but yesterday.

Meantime Back at the Farm!

We hear tales of Mussolini holding out in Northern Italy.

"Wot can he do?" says Gunner White. "I mean he's what . . . sixty? He's screwing this bird, wot's 'er name, Clara Petacci, he's got a few Iti 'erberts in black shirts on two-stroke motor bikes waving daggers on parades outside ruined Roman arches, wot's he think it's going to lead to? Hitler must have been off his nut to have him rescued."

"Well," said Arthur Tume philosophically, "Musso might 'ave owed him money."

There was a long pause, and then the surprised voice of Jack Shapiro chimes in.

"'Ere . . . I never thought of Hitler 'avin' money . . . I mean . . . does he ever have to go into a shop and say 'Ten Woodbines, and have you got change of a quid, and can I have a few shillings for the gas meter?'"

White says, "He has to 'ave his barnet cut, and the barber can't do it for nothin' . . . someone has to shack out for Hitler's haircuts."

"The German people pay for it," said Bombardier Deans.

"The German people???" Edgington laughed. "Haircuts only cost a couple of bob, how do you divide two bob between ninety-five million Krauts."

"They don't," continued Deans. "They take it in turns to pay."

"I wonder who's turn it is this week," said White.

"They never know," said Shapiro. "It's a reign of terror, they never know who's next to pay for Hitler's haircut." Here he stood and dramatised. "Suddenly, in the middle of the night, boom, boom, there's a knock on the door . . . and that's yer lot . . . the haircut payment squad are there."

"I suppose all the Jews left in Germany pray for Hitler to go bald then," said Milligan.

At two o'clock, we arrived at a house. Lt. Walker straightened his hat, and the reason why was soon revealed. A very pretty girl answered the door; from the truck I heard him speak in broken (broken? Shattered) Italian, he was full of smarmy smiling and head wagging, pulling out all the stops. Concluding, she bid him farewell and he lingered till the last view of her was obscured by the door.

"Very interesting, sir," I said as he returned. "But – the piano."

"Ah yes . . . the piano . . . we – er – have to collect that tomorrow," he said, looking dreamily ahead . . . the dirty little devil.

TUESDAY, DECEMBER 21, 1943

MY DIARY: THE PAGE IS BLANK.

Why? Who knows? I usually made up my diary last thing at night, and I am almost sure what stopped me entering in it was an outbreak of Drooling my Spike Deans. I remember, it was late at night, we were in the garage billet, we had got our brazier going, two in fact, and several of us were seated around them, drinking our own brew-ups, and smoking.

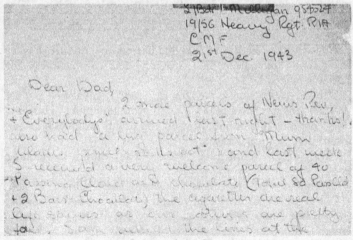

Letter of the Day

Some of the lads were already in bed, among the leaders was Gunner White. He was sitting up, smoking a dog-end and clutching a brown mug. The calm was broken by the entrance of L/Bombardier Deans, Jam-Jar Griffin and a few more piss artists.

"Watch this," said Deans, removed his hat and very carefully aimed it at a distant point, then threw it; it landed anywhere, so we all wondered what we had watched it for.

"What were you aiming at, cunt?" said White.

"I was not aiming it at *anything*," said Deans, "it was just a display of *joie de vivre*."

"Joie de fuckin' vivre?" said White. "What's that?"

"Means, my dearest heart, joy of living."

"There's no fuckin' joy in livin'," was the immediate reply. Deans sat at the foot of White's bed.

"Darling," he said, "have you missed me?" . . . then grabbing White's feet through the blankets, said, "Who's little feetiepoos are these, eh? . . ."

White squirmed uneasily. "Geroff," he said.

Deans, still holding White's feet through the blanket, knelt.

"Ohhhh, dearest is upset, has someone upset my dearest whose little white feet I am holding through the counterpane?"

"Buggerorf," giggled White.

Deans moved his hands up to White's shins. "And whose little leggy poos are these, are they the ones my dearest has been dancing on all day on fields of daisies?"

Deans moves his hands up again to White's thighs.

"Go on, bugger orf," giggled White, who moved uneasily, but not enough to spill his tea, and in this, Deans knew he had White trapped. Nothing will make a gunner spill his Char, it was as predictable as the greedy monkey who couldn't get his food-filled fist back through the bars.

"Darling has been lonely without her diddums to love her, hasn't she?" Deans runs his hands Charles Boyer-like up the blankets on White's thighs.

A small group of interested spectators have gathered around the scene, Deans starts to massage White's thighs, with White himself laughing and saying, "Someone get the bugger off."

"Bugger off? You want your darling, who brings you romance on an Italian farm, to bugger off? . . . Tsu, tsu, tsu," then with a lightning move of the hand, Deans grabs White's cobblers. A great yell from White, who tries to escape and the whole bed collapses sideways to the floor, exposing White naked from the waist down. Deans lets out a horrified gasp, and lunges forward, his quivering finger pointing at White's Wedding Tackle.

"What's this? Ohhhh, while I've been away my darling has been unfaithful to me. . . ."

There ended the romantic interlude.

I might say life wasn't all gaiety and laughter. Alf Fildes' diary of the time mentions:

Boy am I browned off with this God-forsaken army. We have been here a week and still no recreation or trip to Naples. I've had four hours in Naples while others have had days. Doug [Kidgell] is there with the Scammells and some chaps with the guns, lucky devils, but I suppose money won't last long among those thieving bloody Italians, who are still charging four times the value of the goods. I'm sick and tired of this dragging war and dictatorship within this lousy tin-god ridden army. Give me peace or I'll go mad soon. [Soon? He was late. We were already there. S.M.] *And what does this army do to try and cheer us up while the Yanks live in luxury at base kidding themselves they are winning the war and sitting pretty. The whole system stinks!!!*

There you have it. I wonder if Churchill knew all this?

WEDNESDAY, DECEMBER 22, 1943

Battery Orders: the following men have been chosen for GOS's Parade. Santa Maria La Fosse.

Breakfast	0630
Parade	0730
Embuss	0745
Arrive	0815
Parade	0830
March Past.	

Best battle dress. Lanyards will be worn. All webbing to be blancoed. Full FSMO less small and big pack. Rifles will not be carried.

As each one saw his name on the roll he gave a groan and slumped away like a broken man, the one word that destroyed, BLANCO!, it struck terror into all.

In a disbelieving voice Sergeant King reads, "Concert Party *excused guard* in lieu of Rehearsals!"

Morning Parade has gaps in the ranks. "It's the Concert Party, sir," comforts BSM Griffin.

"There's SIXTY men missing," says Major Jenkins. "What are they putting on . . . *Aida*?"

We have sent for Driver Kidgell in Naples. The Guns and the Scammells are at workshops being overhauled; *he's* not being overhauled, no, he and his oily bloody mates are sitting on their fat arses saying "Phew" as they exhaust themselves playing Pontoon, and only move for meals and selling petrol. Half of them are freezing to death as they've sold their blankets, some of them are already in the Mafia.

On the morning of December 22, his lordship Kidgell arrives in a stately three-tonner lorry, he's waving from the window like Royalty and the subjects are returning it with certain signs from the waist down. He drives up to Edgington and I who are trying to make one cigarette do the job of twenty.

Short-arse Kidgell is preparing to leap from the cabin, for this he really needs a parachute.

"It's an insult," he said, "why didn't they send the Rolls?"

"Rolls? You *still* bloody hungry," I said. "Let me take the Royal Big Pack, and count the Royal Cigarettes."

He'd done alright for fags in Naples. "I bought 'em on the black market," he said, as I unearthed ten packets.

Edgington is walking behind, holding up Kidgell's overcoat like an ermine cape. Bombardier Deans spots the entourage, runs forward with his groundsheet and throws it before the dwarf driver.

"'Tis the Virgin Queen," he chortles.

He's timed his arrival well. Lunch.

"Where's the cookhouse?" he said, forming a queue on his own. The sight of our well-prepared stage had impressed him. "Bloody marvellous," said he, "can you eat it? Where's the cookhouse?"

We watch as Kidgell devoured a third helping of duff as

though he'd been adrift with Captain Bligh. Kidgell licks his knife. "My motto is, today I live, tomorrow I die."

"Well, it won't be from bloody starvation."

Meanwhile, back at the stage, Sid Carter and a group of minions are performing miracles, using coloured crepe-paper and bunting; the stage looked splendidly seasonal, even front curtains on runners. "Manglewurzel" Wenham had installed footlights.

"Watch this," he said, and lowered the lights.

"Cor," said appreciative Kidgell, "nearly as dim as you."

"You bugger," said Wenham.

The piano has arrived. It is an aged black upright. Edgington supervises the unloading as though it were a Bechstein, however it was to sound more like a Frankenstein. As he struck the first chord the response was like running an iron bar around the spoke of a bicycle.

"What bloody fool chose this?" gasped Edgington.

"I did," said Lt. Walker. "Isn't it satisfactory? I mean . . . it looked alright."

"Oh, it looks alright, that's all you can do, look at it."

"Oh dear." Lt. Walker was obviously distressed, after all, he was an officer, and here he was being told he was a musical ignoramus. "That piano has set me back to the tune of 800 lire."

"Well, sir, that's the *only* tune you'll get out of it."

That afternoon, armed with pliers, Edgington and I tuned the piano; as he tightened the first string, it snapped with the sound of a bullet ricocheting. BSM Griffin entered at the moment to see us flat on the floor.

Kidgell reads the piano manufacturer's name. "Bertorelli. Milano."

"Bertorelli? Don't they make ice cream?"

"Yes," said Edgington. "They mix it inside."

By sheer effort we managed to tune the piano to a reasonable state. Getting the thing on the stage we dropped it.

"Oh, fuck nooo," groaned a despairing Edgington.

"Don't worry, don't worry," said Shapiro, our khaki Jew. "It can only make it better."

The Concert

We had been overwhelmed with a mountain of jokes, ideas,

202

etc., most of them too terrible to perform; some suggestions were *impossible* to perform – who in God's name would tolerate Gunner Chalky White singing *Ave Maria* nude save for army boots?

"The best we can do is pick the least offensive," I said.

"They're *all* bloody offensive," said Jam-Jar Griffin, who was "Manager" for the Company.

Gunner White gives a soppy grin and says, "General Alexander says we must be on the offensive all the time."

"You can't sing *Ave Maria* in the nude, man. Some of the Iti farmers and their wives have been invited."

"I've got a good voice," said White.

"You've got a big prick as well," I said.

"They don't *have* to look at it."

"How can they miss it."

"Ities like good singing'."

"Not with yer prick hanging out."

Edgington, Fildes and I had "written" a reasonably funny hillbilly act. We set about making beards by unravelling rope, and brushing it into shape. We used boot polish to blacken them.

"Behold!" says Jam-Jar Griffin, holding up four ragged shirts. It was just what we wanted for hillbilly costumes. Where did he get them?

"Pinched 'em off a washing line, keep yer eyes open for four Ities naked from the waist up."

Using miles of adhesive tape, Edgington and Fildes are affixing megaphones to the muzzles of our rifles to give them the appearance of blunderbusses. Sergeant Donaldson prepared blank ammunition by pulling the bullets from their cartridges like teeth.

"Be careful how you point, these will give a flash ten foot long."

"Don't worry, that bastard Jenkins will be in the front row, we'll point 'em at him, ha ha ha," said Jam-Jar.

"A ten-foot-long flash could make some old lady very happy," said Gunner White.

Jam-Jar Griffin is organising the traditional Army seating. "Brass hats in front, rabble at the back."

He had the Battery office working overtime typing and duplicating programmes. The pre-Christian spirit was starting to pervade, and everyone seemed full of bonhomie or alcohol. After lunch a truck is going to Capua and some of us hitch a ride. Driver Sears parks his truck off the road, immobilises it; that is, he leaves it without a driver. Capua! of course. Hannibal and his hairies had knocked the shit out of the Romans just outside. He'd gone but the Romans were now in cafés, selling coffee in cups that looked suspiciously like thimbles with handles on.

"Ort ter bring our own bleedin' mugs," said Sears. "Thirty lire a bleedin' cup?"

"Etta costa thirty lire because eet ees *reala* Braziliana Coffee," said the proprietor.

He should have added, "Stolen from our beloved Allies". However, it was worth it to see the pretty girls seated around. Those *eyes*! Iti girls must have the biggest in the world! To get a smile from one changed the shape of the day; it certainly changed the shape of your body. Helppppp!

The evening ended with a Gunners' beauty contest. The first entrant was Bombardier Milligan wearing a towel and a bra made from two army socks. Deans announced me as "Miss Brockley of 1904, winner of last year's never-been-shagged contest". I am followed by Gunner Devine draped in a blanket, he is "Miss Various Veins of Liverpool, and other areas". Devine turns to reveal a bare bum. "Miss Various Veins is wearing the peek-a-boo skirt with a view of Oscar Wilde." Close behind comes lovely Gunner White in a gas cape. "Miss Conduct of Battersea is wearing the plunging knee-line." White opens the gas cape, he is naked save for an army sock tied round his willy; he wins. Remarks and shouts came in profusion from the spectators, it went on till lights out. As I lay in bed I wondered if we were really going round the bend.

DECEMBER 24, 1943

Christmas Eve Parade

The night before Christmas Eve, after tea, we had all, as was our custom, traipsed across to the Battery office (comfortably ensconced on the top floor of a farm building) to read Part 2 Orders.

"Oh no . . ." says Gunner White, "Oh no, no, no, no." He backs away as though he has seen Dracula. We are ALL to parade on the morrow, to be inspected by GOC 10 Corps.

"Oooo's 'ee?" said Gunner Forrest.

"'Eeee", I explained, "will either be David Niven or someone else."

"'Oooo's David Niven?"

"David Niven", I further explained, "*is* someone else."

Edgington is reading further from Part 2 Orders. "Ohhhh Christ, listen to this, not only an Inspection BUT, we will March Past him."

"That is a total waste of energy, why doesn't *he* march past *us*?"

"Perhaps his legs are in REME," suggests Edgington, doing a Ritz Brothers face, and doing a ridiculous sideways walk. "Come, men," he says, "to La Belle Ballet de blanco." He leaps a clumsy *jete*, sending up a muddy spray.

The morning of Christmas Eve, we awoke to find the dawn blowing but sunny. "Corr, it's parky—" Tired men coming off guard, they rest their rifles against the wall, yawn, and fall on their beds. The Guard Commander, Syd Price, enters, his pipe wafting morning smoke-signals; he hurls his webbing on to the floor.

"Down, you buggers . . ." a change of tone as he sees us all abed. "Come on, you lazy bloody lot, it's Christmas Eve, Father Christmas is on his way with a box of blanco for all good little gunnerkins."

A wave of rude remarks. He chuckles. "You are all rude, nasty little gunners, and I'm never going to play mothers and fathers with you again."

Sensational news, "Eggs for breakfast."

A mighty unshaven rush. I race across the courtyard, Edgington close behind. "Trying to break the four-minute mile?"

"Yes and soon trying to break the six-minute boiled egg."

It's amazing, this spirit of Christmas. Everyone is cheery, there are smiles on the faces of miserable buggers. In a sing-song voice Gunner White recites "Christmas comes but once a year and when it does it brings good cheer".

"Wrong," says Gunner "Dirty Bugger" Bailey. "It's Father Christmas comes but once a year! and when he does

205

his wife has Christmas Pudden Club fear!"

9.00. We are on our transports heading towards Santa Maria La Fosse. We all sing,

> Good King Wenceslas looks out
> On the feast of Stephen
> When the snow lay all about
> Deep and crisp and even
> Brightly shone the moon that night
> Tho' the frost was cruee-ell
> When a poor man came in sight
> Playing with his Tooooo-oooo-lllll.

We are dumped on a raised muddy road without the environs of Santa Maria la Fosse . . . there are Gunners everywhere. We line up next to the 74 Medium, we spot Ken Carter and Reg Bennett, who wave and point to their white webbing.

"Frost," shouts Bennett.

"Stop all that talkin'," shouts a Sergeant.

"It's the only language we know," I said.

"Can we do some mime?" pipes up a voice.

"Silence," says the Sgt.

The GOC walked along the ranks, stopping every now and then and starting now and then. He stops now and then in front of me. I'm trying to stifle a laugh.

"What's your name, Bombardier?"

"I *think* it's Milligan, sir."

He walked on till he was quite a way away from me.

"For Gord's sake," whispered a North Country voice in the ranks behind, "don't upset 'im, he could send us back to t'front."

"What do you mean 'back to front'? . . . make up yer bloody mind."

Ahh! the Royal Artillery Band are striking up. Boom, bang, crash, ta ra ra ra bimmm, the Bass Drummer is so short we can't see his head above the drum, just a pair of legs hanging underneath.

"19 Batteryyyyyyy . . . . . Attennnnnn . . . . . shun! Riiiiiiiiightttttt . . . turn! Kweekkkkkkkk MMMMarchhhhh!"

We swing along the road in the direction of the town and past the saluting base, which appears to be a gunner in the crouching position covered with a blanket. On it stand the

GOC and the OC2 AGRA. As we swing past them, there is a subtle waft of whisky.

"Eyeeeeessssssss Right," roars the command.

We stamp along in fine style, we don't know where we're headed, but we are marching as if we do. The step is getting ragged as the band goes out of earshot, the rhythmic marching becomes a great mass of overlapping steps that sound like we're in an echo chamber. We reach the outskirts of town and are dismissed.

"Now then," commenced BSM Griffin, "there's two hours to see around the town, the lorries will be back 'ere to pick us up at – " he looked at his wrist, realised he'd forgotten his watch but went on " – at 1500 hours. Any late 'uns will have to walk back. Right, disssss . . . misssss."

We repair to a café. Ernie Hart points to a sign saying "English soldiers welcome", in chalk someone had added "and their MONEY". It's the same semi-gloomy interior, a grubby Iti and a mountainous wife.

"Quatro café and Quatro Cognac," I signalled.

We sit at a circular iron-topped table that I seized like a steering wheel and started to make motor-car sounds.

"I'm driving this bar to a better area," I said, crouching over the table. "Brrrrrr Parp Parp."

Italians at other tables are looking at me and smiling, the British don't usually behave like this. We stayed there till we were stoned. We are all decidedly happy as the lorries tumble-dry us back to the farm, where we arrive dead on the stroke of one. Those who aren't dead we carry back to their beds. By six o'clock, after plenty of tea, we were sobering up. All talk is of Christmas. Those who had parcels from home were feeling them, smelling them, tearing little holes and peeping in.

Spike Deans had over the pre-Christmas months been keeping a supply of wine and Marsala in which G and T truck had all paid in so much per week; he, for some reason, had added sugar to the wines, and at this very moment was calling the faithful, "G Truck and T Truck members this way to intestinal trouble."

He had the bottles uncorked, and we presented our mugs for the seasonal cheer. By eight o'clock we were all very merry again; we went to the gun-teams' billets and sang carols. Well-meaning insults were hurled from the windows above. Back in our billet, we went to bed and continued consuming the last of the wine.

There was something grim about going to bed in a coal-bunker on Christmas Eve. As I got in, I remember all those child Christmasses when my mother and my grandmother tucked me up in bed, my face red with excitement at the coming of Father Christmas, the magnitude to the child mind of new toys on the morrow, the trying-to-get-to-sleep-so-as-to-wake-up-early feeling. There was no joy ever quite like that. I tried not to think of all those happy yester-Christmasses, but in the dark they came flooding back to me. I had always wanted toy soldiers, now I was one myself. The billet was mouse quiet. Were they all thinking like me? Outside, a cold wind was playing the trees. Christmas. Somewhere in the rest of this fucked-up world there were still children wide awake. Someone had started snoring, so he had escaped from his nostalgia. Christmas Eve, God, it was quiet, or was I just making it seem that way? No good, I couldn't sleep. I lit up a cigarette. Christmas Eve. What was Mum doing? Dad? Desmond? The Christmas tree at 50 Riseldine Road; we always had a small one in the front room, we bought it from Wheelers at Honor Oak Park. Dad would always buy a bottle of sweet Sherry, a bottle of Port, three bottles of Brown Ale and two large ones of Lemonade, all from Lovibonds, the off-licence on Brockley Rise. All the bottles were saved, as Desmond would take them and get a few pennies on the empties. The Trifle!!! I remember that, I enjoyed it even more than the chicken (we couldn't afford turkey) . . . all that custard, that cream. At some hour during those kaleidoscope memories, sleep must have taken me. Away to the north of us, our sister Batteries were sending out a Christmas message of death and having the compliment returned by an equally unseasonal enemy.

CHRISTMAS DAY, DECEMBER 25, 1943

ALF FILDES' DIARY: *Sgt.-Major Griffin and Sgts. wake us with tea and rum and we're off!*

MY DIARY: LATE REVEILLE, DON'T HAVE TO GET UP. BSM AND SGTS. BRING US TEA AND RUM IN BED.

It was all too much. "Give us a kiss, Sarge," I said as Mick Ryan filled my battered tea mug.

"You'll kiss me arse," he says. An unbearable thought.

All around, smiling gunners are sitting up like old ladies in Geriatric Wards, grinning. "Merry Christmas," they say to each other. We linger over the Rum-laden tea.

"There's a carol service at RHQ, at 11.00, if anybody wants to go."

Why not? It's Christmas, the season of goodwill? Nobody went. A Regimental Parson in a barn merrily sang "The First Noel", all by himself. Fried Eggs and Bacon for breakkers! Wow!!!

The morning was spent fiddling around with the stage and props. All seemed set; we then concentrated on thinking about Christmas dinner.

Soldier and Italians trampling on a German soldier in back of lorry.

"I will eat mine *very, very* slowly. I want it to last as long as possible," said Gunner White.

"They say there's tinned turkey on the menu," I said.

"How do you know?" said Kidgell, his stomach revolving at the thought.

"I heard a rumour."

"Look, mate," said Kidgell, "I don't want a *rumour* of a turkey, I want a *real* bloody one, parson's nose and all." So saying, he ran off to practise eating.

A detail of layabouts had been rounded up and a long makeshift table laid out in an adjacent barn. It consisted of long planks resting on trestles, blankets for tablecloths; someone with a soul had stuck thorn-leaves into some tins to resemble holly. BSM Griffin's voice rings on the air.

"Come and get it!"

We take off like sprinters and collide as we try to squeeze through the door. Thundering ahead is Kidgell, his legs barely touching the ground; pounding behind him is Gunner White, his tongue dragging along the floor. The cry goes up, "For God's sake stop Kidgell before he gets there or we'll get bugger all."

Like a jig-saw puzzle we all fit into place around the table. We sat on an assortment of chairs, stools, tins, logs. We are served, as is the tradition of the Royal Artillery, by the Officers and Sergeants. Lieutenant Walker is the wine waiter; himself having partaken of several pre-lunch drinks he is missing the glasses by a substantial amount. Gunner Musclewhite has a lap full of white Chianti, and Gunner Bailey is getting red wine among his greens. The Sergeants are ladelling out tinned turkey, pork, beef, roast potatoes, sprouts, carrots and gravy. None of our "waiters" are quite sober and there is an overlap at the end of the dinner when Sgt. Ryan is pouring custard over the turkey. As the wine takes effect, the chatter and laughter increase. For duff we have Christmas pudding and custard.

"''Urry up, you buggers," said Sgt. "Daddy" Wilson, "we're waitin' to 'ave ours."

There seemed endless helpings and unlimited supplies of red and white wine, but it was a long way from the Dickensian Christmas around a log fire in the parlour, with Grandma and Grandpa present. However, when you are pissed, all that nostalgia goes out the window. Gunner Smudger Smith stands on his chair and sings "Bang away Lulu".

> Bang away Lulu,
> Bang away Lulu,
> Bang away, good and strong,
> What you gonna do
> When you want a blow through
> And yer Lulu's dead an' gorn.

The Sergeants and Officers are returning, carrying make-shift trays laden with bottles of beer, oranges and nuts. Smudger calls for a toast to "the Orficers and Sarnts". There follow more toasts to the Regiment, the King, and in fact anybody. I distinctly heard, "Gentlemen, the toast is Anybody."

We gave the Sergeants and the Officers a cheer and in that order. We left the table looking like Genghis Khan's horse-

"Daddy" Wilson, eldest member of the battery, aged 93

men had galloped over it. I felt as though they'd galloped over me. There was aught but sleep it all off. We washed our mess-tins in the three separate troughs – WASH, RINSE, DISINFECT, for those interested in detail – these were made from oil drums sawn in half and filled with the requisite liquid. In fact there was to be a "Quickie" in the concert where "Brutarse" stabs Julius Geezer, then proceeds to Wash, Rinse and Disinfect the murder weapon.

Those who had thoughts of getting into Naples were frustrated, as the city was declared out of bounds due to typhus. "Merry Typhus," some of them were saying. The great moment is drawing nigh, the Concert! The audience are arriving early, most of them with bottles of beer stuffed in their coats. The programmes they are reading were as below:

PROGRAMME OF CONCERT

1. Introduction: Spike Milligan and Erbs (Session No. 1).
2. Joe Slater (vocalist, tenor): "As Time Goes By".
3. Sgt. King, normally known as Ross King: "The Green Eye of the Little Yellow God".
4. THE ROYAL HORSE HILLBILLIES (otherwise Milligan, Edgington, Fildes, Kidgell and White).
5. George Shipman (baritone): "Shipmates o' Mine".
6. Jock Webster: Scotland for ever.
7. THE GREATEST ITEM EVER. ALLINSCRAP: Man Mountain Deans (142lb including tin hat & Small Arms) versus The Barnsley Basher (Rollicking Robinson, 156½lb including truck, less tools)
   Referee: The Younger Griff.
8. Community Singing: All the old favourites, led by Spike.
9. BSM Griffin (The Ancient Griff): "The Great Mystery".
10. Douglas Kidgell: Songs you all know and hate.
11. Reg Griffin, assisted by Ken Deans (Spike No. 2).
12. L/Bdr. A. Smythe, otherwise known as Smudger Smiff.
13. Sgt. Lawrence: "Air-burst by Guinness".
13a. Doug mad act.
14. Duke Edgington at the piano.

15. Bags of Back-Chat from Joe Kearns.
16. Spike Milligan and the Erbs once again.
17. Leslie Spence.
18. *Command Post Follies*.
    Scene 1 – the only one!!! Same as before! In the Field.
    Cast in order of appearance.

Gunner and overworked Ack:	Lt. R. D. Walker, RA
Sergeant:	Gnr. V. Nash
1st Subaltern GFC 1:	L/Bdr. Milligan T.
2nd Subaltern GFO 2:	Bdr. Deans K.
Battery Captain:	Gnr. Edgington H.
Battery Commander:	L/Bdr. Griffin R.
Two Signallers:	(Gnr. J. White)
	(Gnr J. Kearns)

19. FINALE – The Whole Shower. "Jogging along to the
    Regimental Gallop" (tune of "Whistling Rufus").

FINIS

Note: Blokes attending Concert will be searched at door for
hand grenades, bad fruit or packets of "Veees". If
M & V is thrown, please retain tin for salvage.

"The Show"

The "artistes" are hidden from view behind a screen of
blankets that have run the length of the hall. Behind it all
the secrets of showbiz are poised to hurl on an unsuspecting
audience. The building reverberates to the buzz of conversation. We open with a chord behind the curtains, then I
shout:

"Ladies and Gentlemen! the 19 Battery Christmas Show!"
The Band swings into "We're the Boys from Battery D",
then switch to our two ocarinas for the Rocamanfina Rhum-
ba. In the absence of a good finish the band all shout HOI!
Curtain down, we dash off to change. We hear Gunner Joe
Slater in his strangled tenor singing *As Time Goes By*.
Edgington is left behind to accompany him on piano. We
keep an ear on the song,

. . . Moonlight and love songs
Never out of date
Songs full of passion
Jealousy and hate . . .

Joe Slater – out of his tiny mind with bullshit.

"I should be singing this," said Kidgell, as he stuck his stringy beard on.

"Harry will have to be quick," said Fildes. "He's only got 'The Green Eye of the Little Yellow God' to change in."

Edgington rushes in while Slater is still taking his applause. "Where's me beard?" he gabbled. We help him into his gear and soon he looks like Zeke MacCoy of Coon County. Sgt. King is on and getting a hard time from the lads.

"He was worshipped by the ranks."

"Was he fuck!" came an authoritative cockney voice from the back.

"You're on," says Jam-Jar.

Fildes, White and Kidgell set themselves up on the stage. Edgington and I wait in the wings.

"Ladies and Gentlemen, the Royal Horse Hillbillies."

Boos, etc. Curtain up. The scene, three hillbillies, seated, drinking Racoon Juice and "Barr's Sweat" from our rum-ration jugs. Gales of uncontrollable laughter. Why? Gunner White is showing a pair of testicles hanging in full view from under his nightshirt. Fildes is paring his toenails with a jack-knife; in his hands he holds a dozen three-inch bolts that he drops as his toenails are pared. Kidgell swigs his "Racoon's Piss", spits, and from the back of the hall comes a Dangggggggggg! as BSM Griffin hits an empty 25-pounder shell-case. BANGGG! BANGGG! Edgington and I let off our blank cartridge muskets. We had never tried them before, so loud was the explosion that a great gasp of "Corrr bloody hell" ran through the audience. At the same time two tin plates dislodged from the roof and covered us in a patina of rust.

214

"Don't fire any more," said a terrified Sloggit, who was working the curtains.

Enter Edgington and Milligan.

Kidgell: "War yew tew bin?" (SPIT AND DANGGGGGG).

Spike: "We dun just kilt a barrrr" (SPIT AND DANG).

Edgington: "Beegest Barrrr I ever seed" (SPIT . . . LONG PAUSE SMALL TING!!!).

Spike: "That barr, when I seed him he dun growl, so Ahhh growls back, he leans ter the laift, so Ahh leans to the laift, he scratches his balls, so Ahh scratch ma balls . . . then that barrrrr dun a shit, and I said Barrrr yew got me there . . . I dun that when I fust seed yew . . ."

A few more gags like that, then we all sing "Ah Like Mountain Music", Fildes on the guitar, me and Edgington on ocarinas, Kidgell on the "Racoon's Piss" Jar. The music was interspersed with rhythmic spits and distant Dangsssss!!! in tempo, and we went off a treat.

'Gunner Shipman will now sing 'Shipmate of Mine'," announces Jam-Jar. " 'Ees never seen a bleedin' ship," heckles a voice.

The curtain goes back to reveal Edgington at the piano in bare feet, dressed as a hillbilly. Shipman has a pleasant baritone voice inaudible in the low register; he insists on walking about as he sings, causing numerous clink-clanks from the stage. His song is frequently interrupted by hissed whispers from the wings, "Keep still." He stops in mid song to ask the voice what it is saying. "Keep still, the floor's squeaking when you walk about." He then continues except that his last position was on the extreme right of the stage, so we have a spectacle of a piano one side, an empty stage, and a singing gunner on the extreme right. He is well received.

Jock Webster follows with a series of hoary old Scottish jokes. "Is anything worn under the kilt? Nai man! everything's in perfect working order," etc. etc.

To the great mock fight 'twixt Deans and Robinson. They appeared in Long Johns and plimsolls. They had been rehearsing this mock fight for a week, but it was all pointless, as in the first few moments Deans took a right hander to the chin that had him groggy, and from then on Robinson had to nurse him along. The crowd barracks, "Kill 'im . . . call a priest . . . send 'im 'ome. . . ." The "fight" went the whole distance and they were given an ovation, especially Deans who now had blood running down his chin. His parting remark, "You want blood, you bastards, well, you got it."

Next, I and the mob in community singing. American officers were baffled by songs like

I painted her,
I painted her,
Up her belly and down her back
In every hole and every crack
I painted her,
I painted her,
I painted her old tomater over and over again.

It's BSM Griffin now, and he's had quite a skinful and does a conjuring act that to this day neither I nor anyone else understands. *He* doesn't even remember it; he sat hidden under a blanket pushing cards out through the slit asking, "What is it?" A member of the audience would identify it: "Ace of Spades." He would take it back inside the blanket and from his obscurity say, "So it is." I think he got booed off, and seemed well pleased with it.

Kidgell next, his old favourites, "Sweet Mystery of Life", "Drigo's Serenade". He has a very good voice.

"He ought to have had it trained," said Edgington.

"To run errands," added Fildes.

Kidgell had announced himself, "I will sing songs you all know and love."

Voices of horror from the back. "Ohhhh Nooo."

When Doug had finished the same voice said, "I didn't love or know any of 'em."

Behind the stage Sid Carter has opened a few bottles of wine to celebrate the show going well.

"We should wait till the end really," he said, "but with this mob there might not be any bloody end."

Edgington is at the piano playing his own tunes with that grim bloody look on his face, as if he expected a shot to ring out from the audience. One of the notes went dead on him and he brought forth laughter whenever he came to the missing note, as he stood up and sang the note himself. Next, from Liverpool, we have a real "Scouse", Joe Kearns. He tells lots of Liverpudlian jokes like "My owd man's got a glass eye, one night he swallowed it, he went to see the doctor, doctor said drop 'em, bend down, and he sees this glass eye lookin' at him out the back and he says, "Wot's the matter, don't you trust me?'"

After him the Band are on again. We play a favourite of ours, "Tangerine", and what in those days was a red-hot number, "Watch the Birdie". We didn't go that well because the boys had heard us so many times at dances. The Finale was a send-up of Major "Jumbo" Jenkins in Command Post Follies, in which we took the piss out of him in no uncertain fashion. He was fuming, but put a fixed grin on his silly face. We conclude with the cast singing "Jogging Along to the Regimental Gallop" to the tune of Jenkins' own favourite, "Whistling Rufus", and by God, we got a mighty ovation at the end.

The officers came backstage to congratulate us, and with consummate skill drink all our grog. We all got pretty tanked up; long after everyone had gone to bed Harry and I sat on the stage drinking and re-running the show. It had been a great night.

"Now what?" said Edgington.

Now what indeed.

News of Amalfi

BOXING DAY, DECEMBER 26, 1943

As if Christmas had not been wonderful enough – out of the line, dry beds, good grub, visits to Naples with free Venereal Disease! – we get *more* good news. It was like hearing you'd won the Irish Sweepstake, the moment you'd just discovered Gold in your garden. We were in bed after our first concert when down the line came the message. The following personnel will proceed on four days' leave to the Amalfi AGRA Rest Camp, and lo! it's the Concert Party.

"Amalfi?" says Edgington, rearranging his cigarettes for the night. "What is an *Amalfi*?" says White.

"It sounds like a high-powered Iti motor car," says Edgington.

But *I*, I, know-all/well-educated-Milligan tell them, "It's an Italian village that lies along the Divine Coast, south of

217

Naples and south-east of Catford, 6,000 miles south-east of Catford I'm glad to say."

Amalfi? There must be some mistake!!! Gunners don't go to the Divine Coast, they only go to the karzi; but folks, it was all true!

9.30, MONDAY, DECEMBER 27, 1943

We were loaded on to our three-tonner, like merry cattle. We were all in cracking spirits; it was December 27, a crisp sunny morning, though Edgington is overcast, cloudy with rain on high ground.

"I had a drop too much last night," he said. "It was a mere thousand feet," he said, imitating W. C. Fields.

I continued in the same voice, "That's perfectly true, my dear, he was making love to Grace on a clifftop when suddenly he went over the side, that's how he fell from Grace." Groans!

From the back we were watching the column of military traffic going up the line, and in between the pitiful civilian transport. There were loads of pretty girls who came under fire from the tailboard. The cries ranged from "I can do you a power of good, me dear," to the less poetic "Me give you ten inches of pork sword, darlin'." It's strange none of the soldiers in Shakespeare talked like this. If Shakespeare had been in the army he would have sounded more like "Once more into the breach, dear friends, once more – cor, look at those knockers – or fill this wall up with our English dead – grab 'old of this, darlin'." We're travelling south down route six, along the line of a Roman Road.

"It's not the Via Appia," said Edgington, "but I have – ha, ha – never been 'appier." Groans. He pretends to hurl himself out of the lorry.

The roads were really a series of holes joined together; we spent the time yoyoing between the floor and the roof of the lorry. Sometimes to ease the jolting we hung on to the roof supports with feet off the floor, making monkey faces and scratching under the arms, all clever stuff. Edgington is demonstrating how he can hang by his insteps. We hit a bump, he goes straight down on his nut.

A few songs to alleviate the boredom.

I'll never forget the day I joined the Army
    on the spree,
To be a greasy gunner in the Royal Artillery.
For my heart is aching and a-breaking,
To be in Civvy Street once more.
Oh you ought to see the drivers on a Friday night
A-polishing up their harness in the pale moonlight,
For there's going to be inspection in the morning
And the Battery Sergeant Major will be there,
He'll be there – he'll be there,
In the little harness room across the square.
And when they're filing out for water
I'll be shagging the Colonel's daughter
In the little harness room across the square!

I'd come a long way since I was Altar Boy at St Saviour's Church, Brockley Rise. We are going through Capua at a speed that would have left Hannibal and his lads a long way behind. Driver Wilson has put a spurt on and we are being shook to buggery. I clasp my legs.

"Ohhhhh."

"What's up?" says Edgington.

"Nothing – just practising."

On, on through Santa Maria, Afrigola, the outskirts of Naples. At the Piazza Dante we get out to stretch our legs and have a slash; we are besieged by Neapolitan Street-Urchins, "Scunazziti", who sell everything from cigarettes to sisters. How could they ever lead normal lives after this? The square is a mass of lorries, jeeps and trucks, large numbers of soldiers drunk and otherwise are either arriving or leaving. The Americans are bumptious. They have a great sense of humour, if you're about five.

"Come on, you lot, we're leavin'," Driver Wilson is yelling above the noise.

On to Amalfi! It's still a nice clear day but cold, the sun shines and bounces off the Gulf of Napoli. To our left looms Mount Vesuvius; white smoke drifts lazily from its crater.

"I wonder who's workin' the boiler room," says Griffin.

Jam-Jar Griffin! He was big, gawky, dark-haired, brown eyes, six foot, when unshaven always looked like the villain in the Mickey Mouse comics. I never saw him down, in fact he was far too often up, a great morale-booster. He had a

Jam-Jar Griffin begging for tobacco on the Amalfi seafront.

huge pipe in which he never seemed to have any baccy. With the greatest guffaw I'd heard, which you could even hear above the guns, he was one of the real characters and therefore invaluable in the run of human affairs.

We had been four hours on the truck, and travel boredom had set in. Lots of the lads were squatted on the floor, trying to doze, and only a few occasional words were heard.

"Bloody lost, ain't we?" says Vic Nash. "Are we lost?" he shouts through the canvas to the driver.

"No, we're not bloody lost," is the reply. "Stop moanin' or I'll go into reverse."

"Is Amalfi in Italy," says Spike Deans, and looks at me.

"It *is* in Italy and we must be nearly there." As I speak we turn off the main Salerno road and lo! we are on a small coastal road with a sign saying AMALFI, MINORI POSITANO.

We all perk up, and the view from the back of the lorry starts to get beautiful, with the sea on the left and mountains to our right. We have many hairy moments trying to negotiate the numerous bends with loony Italian drivers coming the other way. Snuggled along this coast were small fishing villages that looked like those over-syrupy buildings in Disney cartoons, yet they were real. The war had been kind to this coast; the only sign of destruction was our lorry.

"Oh Christ, how much longer? Five bloody hours, you can fly from London to Moscow in that time."

A small squad of unshaven Carabinieri come marching along the narrow road; they are broken up by the passing of our lorry. They reform and continue marching smartly out of step.

The lorry is stopping! AMALFI! Cheers! We pull up on the seafront, opposite is a large barrack-like building. A freshly-painted white sign says "2 AGRA Rest Camp". The whole village is built on steps that ascend up the mountains; the buildings are a mixture of white, sky blue, pink and deep blue; down the centre of the village runs a stream. I could see the odd lady doing her laundry in it and several small boys doing other things in it. The whole place has architectual maturity; there are numerous creepers and vines growing in profusion on the walls and balconies. In summer it must be a riot of flowers, right now it's a riot of gunners, there is a scramble as we dash for the best beds (if any); a Bombardier, all Base Depot smartness personified, says, "Follow me, 19 Battery Personnel."

ALF FILDES' DIARY: . . . *Great! Tablecloths, writing and leisure room, laundry facilities, barbers and SPRING BEDS! in the dormitories. No Roll-Calls! Breakfast from 7-30 to 8.30.*

We were on the third floor in a dormitory of about thirty beds. No pictures, no curtains, no chairs, just beds. Edgington is testing his by his usual method, ten paces back, a run, then hurl yourself on.

"Seems alright," he said.

A "resident" says that the grub here was "not so good", but there were "plenty of cafés in the town". We dump our kit and make for outside. There is a great echoing thumping sound as we "last one down's an idiot" down the stone steps.

The town sloped up the hill from the waterfront. Running along the flanking hills were the remains of fortified walls and crumbling turrets, an echo of the days when the Moors raided the coast. What was unusual was a large Basilica almost on the beach and, more wondrous, sculptures by Michelangelo; an even more important work of art was a sign with the magic words "Eggs and chips". I remember so well that sheer magnificence of smelling food being prepared continental-style, be it only eggs and chips! Through the

Amalfi

café window the sun shone; it was a great feeling, being safe, eating food off plates, and four days of it ahead of us!

"I'd forgotten what it was like to feel happy," said Edgington, as he poked his victuals in.

We had wandered around Amalfi, bought postcards, walked

up and down the seafront, tried to chat the Signorinas, no dice. I thought perhaps when I said "Me Roman Catholic" it might break the ice, but no. I tried "Me Protestant, me Jewish." Nothing.

Chalky White looms up from behind the sea wall.

"I been sunbathin'," he is saying. "What sadist sent us to the seaside in December?"

It's late evening, nightlife consists of going to bed. We troop back to the leisure room to play darts. Dinner is bully beef stew, it's not bad, but somehow eating bully beef in Amalfi is like ordering beans on toast at Maxim's. We are restless, so decide to go for a stroll. It's dark, in the distance we can hear Ack-Ack, God knows where from. It's a remind-er of what we have to go back to. We walked up the steps that ran alongside the stream, and ascended slowly until we reach a café. We entered a small room full of soldiers drinking. Alf and I sat down and ordered a couple of brand-ies; the room was blue with cigarette smoke. A fat-bottomed girl was carrying the drinks to the table, and those whose bottom brushed them seemed well favoured. One drunk was singing self-indulgent songs, "My Mother's Birthday" or some such crap. Ah! the fat bottom is approaching us, she has a lovely plump smiling face, with brown eyes as large as walnuts and glistening like oiled olives. She smiles, places our glasses before us. "Signore," she utters. "Corrrrr," we utter.

"Lets go," said Alf. We picked our way down the steps, no sound save the cascading water running down to the sea. Most of the lads were in bed except! Edgington, he's writing Peg one of his letters. That could mean a three-hour stint ending with swollen balls. I just fell into the bed. Springs! Marvellous. Black out. Zzzzzzz.

DECEMBER 28, 1943

I am roused in the early hours, bitten to death, my bed alive with bugs. I am worried about getting typhus. I report it to the duty Bombardier, he's nonplussed.

"Why you and no one else?" he says.

"Yes, *why* me and no one else," I said. With my clothes off I looked like I'd been sandpapered. I reported to the MO,

223

a 45-year-old Base Depot drunk recovering from last night's piss-up. With eyes like smoked glass windows he examines me and says with authority, "You have been bitten by something."

"Have I?" I said.

"Have you had a typhus injection?"

"Yes," I said very quickly.

"Good," he said. He wrote me a prescription for a bottle of camomile mixture.

"Have a good shower," said the Orderly, "then rub this on."

I retired to the showers. They're ice cold, aren't they!, my screams ring through the building. Covered in pink liquid I dress and join the lads in the rest room. Alf Fildes and I decide to look around the shops; he has already been around and been accosted by two girls who called him "Hello Baby". I thought he looked older. My face a mass of red blotches, Fildes and I appraised the goods in the windows.

"What bloody prices," he moaned.

I was flat broke and living on money borrowed from Edgington, who in turn was living on money borrowed from Vic Nash. It did not deter me from going into the shops just to chat up the shopgirls, all of whom look ravishingly beautiful. We returned to the billets for lunch, an indifferent affair of stew, potatoes, bread, rice pudding, and tea. It tasted best if you mixed the lot together. Still it went down, and you could hear the crash.

"Now what?" says Edgington as we wash our dixies.

"The Ballet? The Opera? Or pontoon al fresco?"

"We're only here for four days, we must act quickly."

"Alright, Hamlet in four seconds!"

The billet notice-board recommended a visit to Ravello. This was at the top of the hill directly above Amalfi, so the gang of us set off, Spike Deans, Harry Edgington, Jam-Jar Griffin, Geo. Shipman, Alf Fildes, Reg Bennett and Ken Carter.

"They say it's very nice up there," says Ken Carter.

"It's a long way to the top," says the Billet Bombardier.

We start walking. The afternoon was bright, with slight haze out to sea. As we ascended I observed profusions of

Soldier pouring sweat out of his boots.

semi-tropical plants growing from the slopes; there were even small Alpine-type flowers growing amid rocks; gradually the view unfolded on to the sea and the Divine Coast; it was superb.

"They say that when an Amalfian dies and goes to heaven, it's just another day to them," spoke Spike Deans.

"Wot if he goes to hell?" guffaws Jam-Jar.

"Well, you'd be able to welcome 'em in, tell 'em one of your scrappy jokes and they'd know the bloody hell *we've* bin suffering from with you!" says Edgington.

Jam-Jar reacts. "Listen, pudden! Where I come from they think I'm in the Noel Coward class."

There is an explosion of disbelieving laughter. He tries to retain his dignity by shouting above it.

"I've sung in D'Oyly Carte."

"You never even sung in a fuckin' dustcart," says Gunner Nash.

More howling laughter. There was nothing so funny as a

225

disorientated Jam-Jar. He realised he was on a losing wicket so joined in the laughter.

"Wot do I care," he roared. "You can't help if it you're a lot of ignorant buggers."

We made it by mid-afternoon. Ravello was magic. It had called the great from many countries, Mozart, Wagner, Greta Garbo, the Duke of Windsor, and Lance-Bombardier Milligan. Ravello was the seat of the Princes of Rufulo. In the centre of the town was the Piazza, with its Cinquecento Chieasa. Inside, one is overwhelmed at the artistry, from the chased silver keyholes in the doors to the magnificent marble-sculptured pulpit turned into lace by the artisan, with the images of the Rufolo family entwined in the facade. A beautiful bust of the Matriarch of the Rufolos (blast! I can't remember her name, was it Rita?, it must be in the Yellow Pages).

The peace inside was shattering. George Shipman, to our

Duomo interior, Ravello.

Ravello - Cattedrale - Parte laterale dell'Ambone
con i ritratti della Famiglia Rufolo

Work it out yourself.

amazement, played three Purcell pieces on the organ, we
had no idea he could play! Neither did he. The music soared,
as only an organ can. I sat in what had been the Ducal Pew,
and gazed at the complex of marble that made up the altar.
Like all worked marble of its day it was a masterpiece. The
vaulted ceilings, however, were free of decoration, just plain
whitewash which caught the light and gave the interior the
effect of sunshine through gauze.

We felt like a cup of tea. In the Piazza we entered a little
café. They made us a pot of brown water with some very
nice Italian pastries.

The place is almost deserted save for a few waiters suffering touristic withdrawal symptoms.

"Beforrrrr warrr, come many a peoples, many, many peoples, English, plenty English, English very rich," said our waiter looking at me.

I stood up and sang "God Save the King", at the same time pulling out the empty linings of my trouser pockets. He understood, and soon he too displayed his empty pockets. We sat him down and he had tea and cakes with us. It was Ken Carter who was flush with money.

"As it appears that 19 Battery are skint, we of the 74 Mediums will pay."

At these words Edgington and I took off our hats, prostrated ourselves on the pavement and kissed his boots. He tried to shoo us off, but we stuck to him like leeches, grovelling to him and shouting "Thank 'ee young master" in a Sussex brogue.

Now what? The place to see, apparently, was the Gardens of the Palace, listed as Belvedere del Cimbrone. Even though it wasn't the flowering season, the gardens were a sheer delight to the eye – shrubs, bushes, trees all placed with the utmost precision to create an atmosphere of relaxation and tranquility. A central ornate marble fountain played watery tunes from its moulded lead faucets, surmounted by stone Cherubim. It was so planned as to avoid any view of the sea until one arrived at the tiled terrace, which was reached through a small replica of a Roman Triumphal Arc, alas now stripped of its marble!

"See?, we're not the only ones who've lost our marbles," said Edgington.

It was sunset. Standing on an abutment of the Villa Cimbrone, we were looking out on to a sea that lay like polished jade. Away to our left, about to be swallowed in an autumn mist, was the sweep of the Salerno coast running away into the distance like an unfinished song. I stood long, next to Harry Edgington. There was no noise, no trains, motor cars, motor bikes, barking dogs. It was a moment that was being indelibly etched in my mind for life. I felt part of past history. Wagner had stood on this spot, what went through his head? From what I hear it was "Vitch Italian Bird can I make vid zer screw tonight?"

"We better get something to eat," said the soft voice of Bombardier Ken Carter.

Belvedere del Cimbrone

"Where?"

"Let's go back to the Piazza," I said. "There might be something there."

"I don't remember seeing anything there," said Edgington.

"You must remember seeing *something*, Harry, if it's only the floor. I mean we were only there half an hour ago."

"Your power to bend words," he said, "will one day end you in the nick, nuthouse or graveyard."

We reached the Piazza as the twilight was touching the adjacent hills.

"You lads lookin' fer sumfink?" A wavery female cockney voice! Standing by the gate of a whitewashed wall was a small, skinny lady of about fifty or a thousand.

"She's speakin' cockney," whispered Edgington from the corner of his mouth.

"Perhaps she's lost," I said. "We're lookin' for *mangiare*," and I automatically did the sign of eating.

"No need to make signs fer me, darlin'," said the amazing cockney voice. "I lived in London forty years."

With the Romans, I thought. She then told us the good news that was to lead to an unforgettable night.

"Come on in, we can fix you up wiv eggs and chips and some wine, that'll do yer, won't it?", she said and gave that

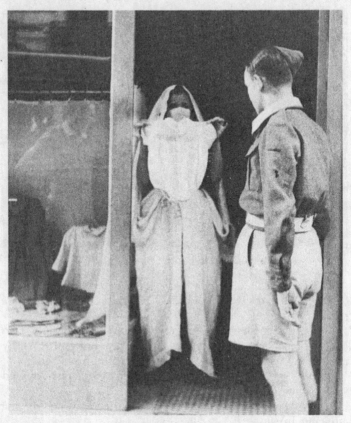

Soldier buying a dress in hopes of an early release, apparently to Arabia.

forced cockney laughter of embarrassment.

We followed her on to a terrace that had a sensational view down a precipitous mountain that concluded with the sea. In a small, plain, wine-coloured walled room, adorned with a few religious pictures and a mixture of stern-faced Neapolitan grandfathers, grandmothers and children in communion white, we sat around a central table with a tablecloth that looked suspiciously like a sheet. I hoped I wasn't at the feet end. Chattering, she plonked down two large carafes of red wine. "There, that'll keep yer goin' till din-dins," and disappeared into the back room where she reverted to broad

Neapolitan and shouting. She was answered by a male voice that appeared to have sandpaper lining his throat, that or his appliance had slipped.

To Edgington's joy, there was a piano against the wall. The first notes of "Tangerine", and we all joined in, a memory of our North African Concert Party days. Outside, twilight was crepuscularly moving along the Amalfian coast. Ah ha, eggs and chips Italian-style, with spaghetti!

"Heavens alive!" exclaimed Edgington, a man brought up on roast beef and two. "Spaghetti with eggs?" he chortled, "that's what Catholicism does for you."

I observed the faces of my comrades, the same expression I had observed a thousand times; it is when for a moment conversation stills at the sight of the food, the communal spirit is temporarily forgotten, and each man is only aware of himself, his stomach, and the pleasant preparatory taste of salivary juices in his mouth. A half-smile was on the face of them all except Jam-Jar. His face took on the appearance of a Cougar about to kill.

"There yer are, me darlins," said our little lady, balancing four plates along one arm.

There followed that urgent rattling of cutlery knives and forks foraging like hungry wolves among the repast. There's the usual English insult to culinary art, snowstorms of salt and pepper. I saw her wince at the request for "Tomato Sauce". Her husband appeared, a replica of Henry Armetta,* short, fat, greasy, amicable; he grinned and made the little nodding gesture of the head peculiar to Italians. On reflection, it would look peculiar on anybody.

"Buona, eh?"

"Si, molto buona," we chorused.

Pressing my linguistic abilities I said, *"Te voglio un becairi de vino?"*

By his facial reaction I could have been speaking Chinese; even worse, he said, *"Scusi, ma Io non parla Francese."*

They had a drink with us. " 'Ere's Victory for the Allies," she said.

That got rid of all the wine. Two more carafes arrived, with

---

*Hollywood support star of the Thirties.

them we drank a "*Salute Italia Viva Il Re*" that got rid of two more. From the bread on the table Jam-Jar Griffin was wiping the last of the egg off the plates.

"Leave the pattern on, mate," said Carter.

"Now, would you like a sweet?" said our Lady of the Food. "We got lots of eggs 'ere and a barrel of Marsala in the cellar and, as a special treat, we could give you all a Zabiglione."

There was the stunned silence of culinary illiterates. Tactfully she explained what it was, how it was made and how it tasted. "It was made in honour of a General Zabiglione, I believe he was one of Garibaldi's Generals." How could we refuse?

In great anticipation we proceeded to destroy our taste-buds with State Express 555. Overwhelmed by my musical ego, I sat at the piano and played a very dodgy version of "Body and Soul", leaving out the difficult key-change in the middle eight.

"That's a lovely tune," said Carter.

"Yes it is," I said.

"Then why play?"

"It's coming," said Edgington cupping his ear in the direction of the kitchen, from whence came noises in the wake of which our Madonna of the seven Teeth came forth with a tray on which were six glasses of yellowish stuff. Slight apprehension, except Jam-Jar who is into it like Dracula into a throat. "It's custard," he said, "That's it, zabiglione is Italian for custard."

It was the turn of Lance-Bombardier Carter to play.

"They laughed when I sat down to play the piano," he said. "But when I played . . . they became hysterical."

We all giggled and laughed, mind you, at this stage we would have all giggled and laughed if we'd been told we had a week to live. He played his own composition, called "Candlelight".* I still, to this day, sometimes find myself humming it.

*Strange, when I was writing about this particular incident, I phoned Ken and asked if he remembered the words. He said, "Yes I've got them somewhere. I'll dig them out and let you have them." That night Ken died in his sleep.

The man on the right is Bombardier K. Carter and the man on the left isn't – but with promotion could be!

We were now introduced to an exotic Italian after-dinner drink, Sambuca, which is set alight.

"Christ," said Edgington, "how do you drink that without first-degree burns?"

Outside, night had fallen along the Amalfian coast. With Ken still playing those incredibly romantic tunes of the Forties, Harry and I went and looked at the view outside. It was a vast, velvety panorama. The moon lit the whole scene, the clarity was startling, like sunlight through a blue-tinted glass. I could hear distant singing drifting upwards from the sea. I noticed boats with tiny yellow lamps like fairy lanterns on the water, and a rhythmic beating, of course! it was the *pescatores* attracting the fish. It was like a magic canvas.

I include Harry Edgington's recollection of that evening, written in 1977!!

But to the memories of the evening of that day, which as I've already said are not continuous or consecutive in their order. How we got to that establishment virtually on the brink of a 2,000-foot-high coastline, I haven't a clue. Whether it was a private house or a café I couldn't tell you. I can recall that we sat out on that stone-flagged terrace with disconcertingly thin wrought-iron railings; we were there for perhaps an hour while evening gave way to twilight and eventually to a fine calm night over which mistress moon queened it in spectacular fashion, cutting a massive fan-shaped swathe across the millpond calmness of the Med., directly towards us so it seemed.

We were too overawed by the scene to talk much. Far below the fishermen's boats were intriguing us, lanterns on the prow; the singing of the fishermen came wafting up the 2,000 feet as they banged on the sides of their boats with pieces of wood. The sounds and sights came to us perfectly focused, so clear was the moonlight, so we just drank in the scene, which I would say was starkly rather than restfully beautiful.

Back in the little dining-room the romantic mood had gone, and Jam-Jar Griffin was in the middle of a magnificent rending of "Poor Blind Nell", who in thirty-two bars of music had more perversions committed on her than a victim of Caligula. Reg Bennett played "Blue Moon", then "Follow my heart my dancing feet", while I danced with the hat-stand, and Edgington a chair.

The dénouement. Rosie says, " 'Ow about some Iti champagne?"

Champagne??? Gunners drinking Champagne? It was called Asti Spumanti, more like Proof Lemonade, but the sheer feeling of luxury made it even more heady.

"Cor. Champagne," said Edgington, making it disappear at a great rate.

He was at the old piano again; we stood around and sang tunes that put an emotional seal on our generation. Along about two in the morning we paid the bill, bade noisy good-nights to Rosie and her husband, and started down the long winding road to Amalfi. It looked like a silver river. No one was drunk but we certainly weren't all that steady, there was a lot of sliding and slipping on a sharp gradient. . . . It was a mile to the bottom, and I think our gyrations added another three. The seafront was quiet, a few chinks of light showed through late windows. I slept to the sound of the sea and a tide of thunderous snoring from a Neolithic gunner in the next bed who was fully clothed and sick down the front of his battle dress, a perfect end to a memorable night.

Jam-Jar Griffin and Reg Bennett appearing as extras in a picture featuring a horse and driver.

WEDNESDAY, DECEMBER 29, 1943

MY DIARY: NOTHING.

FILDES': *Memorable because saw the remains of Pompeii.*

This day *was* memorable. All the lads left early for Pompeii; having seen it I opted to stay in bed. It's a cold sunny day on this delightful coast. I miss "official" breakfast, so go to the little café by the Cathedral steps; inside I find Gunner White, and a drunken Scot from 64 Mediums. I joined them.

"Aren't you seeing Pompeii?" says White.

"Not from here – anyhows, I hate conducted tours."

I order two eggs-a-cheeps from the Signorina.

"This place gets a bit boring after twenty-four hours," says White.

For the first time the drunken Scot talks. "Aye – fookin toors – nae bloody gude – s'better here, ah fuck."

Let me describe him. Short, stocky, black hair, red face

Left to right: *Edgington – Bennett – Iti Guide; behind them Ken Carter and Spike Deans. They are outside Pompeii Cathedral, where they belong.*

and staring blue eyes in a sea of red veins, he had no mouth as such – it looked more like an incision. He reeked of alcohol. The front of his battle dress was a mass of red wine-stains – his teeth were Van Gogh yellow – he hadn't a penny, and sat with anyone who could stand the smell.

"I can't get rid of him," said White.

I ate my eggs and yarned with White. The drunken Scot kept interjecting, with unintelligible Scots rubbish. "Yerur – nae – narraer – getar – arrr – Glasgae arrhh – fuck."

We get on to the beach and hire a boat. "Yem – nae ach – aye, Glasgae – abl – fuck." I took the oars and we pulled gently from the shore. Out loud I quote, "All in the lazy golden afternoon – full leisurely we glide."

"Yer nae sael ger – Glasgae – ah – fuck."

A hundred yards offshore, I stack the oars and we just drifted – wonderful! peace! smoking, with our feet up. The sun is warm, the air balmy, the waters calm, the terrible Scot is sick – not in the sea, in the boat. We rowed back hurriedly, with him downwind. "Arragh – wae gal – ferrr – Glasgae ah fuck," he said.

Left to right: *Jam-Jar Griffin*, *Vic Nash*, *Spike Deans*.

237

We climbed the sea wall and ran away from the reeking Scot. The afternoon we walked along the coastal road towards Positano – the afternoon sun was like a warm caress, we slung our jackets over our shoulders.

To our right are granite cliffs – "What's caused that?" White points to a great cleavage in a hill.

"That's a fault."

"Fault? Whose bloody fault?"

Carefully I explain its geological origins.

"Oh," he said.

It was a waste of bloody time. If I had answered "Mussolini's fault" he'd have been satisfied.

"Agh – ah – weel – Glasgae – ah fuck," he'd caught up with us. We watch men catching octopus along the shore, to kill them they pulled them inside out. It was obscenely cruel, but then Man is.

"Do they eat those bloody things?"

"Yes."

White shuddered. "Ugg – like eatin' bloody worms."

The Anglo-Saxon will devour stale bread, bully beef, hard rolls, food boiled to death and obliterated with artificial seasoning – yet delightfully cooked octopus in garlic, No. You are what you eat, that's why we all look so bloody ugly. Back to billets to see if the showers are hot. Yes! But oh God! the news has got around, crowds of steaming red naked men cram the bathrooms – there's five men to a shower.

"It's every man fer 'ees bloody self." So saying, White and I charge our way in; the bodies are so compressed, I'm sure someone else washed my legs by mistake.

"Arrgg, yer sael nay fuck," the Scot; he's under the shower, but still in his underwear.

All clean and glowing, smelling of Wright's Cold Tar, we are ready for the evening. We're nearly skint so we have to eat the Army grub; we needed every penny to get pissed.

"Let's look fer somewhere noo." White is looking up the steps that run up the centre of Amalfi. "Thank fook we got rid of that bloody Jock."

It's evening now, above I spot Hesperides; I didn't mention this to White, he was already baffled enough by the Geological Fault lecture. All the way up the stairs at intervals were little Trattorias; we ascend half-way up the town and a

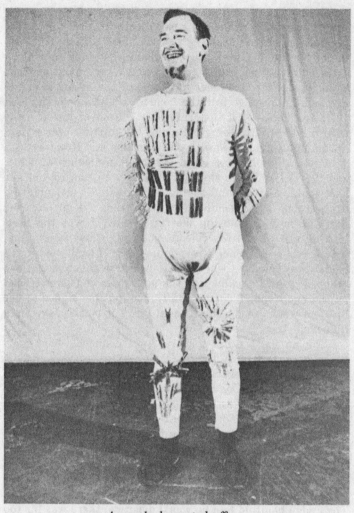

A much decorated officer

pretty girl is standing invitingly outside of a house.

"You wanna drinka wine, bebe?"

White needs no second invitation, we go inside; it's a one-woman brothel. Now these weren't regular whores, but working-class girls who had fallen on hard times and were doing it just for "the duration". Inside is a square whitewashed room with a charcoal burner in the middle; there are simple wooden chairs with rush seats around the walls; several soldiers are drinking red wine from a large bottle on the centre table. There a large middle-aged lady in a black dress, and another young girl of about fifteen, pour us some wine. The girl from outside has come in and points to one of the soldiers; they go into the next room and I hear the lock go in the door. I felt uncomfortable, I'd never had it away with a whore, and being a Roman Catholic by upbringing, the thought of doing it with one horrified me. However. . . . A couple of hours later I had blown all my money on wine, and the girl had been through about six customers, but she kept looking at me and saying "You want?" and pointing to the room. I had declined, and each time she got angrier; she was in fact fancying me. (Why not? I was the best-looking one there.) My rejections finally drove her to say, "You, you no-lika-me. Why you no say?" I explained that I hadn't any money, whereupon in my drunken state she grabbed me, ushered me into the next room and screwed me. At the end I said, *"Niente Soldi"*, she put her finger to her lips and went "Sushhhhh", then, wait for it, she gave me a thousand lire.

"You no speak other soldiers," she confided, "you come back again, domani notte, eh."

Well, well, my male ego was bursting, after all she was not a common whore. Common whores wouldn't rate me at one thousand lire a go, no! This girl had a fine sense of values and a remarkable understanding of currency. Would I catch something? That's the question that haunted me in bed that night; however, I had broken the back of my Roman Catholic inhibitions. What would the Pope say? It all reminded me of the story of a fifty-year-old Pioneer Corps soldier who was caught having a knee-trembler in a doorway in Bradford. The Judge had told him he was a disgrace, there was far too much of this thing going on in Town etc., he was going to make an example of him and give him three months for indecency. The comment from the Pioneer soldier, "I tell thee summat, you'll never stop fookin' in Bradford."

White is laying back in bed, ecstatic with the evening.

"Oh Mummy," he suddenly says, "I don't want to go back to school."

240

DECEMBER 30, 1943

DIARY: GOT PISSED ALL DAY.

As requested I went back to the girl the next night, she was delighted and screwed me again. As I dressed I awaited my rightful payment.

"That will be a thousand lire," she said.

The woman was nothing but a common whore. If she weren't careful I'd become a practising Catholic again.

WE LEAVE AMALFI

DECEMBER 31, 1943

"All good things must come to an end." So saying, I slammed the tailboard up, climbed aboard, and we commenced our journey along the muddy Route 6, back to the farm. Ah Amalfi! Ravello! what terrible withdrawal symptoms is produced. We arrived back just after dark, the Sentry challenges us.

"Halt, who goes there?"

We give an incredible mixture of replies. I said, "Hiawatha and Co. Limited", *I think* Edgington said, "W. C. Fields, my deeer."

White dumps his big pack on the deck, flops on to his bed, lights a fag: "Comin' back to this fooking place – it's like being taken to the ballet then asked to empty the dustbins."

Harry starts to sing "Cuore Napolitano", a song we had heard in Amalfi. It had all been memorable.

JANUARY 1/2, 1944

A muddy field, a rectangular pitch, at each end goals made from a bric-a-brac of telegraph poles, logs and branches of trees fresh-painted with whitewash. Around the touchlines are foregathered men of 19 Battery, they have come to see 19 Battery "wipe the bloody floor" with a team from RHQ. "We'll teach 'em to live in dry bloody billets," said Dai Poole as he took the field to captain our team. Great cries of encouragement, as against the boos that greet RHQ. The referee is Sgt. Donaldson, the two linesmen Jock Hall and Bdr. Marsden: so biased is the referee that the

Correct uniform for officers sleeping on duty.

entry of RHQ is greeted with a blast on the whistle and a cry of "Offside."

The game didn't seem to bear much relationship to football. Rather mud-ball. At times it was buried a foot under the surface, and after ten minutes both sides looked identical. Thereafter all the players ran around the field identifying themselves by shouting "19 Battery" or "RHQ". It sounded like a lunatic Eastern bazaar. All attempts at positional play were abandoned in favour of a mass concentration of wherever the ball was. I swear to God the first goal for 19 Battery was scored by the referee, and when the ball came where the touchline *might* have been, several spectators joined in the dribbling. The interval was resplendent with two huge containers of tea, and a seasonal "gift" of rum. The spectators were into it first, and the players got bugger all.

The game is about to be resumed, but stops when three 19 Battery players were found hiding among the RHQ team. The game ended in a 2-0 win for us. Our second goal was unique; RHQ goalie stopped a shot and was standing holding the ball on the goal-line, when Gunner Devine shoved him in. There was a hell of an argument but the goal was allowed, some say only after the referee had promised the goalie fifty lire.

That night we had news from the front, 18 Battery in a duel had blasted a Jerry gun off the face of the earth with an observed direct hit (from an Air OP), and 15 Battery had destroyed a very dangerous MG pill-box. Happy New Year!

Search for AFN Naples

JANUARY 2/3, 1944

I wanted to get the Band a broadcast; with this in mind I skidaddled to Naples, hitching all the way. After much searching, I finally located the offices of the Allied Forces Network. They were located on the first floor of the San Carlo Opera house. I passed along a corridor of Baroque doors. Signs – "Cappo de Ballet", "Maestro del Orchestra", "Prima Ballerina", and "Viatato Ingresso". Finally a piece of true British enterprise, "AFN Liaison Officer", written on a piece of cardboard with a three-inch nail through it. I knocked politely – the door was opened by a tubby ATS girl who greeted me with "Yes?"

"I'd like to speak to someone about doing a broadcast."
"Oh yes?"
"Yes . . ."
She stood there like a dummy.

243

"Well – could you tell me who to see?"

"Well, there's only Lieutenant Mondey."

"Can I see only him?"

"Does he know you're coming?"

"Not unless he's an extra-sensory perceptionist."

"I'll tell him you're here."

She waddled off to a door directly behind her. Her bottom wobbled as though operated by an invisible hand. She reappeared blushing as though she had been interfered with. If this was the case her molester must be blind.

"Lt. Mondey will see you now."

I walked into a room that had obviously once been a broom cupboard. The desk took up most of the room, the walls were barren save for a nail with a hat on. On the desk was the stub of a pencil, a telephone and a copy of the *Union Jack*. Behind it sat a minute, sallow-complexioned man; he was either a dwarf or sitting on a milking stool. If the latter was the case, the pained expression suggested the stool was inverted. He looked at me as though I had come from Mars.

"Yes, what is it?" he said, shifting his seat.

His demeanour gave me the same feeling Edith Cavell got on the dawn of her execution.

"I'm Lance-Bombardier Milligan, sir, 56th Heavy Regiment."

He received this announcement as though it was an eviction notice.

"Oh yes," he said.

"I'd like to get a broadcast for a Jazz Quartet."

An eviction notice plus seizure of all assets. This was all new to him; by the silly look on his face, *any*thing was new to him. He squirmed and said, "I see." He didn't really. "Are you professional musicians?"

I thought the answer "Yes" a good one.

"Do you earn your living as a musician?"

"No. I earn it as a Lance-Bombardier."

"I better make a note of the Band's name," he said. "It's – er? – er?"

"It's – er – D Battery Dance Band."

"E Battery?"

"D sir."

"What?"

"It's D, sir."

"D? D what?"

"D Battery – you were writing E."

"Oh," he scribbled out the E and wrote D. "There," he said as though he'd climbed Everest. "Now!" He placed his pencil tidily on his deck. "Anything else?"

Anything else? What was he talking about?

"Yes, sir . . . when?"

"When what?"

"When can we broadcast?"

"Broadcast? Well . . . we don't know what you sound like, do we? ha ha ha."

"Well, how about an audition?"

"Audition?" It was like checkmate. "Ah yes – an audition – now when?"

"Any time."

"Any time – when would that be?"

God! there was only one way he became an officer, he was baptised one.

"I think my boys could make it day after tomorrow – the afternoon."

"Let me check my diary." He opened a drawer which was empty, he pretended to write something, closed the drawer. "Well, that's that," he blinked.

I saluted, he didn't. I don't think he knew how to. I walked out past the ATS girl, who was preparing for the next groping session.

Outside I rubbed my hands with glee. (I always kept a tin handy.) Wait till the lads hear the news!

"Now what songs will I sing?" were Kidgell's first reactions. "I'll be a hit on radio – for a start they can't see what a short-arse I am."

"It took a bloody war to get us on the air," Fildes says, "we owe it all to Hitler."

"Gentlemen," I said, "will you all stand for Adolf Hitler."

JANUARY 4, 1944

MY DIARY: NIGHT OF FOURTH. NEWS THAT WE ARE ABOUT TO MOVE ''SOMEWHERE'' AT ''SHORT NOTICE''. THIS HAS

It was a coldish night, so most of us were in bed, some with
bottles of vino, some reading old newspapers, some writing
those feverish letters home. I was reading letters from Bette,
Beryl, Lily, Ivy Mae, Madge, and for some inexplicable
reason, Jim. I would read all the best bits out to the most
frustrated Gunners. White is sitting up in bed, with Happy
New Year chalked on his tin hat.

Enter Bombardier Fuller. What's he doing up? He is fully
dressed, looking very alert, and bearing down on us. It looks
bad. It is bad. He says, "Listen fer yer names." He calls out,
"Nash, Milligan, Deans", he drones on for about ten more.
My God, they've found us, we were going to war again – a
new position. We are the advance party to dig gun-pits,
Command Posts, cookhouse, shit house, etc. etc.

"You've got to be packed and ready to leave at 0530
hours."

Christ. Breakfast at 4.30. Bloody hell!! Why don't they
make sleeping a crime and have done with it?

"I suggest we sleep with our eyes open," I said.

"Shut up, Milligan," says Fuller.

He tucks his papers back into his pocket. He tells us we
have to prepare our trucks and load them "tonight". We
swearingly drag ourselves from our beds. The rain outside is
torrential, and into it we go. We have to test the batteries for
the wireless set, then test the set, pack all the Command
Post equipment. Who invented bloody artillery boards???
What idiot invented drums of cable, what fool made dead-
weight telephone exchanges, that had twenty subscribers
and also subscribed to double rupture? Like drowned rats we
humped all this stuff into the wireless truck, and you HAD
to pack it very carefully or you couldn't get in yourself. My
companion in the back was to be Gunner Birch, who had
Space Cancer – with a minimum amount of possessions he
could fill a room. Every flat surface for a hundred feet
around was covered, every chair, table, box, floor, shelf,
hook, nail he managed to cover with a mess of possessions,
and *me*, *I* would make space by *careful* packing. In would
come this lumbering idiot and fill every bit of that. Even

Lloyds Bank move in on D+1 using a Banco di Napoli sign.

then his pockets bulged with stuff he could find no room in his kit for. Underpants and vests poked out of his pockets, vests he could find no space for he wore, his gas mask was full of socks and handkerchiefs. He was a walking disaster, and worse, he was walking with me. As fast as I packed something in place he would throw something on top. By eleven I told him: "Look, go away, lie down, *stay* away, don't come back and I'll do it all."

He walks squelching back to his bed. By midnight I had unpacked the truck and repacked it, making a mental note to get into my seat next morning before he managed to pile it with his rubbish. I returned to the shed, and was delighted to see that someone had lit a brazier that glowed lovely and red in the dark.

"Finished?" It was Spike Deans speaking.

"Yes, I'm finished," I said, warming myself by the fire.

247

I took off my soaking boots and socks, and changed into dry clothes, leaving my wet ones to dry in the heat. Deans looms from the dark with a cup of hot tea. "God bless you, sir," I said, "God bless you."

"Just made it before you came in, there's a whole tin of it still hot."

"Good luck, sir," I said.

I wearily slid into bed and sipped the tea. It was quiet now. Better get some sleep. I drained the tea, rolled myself into my blankets, got *really* comfortable – warm – cosy – drowsy – had to get up for a slash! As I lay there the others came dripping in at various intervals. Little Vic Nash is swearing enough for a Company of drunken Scots Guards. "Fuck 'em," he says, "fuck-fuck-fuck-fuck-em," and I think that about summed it all up. I fell asleep to his gentle swearing.

4.20 AM.! Please God, why didn't you take me in my sleep!

Pitch-black cold, and a howling gale. As I dress I hear a tree crashing down, why couldn't it fall on me?, some distant shouts; it all sounds like we're on the moon. Breakfast helped. The duty cook, Ronnie May, served it up like a zombie, then went back to bed. At 5.30 sharp our small convoy moved out. The destination was a place called Lauro. In the back of the wireless truck, by the light of the operation lamp, I found the place on the map, a small village on the foothills that ran down to the Garigliano plains. Across the brown Garigliano were towering mountains – in these Jerry was waiting, among them a Jerry who was going to do for me. Slitheringly, we pressed forward on our muddy narrow road. First light was eeking through overcast skies; the wind was at gale force, coming from the south-west; we could feel the truck take the impact as strong gusts hit us broadside. Behind us was a three-tonner with the digging party. Stark winter-black trees lined our route in inordinate patterns. The road was deserted except for a gradual increase of military traffic going the other way. I hoped they weren't retreating. One never knew in war. More than once have I seen an infantryman run out of his tent down a slope to do a "pony", and heard anxious voices saying to him, "Are we retreating?" In this case he was evacuating.

I was directly in front of the wireless set. I switched on and got early-morning music from AFN Naples. I cursed the luck that had spoiled the Band's chances of doing a broadcast. News is good. The Russians have advanced across the Polish border and are now ten miles inside. It seems they might win the war before us. If the Allies know what they are doing, they must occupy as much territory as they can before it is annexed by Russia. Otherwise, the post-war border of Russia will be somewhere near Tunbridge Wells. Every day we don't land in France is a bigger headache for us after the war. It's frustrating to know that this war will make Russia a post-war giant, and that all our Military energies would be spent on a peacetime build-up to meet the Red Threat. It seems that like Hollywood endings, wars went on for ever. As my dear father had once said, "The only way to get rid of wars is to have them." Right now we were having one. "Wot are we supposed to be doin' at this place?" says Birch, who is not the brightest. "We have to prepare gun positions by the 10th, a big do is going in."

"What have we got to do?"

"You and me?"

"Yes."

"We do what the rest of them are doing. Digging bloody great holes in the ground for bloody great guns."

He didn't answer, he lit up another cigarette. Then spoke, "Why don't the bloody Pioneer Corps dig our holes?"

"Because they are all home in bloody beddy-byes."

I explained the Pioneer Corps only did roads and buildings, not "makin' 'oles in the ground".

"We do the bloody lot. I've dug 'oles, filled sandbags, chopped trees, put up tents, officers' messes, karzis, Nissen huts, the bloody lot."

"So? What are you complaining about, you could be right now with the PBI, being shelled, mortared and machine-gunned, and here you are safe and sound in a luxury wireless truck that would be much more luxurious if it weren't for your packing, you loaded this truck like it was a bloody dustcart. No, Birch, you have nothing to grumble about, but everyone has a right to grumble about you! What were you before the war?"

"Happy," he said. The standard funny answer to that question.

"See? You can't even think of an original reply. What were you really before the war?"

"I was a trainee sluice operator at a Sewerage Farm."

"And you call that happy? You must be a pervert."

"Pervert? What's a pervert?" he said, his dull eyes blinking.

"A Pervert is a trainee sluice operator on a sewerage farm."

By eleven, we arrived at the hill village of Lauro – through it ran the road to the 5th Army west front.

Bren carrier of London Irish Rifles going to the front.

250

JANUARY 5, 1944

The roads in Lauro are all the same. Built and paved about 1870, they had remained the same width ever since. A Sherman tank filled the whole road, the only way to let it pass was to run over you. In the main street of Lauro was the Police Station; at the most, it could hold about ten prisoners in its two separate cells, really each cell was for four people. Off a central room, which was entered from the road, were three other rooms, two as bedrooms for policemen on night duties, one room for cooking; it was all on one floor, all adobe walls.

That morning when we arrived, the place was pretty hairy; in the central room at a table sat an Intelligence Corps Corporal, who must have got there by reason of his speaking the language. As we entered, there were angry shouts, babies screaming and women crying. Both cells were crammed with civilians, so much so we nicknamed it the black hole. They were civilians who had crossed through our lines to avoid the fighting, but all had to be screened in case spies were among them. The Corporal was talking to an old Italian man who wore banded leggings around his trousers, and skin shoes. He could have walked out of the eighteenth century. The smell inside the prison was hell. The prisoners had no facilities and they had had to defecate in the cells. Why this situation was allowed to exist can only be put down to the wonderful "I'm alright, Jack" attitude of the British. We are not cruel, but, Christ, sometimes we come very close to it.

The man in charge was the Commandante of the Carabinieri. A man in his fifties, grey wavy hair, wearing a crumpled grey-blue uniform, he was an out-and-out "Fascisti"* and made it very clear by his surly attitude. He unlocked a room which was to be our billet. It was large enough for twelve to fifteen beds. He grunted "Qui." We all trooped in and chose our positions, mine near a window; I always did this in case of a direct hit blocking the door. (But silly! supposing one hit the window?) I was immediately made "Room Orderly" for the day, by me. Vic Nash had to start up a cookhouse in one of the adjacent rooms,

*Our Colonel gave him six months in Sessa prison for not co-operating with the Allies.

The Commandante of the Carabinieri

alongside an Italian lady cook, one Portence, a middle-aged lady, all very willing and smiling and amused at seeing a man doing the cooking. She cheeerily helped Vic Nash, and was quick to learn the benefits of making tea, and the rewards to be had in the shape of cigarettes and bars of chocolate. She seemed to be eternally on duty, from dawn to one in the morning. When I think of some of the soppy females of today who get a charlady to clean their flat of three rooms while they phone their friends and eat chocolates, I realise the change in the quality of ladies' working lives.

Howling gales continued blotting out any sound of gunfire. It was a gorgeous easy day. I was able to renovate my kit, sewing up socks, putting buttons on trousers that had been held up with knotted string and signal wire! (Any message for my trousers today?) At eleven o'clock Portence brought me a mug of tea! I lay back on my bed sipping it and reading from an Anthology of English Poets I had bought in a shop at Castelemare. I read the Love Sonnets of Henry Howard (Earl of Surrey), who apparently imitated Petrarch. I had enough trouble imitating Al Jolson. Somewhere outside, the Gunners were digging in heavy mud and a howling gale. When they returned that evening, soaked, muddy, tired, I just didn't have the heart to tell them I'd been reading,

"The sweete season that bud and bloom forth brings
    With green hath clad the hill and eke the vale."

Soon the room filled with cigarette smoke, swearing, moaning, and an occasional snatch of song. After a hot meal, there was aught to do but get into bed. A last gesture of sociability, I went outside to the wireless truck, listened to the BBC News, jotted down the main details, and from my bed read it out to the lads. The best received was the unstoppable grinding advance of the Russian Army, who were well inside the Polish border, the announcement of which brought a small tired cheer. Birch was sitting up in bed, his arms folded, a cigarette embedded in his face.

"I'm too bloody tired to smoke," he said.

"Try steaming," I said. "It's easier."

Bombardier Harry Holmwood chips in, "It's alright for some, Milligan, sittin' on their arse all day, playin' their bugle."

"I swear on the Pope's legs I have not touched the bugle all day."

I slept soundly that night.

THURSDAY, JANUARY 6, 1944

ON THE JOB AT 8.15. BITTER COLD. THROUGH THE BUSHES MASKING OUR POSITIONS WE CAN SEE THE SNOW ON THE HILLS ACROSS THE GARIGLIANO.

We were supposed to dig a Command Post, but No! No, we find a super cave right near the gun positions. So, instead we have to dig a cookhouse; this took most of the day. We dug into a bank under the supervision (Super?) of Vic Nash. There is nothing so invigorating as an ex-Old Kent Road pastry cook tellin' you how to dig a hole.

Hands and feet are freezing, the only way to get them warm is dig. By five o'clock it was too dark to see. We returned to the billet and luxurated in the warmth inside provided by an old Italian device, a large stone the size of a millstone, with a countersunk hole in the middle filled with charcoal, that burnt brightly with a minimum of smoke. It was all very quiet here, but at night we hear how close our infantry were by the night exchanges of machine-gun fire, just over the brow of a hillock behind us. At night we would hear the grumble of vehicles bringing supplies for the "build up", and a sound that always made me feel ill, infantry men coming up the line, the unending trudge of what sounded like hollow boots and the occasional clank or clink of some metal equipment, and most distinctive, that ring of an empty metal tea mug. I used to wonder how in God's name the High Command could keep the movement of a quarter of a million men secret. . . . I always had the feeling that Hitler knew exactly where I was all the time.

On this the coldest day of the year, we hear that bitter fighting is going on for Vittori, and we are now only five miles from Cassino.

The days that followed were all the same, digging. To speed up the process more gunners arrive to dig at night! Mail is slow in coming up here owing to the traffic congestion and the one-way road system.

FRIDAY, JANUARY 7, 1944

What's this mess approaching at dawn. It's a fully shagged-out Gunner answering to the name Edgington. "Argggggggggggg," he collapses into our billet. "What a bloody caper . . . up at four o' bleedin' clock, half a mug of cold tea, a spoonful of egg powder and now this bleedin' crap hole." He drops his kit.

"Welcome home, young massa," I said. "De plantation ain't bin de same widout you."

"Ohhhhhh," he groaned as he fossicked in his pockets for fags. Seeing him nigh to death my heart was sore afraid, so I scrounged an extra mug of tea, then sat him on his big pack. "Now tell mummy, was there a rude boy at school today?"

"I refuse to be cheered up," he said. "There'll be no smiling Harry till about mid-day."

"No? let me help you keep that way – there's bloody great holes in the ground to be dug, and *you* have to dig 'em in the crippled position otherwise Jerry can see you."

He is soon with shovel, and the wind whistleth through the seams in his underpants, and he liketh it not. A young Italian boy from the village came up and did some digging for us – as a mark of apprecation we gave him a few V cigarettes that would stunt his growth. We get a visit from the village barber; in an immaculate white jacket, he cut the hair of the entire mob. He was very thorough, snapping hairs in ears and noses. He went away, his pockets bulging.

"It's mad," said Edgington, "paying for something you don't want."

Captain Sullivan comes up to poke around. "Mmm – yes," he said. "Was it worth the journey?"

JANUARY 8, 1944

MY DIARY: WEATHER WARMER. DIGGING.

JANUARY 9, 1944

MY DIARY: DIGGING AND SWEARING.

JANUARY 10, 1944

MY DIARY: DIGGING AND SWEARING.

JANUARY 11, 1944

MY DIARY: DIGGING FINISHED. SWEARING STOPS.

At last. We could relax, but still all movement had to be minimal and carried out under cover. Nash used to hold a piece of cardboard over his head. He was desperate for an officer to ask why, but it never came to pass. One fine morning he says, "I must have a look at Jerry's lines. It's a nice clear day, the view ought to be good."

He was right, the view was so good he got a Jerry bullet over his head, and a terrible telling off from Sgt. Jock Wilson.

"You want tae giv awa' oer position? You stoopid little cockney cunt!"

We had done all the digging and were now to excavate our own G truck billet. Down a small bank we find an ideal spot, and start to dig. We make it almost a room-size excavation, we roof it with corrugated iron, prop it up with poles, some canvas to waterproof it, a camouflage net on top along with dressing of bushes and branches. With loving care *I* (*me*)

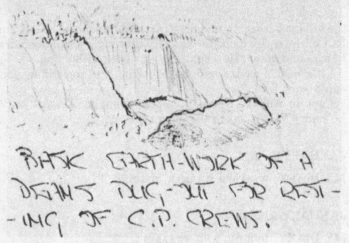

BACK EARTH-WORK OF A
DEAN'S DUG-OUT FOR REST-
-ING OF C.P. CREWS.

Method of digging a dug-out

tunnelled out a large chimney, and had a fire going to dry
out the interior. Edgington's sketch shows the method of
excavation at that site, and my drawing shows the finished
job. What I needed for a bed was a good piece of wood. Now,
Gunner Nash had mentioned a ruined church across the
road.

"There's catacombs, you can see 'em through the floor."

Yes indeed, Nash saw Milligan disappear down that hole;
soon hurling upwards were numerous bones, skulls, rocks,
etc. as I searched for a coffin lid. Eureka! I got three, and
soon I was lying on it in grand style; the others I gave to
Deans, and one to the telephone exchange for the duty
signaller to lean against.

JANUARY 12, 1944

Troops in front of us are our old friends the Berkshires and
a new mob, The London Scottish. Heard ITMA on Radio this
evening. Corny bastards. Heard Henry Hall, corny bastard.
Have laid in a good supply of firewood. Made two more oil
lamps, now in niches inside of our dug-out. Knocked off drum
of Derv Oil from parked lorry. Enough to last us a month.
Swopped soapy cigarettes with Italians in exchange for eggs.
Had a marvellous evening meal, boiled the eggs and floated
them in our beef stew and potatoes, ate it sitting on my coffin

lid. I gazed long in the fire, and listened to Deans holding forth about the war! "It *must* end soon," he says.

"Why?"

"Because I *want* it to."

"If *wanting* to is going to end it, I wanted it to end the day before I bloody joined."

"I'll tell you when it's going to end," said Fildes in between mouthfuls. "When we've flattened every German city and every German, that's the way it will end."

"I think he's going to lose, but we can't afford to let up here, he knows he's going to go on retreating, but the bastard only wants revenge in the form of our blood. The blokes running their war would rather burn Germany to the ground than surrender, they'll only surrender when they have to, and that goes for those little yellow fucking creeps the Japs."

"Oh Christ," said Deans. "I'd forgotten about them, it'll be just our bloody luck, when we've finished Jerry off, we'll be shipped off to the bloody jungles . . . it's never going to end."

Down on the plain there is a burst of MG fire, trained ears recognise it as Jerry's, there's response from tommy guns, two patrols have clashed, life and death, more shooting, and I slide another spoonful of dinner in. I really can't get it all together, us dining, them dying. . . . A head pokes through the black-out, it's gambling-mad Bombardier Marsden.

"Pontoon?"

"Piss off," we said.

The head disappeared. We could hear him visiting all the dug-outs around.

"How come he always seems to win?" I said.

"Never mind that," said Fildes. "How come we always seem to bloody lose?"

THURSDAY, JANUARY 13, 1944

MY DIARY: SUNNY, SPRINGLIKE MORNING. VERY QUIET. WOKEN BY STARLINGS SQUABBLING OVER SCRAPS I'D LEFT OUTSIDE DUG-OUT. NO WORK. PARADE AND THEN DO AS WE LIKE. EXCHANGE MANNED BY MONKEY TRUCK MEN. WILL CHECK COMMAND POST TO SEE ALL SIGNAL STUFF WORKS.

FILDES' DIARY: *Cushy now digging is finished. We all had bath down at village hot showers in front line. Fifty casualties in last night's attack by Berkshires and London Scottish.*

Oh yes, those hot showers; there were the infantry blazing away just outside the town, but what Fildes *doesn't* say in his diary was that when it was L/Bdr. Milligan's turn to have a bath, he and a score of the other great unwashed are suddenly divebombed by Jerry, five ME 109s. A goodly sight the folk of Lauro village were treated to, as a crowd of naked pink men scooted out the shower rooms and dived for cover in adjacent slit trenches. As I sat naked in my muddy pit my one thought was for my money in my battle-dress jacket, no sooner the bombing over and people sorting themselves out than L/Bdr. Milligan was seen to sprint back to the shower unit. Thank God! Money was safe! I must have Jewish blood. It was only after checking my wallet that I asked if anyone had been hurt. We restarted our shower as we were now all muddy. This time there is no singing, all ears were tuned to listen for any further planes. Pink and rosy and smelling of Lifebuoy soap I took me to my dugout, rolled up the canvas flap and let the sunshine in. The fire was going nicely, so I took out my trumpet and played away at the jazz for an hour.

"Hello, hello, what's this, then?" Through the sandbagged portals steps Gunner Edgington.

"I heard the tune of a fairy piper and I couldn't stop a-dancing." Then in a ridiculous voice, "I've danced allll the way here, me dearrrrr."

We yarned nostalgically about our "gigs", all that happy playing together that had now all stopped.

"It's not the same without people dancing," he said. "Dance music needs dancers."

I brew up some tea, and he talks about tunes he's got going in his head. He had the great gift of writing a tune that you almost immediately remembered, and he still does; it's a great waste of great tunes that he doesn't try to sell them. I'm privileged to be the only one who hears them, it's like having your own pet composer. He whistles a new theme,

Lauro gun positions, January 1944. Two officers (Lts. Pride and Walker) are on their knees through lack of food. Also on his knees is Vic Nash, who is the same height standing. Standing on the left is Ron Sherwood, and pointing is Jam-Jar Griffin.

"It's called 'The Angels Cried'. I had it in mind when you first told me that you loved Lily Dunford and she'd gone off with some other twit, and I think I've just about got the tune right."

I'm honoured! a song about my love affair. Wow!

Bombardier Marsden is up with the Naafi and Free Issue, he's on the fiddle again and is going to raffle a bottle of whisky.

"Ten lire a ticket." We all buy one. "Ten lire for a bottle of whisky, that's cheap," he says.

259

"It's ten lire more than you paid for it, you thievin' bugger," says forthright Gunner Devine.

"Watch it, watch it," threatens Bdr. Marsden.

"Watch *it*," laughs Devine. "Watch *it*." Whatever that meant.

Marsden has that sharp look, anything that's going, he'll have. His type always seem to get into the Q stores or something to do with the rations, and carry a Housey-housey kit or a Crown and Anchor board up their shirt. He is more than keen on knowing if there's been any casualties; if there are, that means all their bloody rations go into his pocket. We carry our rations back to the dug-out, and start stuffing ourselves. It was almost a psychological need, a substitute for happiness.

"I suck mine until there's only the raisins and nuts left in me mouth then I manipulate them into a ball and chew them." This was Edgington revealing his method of chocolate mastication. Were there no secrets left? He groans at the call of his name.

"Bloody Exchange duty, when will it all bloody end, when, when?" With hands raised in heavenly appeal he leaves.

I forage among the olive trees and gathered wood for the fire. Wrote home to Betty with a thousand improper suggestions. The sun is waning, I light the oil lamps in the dug-out, and I thumb through a book of British poetry, some of Wilfred Owen's poems – they are woefully sad, full of anguish. . . .

SATURDAY, JANUARY 15, 1944

I woke up with a feeling of foreboding, had it all day. I remember on duty in the Command Post. In the darkness men, machines and guns are moving, moving, moving, an occasional mule brays out a protest; this luxury is not afforded the men, it's uncanny how we hear no utterance from them. It's as though they are struck dumb. To add to the depressing atmosphere a lone piper wails in the rain-filled dark "The Skye Boat Song".

"It's the London Scottish, they're buying their dead," said Bdr. Fuller, who had come in to replace the batteries in the telephone. "Poor bastards, buryin' 'em in the bloody rain, their graves are 'alf full of bloody water.''

The air above the gun position is an overlay of Jerry shells. ''They're after something behind us.''

We hear the shells exploding, and I wonder if they're on target. Grapevine says no. 0350 hrs, more fire orders, no one sleeps tonight. 0500 hrs. The rain has stopped. Through the cave mouth I see the trees growing in the morning light; among them I see the muzzle bed. In comes Tume.

''Oh, here we bloody go again,'' he puts his mug of tea down, no time to drink, more fire orders. I leave the cave; outside it's guns guns guns! There's a frost. I feel it crunching underfoot. I descend the ladder to our dug-out. Deans is asleep . . . the fire is just alive, I throw a handful of wood on, the noise awakens him.

'''Ello,'' he yawns, ''what's the time?''

''Just gone five . . . bloody cold.''

I automatically prepare my bed. I'm off to collect grub, I wobble across the hard ground, balancing my dixies, powdered egg and mashed potatoes; as I walk I sip the life-giving tea – why do we dote on tea? It tastes bloody awful, it's only the sugar and milk that makes it drinkable. It's like fags – we've got hooked. Weary, I climbed into my bed, three dark

7.2 being laid by Bdr. Fordham (eh?), Lauro, January 1944.

Lt. Stewart Pride awaiting a call to stand in for James Mason.

blue blankets, and one grey, funny how I should still remember the colours. . . . As I closed my eyes, the sun was stream-
ing above my sand-bagged wall; it cut a golden swathe into
our dug-out, illuminating Deans' legs. He was shaving into
a metal mirror and humming a tune.

"Sorry mate," Sgt. King is peering down on me, "we're
fresh out of signallers, you'll have to go back on Command
Post at eight."

What was it now? 6.40. "OK, Sarge, I'll kip till then.
You'll wake me, won't you?"

No he won't. I sleep fitfully, casting glances at my watch.
I'm back in London – no I'm not, I'm in Italy. My mother is
making banana sandwiches. I'm off to work – no I'm not,
I'm in Italy at five to eight. And I was washing in Spike
Deans' dirty water; a fag, and I'm back in the Command
Post. Lt. Stewart Pride is duty officer. Christ, I'm tired.

"I'll get you a relief at mid-day," said Bombardier Fuller; the bugger looked clean-shaved and fresh. He'd been getting his quota of kip.

"A moment of cheer." Edgington just off Exchange duty comes in. "Some mail, up, mate."

I recognise my brother Desmond's terrible handwriting, that or it's been written during a violent earthquake. He is seventeen, working as an errand-boy in Fleet Street for fourpence a week, he gets up in the dark, travels on a smoke-filled blacked-out third-class carriage to all-black Black-friars – then to some grim office, runs around the streets with messages and packages that are now forgotten, meant nothing, left no trace and changed the world not one jot, he then came home in the dark on a blacked-out train to a blacked-out house, no wonder he went to Australia. He tells me he's doing lots of drawings, and follows the course of the war with teenaged fervour – he has a paste-up book – and numerous drawings. He sends me one of "German Bombers over Riseldene Rd, SE 23". Shall I send him one back of German bombers over my dug-out?

SUNDAY, JANUARY 16, 1944

I have no entry in my diary, but in a small pocket-book I had written this. "On road to OP. Wherever that is. It's going to be a big 'Do'. Everything secret. With me are Lt. Budden, Bdr. Fuller, Driver Shepherd. It's a glorious evening, blue sky, sunshine so unfitting for a bloody battle – here goes – long live Milligan. Wait, we are to go back to the gun position for the night and await further orders. So to bed. Did not pleasure any lady with my boots on."

I remember dumping my Arctic Pack on the OP jeep, and made my way back to the dug-out. Spike Deans was still awake. He was scribing to some bedworthy female on Anglo-Saxon shores, "If only she was on the bloody phone it would save all this burning of midnight oil."

"Yes," I said wearily.

"Here," he stopped writing, "weren't you supposed to be at the OP?"

"Change of plans, Churchill didn't want to risk me, so he's called it off . . . until tomorrow."

"What a bastard, getting you all worked up and then call it off . . . Where's Fildes?"

"He's already gone on ahead . . . with the first party."

"Sod his luck."

He continues his lovelorn missive. "Christ, it's quiet," he says. "I can hear the nib scratching on the paper."

"Haven't you got a silencer?"

"Good night, kind sir."

MONDAY, JANUARY 17, 1944

REGIMENTAL DIARY: *Regimental OP established at 882960 and line laid by 10.30.*

FILDES' DIARY: *This was the hottest time I've ever had when we crossed the Garigliano. Shepherd and I in jeeps were two days behind the advance carrying party, who footslogged to the river then crossed in boats. We joined them at 167 Brigade HQ.*

MY DIARY: BREAKFAST AT 0800. OP PARTY FOREGATHER AT 0900. WE ARE ISSUED WITH ARCTIC CARRYING PACKS. WE HAVE A "DRESS REHEARSAL", FULLY LOADED, THEN BREAK OFF TILL FURTHER ORDERS, IN WHICH TIME I AM WRITING THIS.

I had made a note in my diary at this point saying, "I died for the England I dreamed of, not the England I know." I had a terrible foreboding of death. I'd never had it before. We hang around all day. The waiting is the worst part. I oil my tommy gun, I don't know why, it's already oiled. Word that our Major and his OP party are at 167 Bde HQ at Santa Castrese.

"I suppose", says Fuller, " 'ees the patron saint of Castration."

"They make a damn fine stew," I said.

"What do?"

"Bollocks."

I had a great urge to go to the ballet. I had always loved ballet, and was forever in love with ballerinas; it's something I still suffer from. Somehow I couldn't see myself going to the ballet today. Going to the Major, under fire, crawling forward to him and saying, "Excuse me, sir, could I have a

264

24-hour pass to see *Coppelia*?" It wasn't on.

"You're not going, Milligan, you're wanted on the WT at the Command Post." Bombardier Fuller gives me the news. Birch is to go in my place. Christ, what game are they playing? That's twice! This will drive me bloody mad. Still I was going to be safe. Why was I grumbling? It's still evening. It's sunny, and, it's good to be alive.

"Christ! You back again," said Deans.

"Is it bothering you?"

"No."

"Well, it's bothering me."

I flopped on my bed and dumped my small pack down. Five o'clock. Time for Command Post. I've got a sore bottom. The dreaded piles!

The evening in the Command Post was enlivened by some Coon-type singing. Lt. Stewart Pride, Edgington, Deans and I were given to spirituals. Our programme was "Swing Low, Sweet Chariot", "I looked over Jordan", "Old Man Ribber". At eight o'clock I flopped on to my bed. I knew there was a barrage going over at 2100 hours. I didn't want to miss it, so I read a collection of *Tit-Bits* and *Tatlers*. I must have dozed off but I was awakened by the Boof boof boof of Beauforts blazing away about four hundred yards from my dug-out. In my diary I write, "Barrage not very intense.

Alf Fildes on the path just outside our dug-out in Lauro. His hands are tied behind his back to stop him going blind.

Beauforts using one in five tracer, I think it's more a marking barrage for the infantry. Better get my head down, I'm on at 0500! Piles giving me hell."

JANUARY 18, 1944

Somewhere in the small hours I heard explosions in that distant sleep-ridden way; I hard Spike Deans say in a sing-song voice like Jiminy Cricket, "Oh Spikeeeee, we're being shelleeddd."

I remember my reply, "Fuck 'em", and dozed off but then . . . my diary tells the story:

0220 HRS: AWAKENED BY SOMEONE SCREAMING COMING FROM THE GUNS, PULLED BACK THE BLACK-OUT AND COULD SEE THE GLARE OF A LARGE FIRE, AT THE SAME TIME A VOICE IN PAIN WAS SHOUTING "COMMAND POST, FOR GOD'S SAKE SOMEBODY, WHERE'S THE COMMAND POST?" IT WAS SOMEONE WITH HIS HAIR ON FIRE COMING UP THE PATH, HE WAS BEATING IT OUT WITH HIS HANDS, I JUMPED FROM MY BED SANS TROUSERS AND RAN TOWARDS HIM, IT WAS BOMBARDIER BEGENT. I HELPED BEAT THE FLAMES OUT. HIS FACE AND HANDS WERE BADLY BURNT, I HELPED HIM UP THE LADDER TO THE COMMAND POST AND I BLURTED OUT TO THOSE WITHIN, "THERE'S BEEN A DIRECT HIT ON THE GUNS." I REALISED THEN I WAS LATE WITH THE NEWS, WOUNDED GUNNERS WERE ALREADY BEING ATTENDED TO. EVERYBODY LOOKED VERY TENSE, BEHIND ME FLAMES WERE LEAPING TWENTY FEET IN THE AIR, I RUSHED BACK TO MY DUG-OUT DRESSED IN A FLASH. TOOK MY BLANKETS BACK TO THE COMMAND POST TO HELP COVER THE WOUNDED. I THEN JOINED THE REST OF THE BATTERY, WHO WERE ALL PULLING RED-HOT AND BURNING CHARGE-CASES AWAY FROM THOSE NOT YET AFFECTED. THEY WERE TOO HOT TO PULL BY HAND SO WE USED PICKAXES WEDGED IN THE HANDLES. LIEUTENANT STEWART PRIDE WAS HEAPING EARTH ON THEM WITH HIS HANDS. GUNNER DEVINE SEEMED TO BE ENJOYING IT, HE WAS GRINNING AND SHOUTING, "THIS IS THE FIRST TIME I'VE BEEN WARM TODAY." IT NEVER OCCURRED TO ME THAT SOME OF THE BOXES THAT WERE HOT MIGHT STILL CONTAIN UNEXPLODED CORDITE CHARGES, FORTUNATELY THEY DIDN'T GO OFF AND THAT'S WHY I'M ABLE TO WRITE THIS DIARY TODAY.

Bdr. Begent in a romantic mood or with heart disease.

It was a terrible night, four Gunners died and six were wounded. All suffered burns in varying degrees. The work of subduing the fire and tidying up went on until early dawn. It was terrible to see the burnt corpses. There was little Gunner Musclewhite, he'd been killed sitting up in bed. He was burnt black, and his teeth showed white through his black, fleshless head. Sgt. Jock Wilson too, Gunner White and Ferrier. . . .

A burial party under BSM Griffin were starting to dig as dawn came up. I went on duty at the Command Post. I wondered where Edgington was and wondered if he was a victim.

"No, he's on Exchange duties," said Chalky White.

I had run over to him just to verify. I pulled back the black-out that covered the little cave that the Telephone Exchange was; I could see he was visibly shaken by the affair.

"Just seein' you was still alive," I said and rushed back to the chaos.

What had happened need never have been so bad had we all not become careless. The Gunners had dug themselves a dug-out and covered it with a camouflage net, but they had surrounded their dug-out with Charge Boxes. The first shells must have hit the charges, which blew up and ignited the camouflage net that then fell in flames on top of those trapped underneath. . . .

1605 HRS: Lauro dive-bombed by seven enemy fighters. The all-night standing had made the piles worse. They started to bleed, it's all I needed for a perfect night.

Yes! I have what is called the curse of the Milligans – piles! My father had them, my grandfather had them, I was *born* with them. I thought they came along with legs, arms and teeth. They were bloody painful, and mine were bleeding down my legs. My father *hated*, personally hated, his piles; he, a great *romantic* of all the ailments! *he*, good-looking tap-dancing he, had to get piles. Why piles? he would rage as he squatted on two bowls of water, dipping his end alternatively into the hot and cold. Why – why like Chopin could he not have the romantic scourge? Consumption – "Look at the *sympathy he* got, lucky swine! – he could sit at his piano in a cell of the Carthusian Monastery, composing his Nocturnes, coughing gently: *that* was music and disease at its romantic best. But how, he asked, how could Chopin, in the sight of his beloved George Sand, sit at his piano, strike the first chords of the E Minor Nocturne, clutch his backside and say, "Oh my piles" – he wouldn't have got very far like that! My poor father – how he suffered, it wasn't the piles but his *pride* that hurt. When he had to cancel a performance at the Poona Gymkana special show for Sir Skipton Climo MC in 1925, he wrote, "Dear Lady C, I'm afraid I have been confined to bed, an old war-wound from Mesopotamia, a Turkish sniper got me", etc.

When I said to him, "Why don't you have them out?" he said, "What? and let them escape! Never! when I die I'll go straight to hell and I want those bastards to come with me and SUFFER."

We drove in a 15-cwt back to the Wagon Lines, and waited outside Dr Bentley's tent – came my turn.

Duck into the tent. Dr Bentley. He smiles as I enter.

"Ah Milligan – haven't seen you for a while."

"It's not for the want of trying, sir."

"You look alright."

"You're looking at the wrong end."

"What is it?"

"Piles."

"Piles! At *your* age."

"Yes, sir – I'm advanced for my years."

"Yes – they look very sore – "

"They're bloody sore – it's painful to walk."

"Well, I've no medication for them – I'll give you bed down forty-eight hours – attend B."

Bed! Forty-eight hours! A fortune-teller said one day I'd be lucky!

JANUARY 19, 1944

MY DIARY: SORE ARSE. GOOD MORNING, EVERYBODY. ALL VERY DEPRESSED ABOUT THE LOSS OF THOSE POOR BLOODY GUNNERS.

It was a sunny morning again. I could hear some birds singing in the olive trees. Wish I had something to sing about. Can't sing about a sore arse. Thank God, I'm bed down; but no, here comes bed up, it's Sgt. King.

"Sorry, Milligan, you'll have to go on Command Post, we're stuck for signallers, that cunt Jenkins took enough of them with him to start a regiment."

"But I'm bed down, Sarge."

"What with?"

"Piles."

"Piles? That all? I'm not asking you to use that end, just answer the phone and work the wireless, that won't affect 'em."

I couldn't say no, we really were short of men. So, with my backside hanging out, I sit on it in the Command Post. Situation reports are coming in, the battle up front is raging; I can't understand why the guns are so quiet. It must be close fighting. Deans is on duty and so is Lt. Wright.

"They've forgotten about us," he says, stands up, stretches himself and sits down, a masterful exercise in control. Deans scrapes some chestnuts from the fire and hands them around from his tin hat. "Farm Fresh," he said. "Laid this morning."

The phone goes. "Command Post . . . it's for you, sir." I hand the phone to Mr Wright.

"Wright here . . . yes . . . yesssss." He hangs up. "That was Regimental OP . . . they were checking that the line was through."

"Of course, I couldn't have told them that, sir."

Wright grins, he's one of the lads. "Well, Milligan, that's one of the perks of being an officer."

"One day I'll be an officer, sir," I said in shining tones, "and *I'll* be able to pick up the telephone and say, 'Yes, I can hear you.' That will be a wonderful day."

The phone buzzes, I snatch it up and shout, "I'm not an officer but I can hear you and that means that the line is through!"

It turns out to be some poor lost bloody signaller from another field regiment, he's been following the wrong line.

"Whose line are you then?" he says.

I can't tell him, that's security.

"Oh fuck," he says, and then I'm sure he's one of us, but I give him a quick security test. "Who says 'This is Funf speaking'?"

There's a giggle on the line. "That's ITMA."

"This is 56 Heavy Regiment so we're no use to you, mate."

"Ta," he says and is gone.

Lt. Wright is looking at me. "What was that ITMA stuff all about?"

"I was checking a signaller's bona fides, sir."

"Were they in order?"

"Yes, sir, he knew exactly what the answering code-word was for ITMA."

"And what was it?"

"Bloody awful, sir."

The phone rings again. "19 Battery Command Post." It's the RHQ OP. "Take Post." I rattle down the Tannoys, "Right Ranging." Soon we are all immersed in a two-hour Cannonade; we have no time other than to snatch a drag at a fag.

"Christ, someone's copping it," was Lt. Wright's remark, based on the fact that the target remained static and we just rained gunfire in it. "It's a crossroads with ammo lorries trying to get through," he informs us later.

The OP tell him that several trucks have been blown up and they are trying to detour over adjacent fields, where the 25-pounders plaster them. It ends with most of their trucks blown up and they pack it in, but it took a lot to stop the bastards. They were a tough lot OK. At mid-day I am relieved by Sgt. King himself.

"Off you go, Milligan, get lunch and be back at – " he looks at his watch " – two o'clock."

"Right."

"'Ow's yer backside?"

"Out of bounds."

I have lunch, then lay on my bed in total discomfort and very depressed. I think I'd better have the operation, yes, I'll see the Doc in the morning and have the damn things out. Guns are going all around me; in between, birds try and sing, what do they think of all this lunacy? I have a stab at reading a book by another loony, Lord Byron; it's appropriate, *Childe Harold*, and it's being read by Child Milligan, he goes on about Italy and Rome,

> Thy very weeds are beautiful, thy waste
> More rich than other climes' fertility.

Have I got news for him! No I couldn't stomach Byron today, so I read what must be the most up-to-date newspaper in Italy – the *Daily Express*, January 7, 1944. It was flown here on an RAF with a contingent of officers, one of whom met Lt. Mostyn at base depot, and in turn it had ended up in the Command Post.

"It says we have 'Fighter with no propeller'," I read aloud. "Ah, well that's due to shortage of parts," said Vic Nash. "I myself have a razor with no blades, it's part of a

Lt. Joe Mostyn – an identification photo was given to each member of the battery with warning not to lend money.'

plan to drive us all bloody mad.''

I read that there is a "Test lighting of street-lamps in Malpas Road, Deptford, a Councillor Coombs pressed a button in a controlling sub station and the lights came on."

Nash looks up from de-mudding his boots. "A lot of fucking good that's going to do for winning the war."

"I've looked through this paper and there's not one bloody mention of us."

"That's it mate . . . we're the forgotten Army."

"Forgotten . . . FORGOTTEN? Don't make me laugh . . . they've never bloody heard of us."

Smudger Smith and Spiv Convine from B Sub have arrived. They are definitely scrounging. "Got any fags, Milly?" (Smudger always called me Milly.) He's moaning about not having enough mail.

"They must all be bleedin' crippled from the shoulder dhan, I written a dozen bleedin' Air letters and nuffink back, last one was Christmas . . . Huh . . . women . . . Huh!"

He was right. "Women huh!", that summed them up. "Huh."

"Good news, Smudger, according to the *Daily Express* there's no war in Italy."

He borrows the paper; I never saw it again. It would come to the same terrible end that all good newspapers came to in this army, even *The Times*. At that time, I was dreaming of after-the-war ventures, and I had decided that I would like to have a Club on the river. Edgington, Deans and myself had discussed being partners with Dixie Dean* from Hailsham. It would be called either Holiday Inn or Ravello's: Deans would see to the catering, I would have a band, and Harry Edgington would play the piano in the lounge. I had a pad and I was writing down what the requirements of the place were – plates, chairs, etc. Dreams. Dreams. Dreams.

"Come on, you're bloody late," Sergeant King has bearded me in my lair.

"Sorry, Sarge, I was miles, miles away."

"We're *all* bloody miles away," he said. "They're having a bloody hot time across the river. We're through to them on the wireless; they're at Tac HQ where "Looney" is. Lt. Budden and party are up Dimiano trying to establish an OP."

*He used to play drums with us when we were stationed in Hailsham.

Lt. E. Wright holding up a set of railings willed to him by his mother.

We are walking together to the CP. He leaves me at the entrance.

'Hurry up, Milligan,'' says Lt. Wright, ''we're off again.''

Bdr. Edwards has been working the phone, the wireless and the Tannoy.

''What's it feel like to be fully employed, Eddy?'' I said, taking over the earphones.

Bombardier Edwards was a gift to the army. He did his job to full measure, never complained, first class at his profession of Specialist, clean, shaved every morning even in cold water, about five foot ten, black-haired, not in any way good-looking, prominent teeth, never said much; when we were all getting pissed out of our tiny minds, Eddy would be doing water-colours and sketches of the landscape. We noticed at dances, whenever he took the floor, he appeared to be on wheels and his lady partner pushing him around. At OPs he was very brave – well, braver than me – he wouldn't flinch when one dropped near, and I did, I flinched when they didn't drop near. I even flinched when nothing was happening, I was an inveterate flincher. I flinched after the war whenever a car backfired.

The weather now is glorious, a faint promise of spring

273

warmth is in the air, the sun is in a cloudless sky, and the Germans must be cursing it as the RAF and the USSAF pound the daylights out of them. Suddenly there are no more fire orders. All round, guns are going, all except us, is it because we're Jewish? We all stare into the Command Post fire, it stares back, we are all pissed off, and trying to find comfort in dreams.

"I think I'd like to be walking along the front at Brighton with Margaret," said Edwards.

At the hour of five I was glad to see Sergeant King come and take over. I go straight to my bed. My backside is on fire. I swallow six aspirins to try and kill the pain.

MY DIARY: FILDES ARRIVED BACK FROM OP WITH ERNIE HART ALL BADLY SHAKEN, HART IS ALL IN AND CRYING. "THOSE POOR BASTARDS UP THERE," HE SAYS.

Lt. Wright calls the few remaining signallers together. "Look," he sounds uneasy, "they need a signal replacement up at Tac HQ . . . any volunteers? . . ."

There is an embarrassing silence, I can't stand it.

"I'll go, sir," I heard myself say; I was the only NCO there, I *had* to say it, example and all that. "So, Mr Fildes, you have come to take me for a nice little ride."

Alf Fildes smirks. His eyes tell a different story.

JANUARY 20, 1944

Going to Dimiano OP

I get into the jeep next to Alf and we set off; he didn't say much until we got through Lauro and then on to the railway track, now denuded of rails and used as a communications road. It was a lovely day, sunny. Suddenly Alf said, "This is beautiful! Sunshine – birds singing, I could do with more of this."

He told me the OP and the Major's HQ were both in "dodgy" positions. Hart had been up the OP, and it had finished him – Jerry was ramming everything on to them. It all sounded grim, and I wondered what my lot would be. The sounds of Artillery faded as small arms, automatic weapons and mortars increased. We were passing a steady stream of ambulances; one I notice had shrapnel holes in the sides.

274

Recce scout car coming out of smoke being laid to obscure pontoon bridge over the Garigliano.

We turned off the railway embankment on to a country "road", really a cart track; a one-mile sign read "Castleforte 5 kilometer".

"How's Jenkins been behaving?" I said.

Fildes smirked. "He sends everyone up the OP except himself. I think he's shit scared, that or balmy."

I didn't fancy being in any way mixed up with Jenkins, he was humourless. I didn't understand him at all, no one did; God help me, I was soon to find out what a lunatic he was. I was already tired having been awake for two nights, and the piles were giving me hell. We approached the ferry bridge over the Garigliano. Jerry was lobbing occasional shells into the smoke that was being used to obscure the crossing. From the smoke loomed the Pontoon Ferry bearing its load of wounded. Some looked pleased to be out of it. Others looked stunned, others with morphia were just staring up from their stretchers.

"Any more for the Woolwich Ferry?" says a cheerful cockney voice. We and several other vehicles move forward, among them a truck loaded with ammunition – a few more Jerry shells land in the river. By the sound they are close, can't see for smoke – we stop. Through the smoke, a figure with outstretched arms to stop us going off the end as apparently had happened earlier. A jeep driver, thinking it was a continuous bridge, roared off the end, surfaced swearing. "Where's the rest of the bloody bridge?" More shells. We are moving.

275

Pontoon bridge over the Garigliano during a lull in the shelling. Men with ugly faces were told to look away from the camera.

We pull off the other side; to our left looms Mount Dimiano.

"That's what all the trouble's about," says Fildes, "our OP's on there somewhere."

Off the road to our right is a cluster of farmhouses, some shelled, some intact.

"This is it," says Fildes, as we turn right into them.

We pull up in front of the centremost one. A two-storeyed affair – all around are dead Jerries. MG bullets are whistling overhead as we duck and run inside.

It was a large room. On a makeshift table was a 22 Set. There was Jenkins. Laying down at the far end of the room, "Flash" Gordon, Birch, Fuller, Howard, Badgy Ballard, Dipper Dai – all looked as gloomy as hell.

"It isn't the war," said Birch, "it's Jenkins."

"Milligan – you can get on the set right away," says Jenkins.

I took over from Fuller; immediately, Jenkins sends RHQ a series of pointless messages. "It's very stuffy in the room." "There are eight ORs, two NCOs and myself." "Thornton coming back." "The Germans are shelling us." "The Germans have stopped shelling us."

I don't exactly know what his job was supposed to be. The people who were taking the stick were Lt. Budden and party, who were being "stonked" unmercifully. In the room, save for a direct hit, we were comparatively safe. From the time I arrived (about 4 pm) the bastard kept me on the set all night, a total of seventeen hours with the headphones on. It was my third night without sleep, just the noise of the interference was enough to drive you potty. To get a break I said, "Do you think, sir, under the Articles of War, I could be relieved, so I can relieve myself?" Even then he said, "Well, hurry up." I felt like saying, "I will piss as fast as I can, sir – would you like someone to time me in case I loiter?"

Outside a young Lieutenant was talking to a Sergeant. ". . . Then why didn't they stay inside. I mean those inside didn't get killed." I presume he was referring to the unburied dead who lay without the walls. It was dark. A stream of MG bullets whined over the roof, God knows what he was aiming for – there was nothing behind us.

Overhead, stars shone. Back in Major Jenkins' Salon for the Morose, I went back on the set. At that moment a terrific explosion shook the farm; it was a Jerry 155mm shell, and he continued to carry out harassing fire throughout the night. I think it was the road to the ferrybridge he was after, but he moved around a bit. I continued to relay our lunatic's messages. "The Germans have started shelling us", "There's an interval of two minutes between each round", this his most unbelievable one. "Every time we transmit a message – he shells us."

The idiot was implying that Jerry had a device that made it possible to locate the position of a wireless set by its transmission. Of course, there was absolutely no truth in his statement – when we didn't transmit Jerry shelled us – so how did he become a Major? Mens' lives were in his hands. Like all lunatics he had unending energy – as dawn came he got worse. I was almost numb with fatigue, and my piles had started to bleed. I should never have volunteered. One of the lads makes breakfast – while I'm eating it Jenkins tells me, "Bombardier, I want you to take Gordon, Howard, Birch and Ballard to the OP with fresh batteries and a 22 set." Great, all I have to do is carry a 50lb battery to the top of a mountain, anything else? Like how about a mile run before in medieval armour?

Ballard apparently knows the way. At 9.00 we put on Arctic Packs and strap on one battery each. We set off single file on the road towards Castleforte, which sits in the near distance on a hillside full of Germans. We turn left off the road into a field; we pass a Sherman Tank, a neat hole punched in the turret; a tank man is removing kit from inside. Laying on a groundsheet is the mangled figure of one of the crew.

"What a mess," says the Tankman in the same tones as though there was mud on the carpet.

I grinned at him and passed on. Above us the battle was going on full belt; coming towards us is Thornton, dear old 35-year old Thornton; he looks tired, he has no hat, and is smoking a pipe.

"Hello, what's on?"

He explains he's been sent back. "I'm too old for that lark. I kept fallin' asleep."

I asked him the best way up. He reaffirms, "You got up a stone-lined gully; when it ends start climbing the hill, it's all stepped for olive trees. Of course," he added, "if you're in the gully and they start mortaring, you've had it."

"Thanks," I said, "that's cheered us up no end."

He bid us farewell and we went forward, we reached the gully. In a ravine to the left were Infantry all dug into the side; they were either "resting" or in reserve. So far so good. We reach the end of the stone gully and start climbing the stepped mountain – each step is six foot high, so it's a stiff climb. CRUMP! CRUMP! CRUMP!, mortars. We hit the ground. CRUMP CRUMP CRUMP – they stop. Why? Can they see us? We get up and go on, CRUMP CRUMP CRUMP – he can see us! We hit the deck. A rain of them fall around us. I cling to the ground. The mortars rain down on us. I'll have a fag, that's what. I am holding a packet of Woodbines, then there is a noise like thunder. It's right on my head, there's a high-pitched whistle in my ears, at first I black out and then I see red, I am strangely dazed. I was on my front, now I'm on my back, the red was opening my eyes straight into the sun. I know if we stay here we'll all die . . . I start to scramble down the hill. There's shouting, I can't

278

recall anything clearly. Next I was at the bottom of the mountain, next I'm speaking to Major Jenkins, I am crying, I don't know why, he's saying, "Get that wound dressed."

I said, "What wound?"

I had been hit on the side of my right leg.

"Why did you come back?" He is shouting at me and threatening me, I can't remember what I am saying. He's saying, "You could find your way back but you couldn't find your way to the OP", next I'm sitting in an ambulance and shaking, an orderly puts a blanket round my shoulders, I'm crying again, why why why? Next I'm in a forward dressing station, an orderly gives me a bowl of hot very sweet tea, "Swallow these," he says, two small white pills. I can't hold the bowl for shaking, he takes it from me and helps me drink it. All around are wounded, he has rolled up my trouser leg. He's putting a sticking plaster on the wound, he's telling me it's only a small one. I don't really care if it's big or small, why am I crying? Why can't I stop? I'm getting lots of sympathy, what I want is an explanation. I'm feeling drowsy, and I must have started to sway because next I'm on a stretcher. I feel lovely, what were in those tablets . . . that's the stuff for me, who wants food? I don't know how long I'm there, I wake up. I'm still on the stretcher, I'm not drowsy, but I start to shiver. I sit up. They put a label on me. They get me to my feet and help me to an ambulance. I can see really badly wounded men, their bandages soaked through with blood, plasma is being dripped into them.

When we get to one of the Red Cross trucks, an Italian woman, all in black, young, beautiful, is holding a dead baby and weeping; someone says the child has been killed by a shell splinter. The relatives are standing by looking out of place in their ragged peasants' clothing amid all the uniforms. An older woman gives her a plate of home-made biscuits, of no possible use, just a desperate gesture of love. She sits in front with the driver. I'm in the back. We all sit on seats facing each other, not one face can I remember. Suddenly we are passing through our artillery lines as the guns fire. I jump at each explosion, then, a gesture I will never forget, a young soldier next to me with his right arm in a bloody sling put his arm around my shoulder and tried to comfort me. "There, there, you'll be alright mate."

279

Wounded coming across the bridge, January 20, 1944. I was to come across the same bridge the next day.

We arrived at a camp. I was put into a tent on a bunk bed. An orderly gave me four tablets and more hot tea; in a few seconds they put me out like a light. I had finished being a useful soldier. I've had it. Here is "Dipper" Dye's version, though it differs a lot from mine. However!

All this time Jerry was belting away at us, so even getting the rope across the river was no mean feat by whoever had managed it. Once on the other bank of the river there was still a good march to the base of "Damiano", and Bombardier Milligan and I were given the job of carrying a large coil of telephone wire attached to a drum which took two men to carry by holding a pole through the centre of the drum. What with packs on our back, carrying tommy gun and the wire and the state of the terrain, I was beginning to wish I was back at base with my gun-towing Scammell and Doug Kidgell, who was my co-driver. Spike and I trudged on until we were nearing "Damiano", and at the foot of the hill we came to a gully. Suddenly mortar shelling became really violent and I dived for cover in a cranny at the side of the hill. Spike fell to the ground and seemed very badly shellshocked and affected, especially in his backside area.* I helped him to his feet and carried him to the best of my ability to the First Aid Post, where I left him. [Thank you, Dipper!]

I wake up, it's very early, am I now stark raving mad? I can distinctly hear a brass band, right outside the tent, they are playing "Roll Out The Barrel" at an incredible speed. I get up, look outside. There in a circle stand a collection of GIs, all playing this tune; they are in a strange collection of garments, some in overcoats with bare legs and boots, some in pyjamas, others in underpants, unlaced boots and sweaters, an extraordinary mixture.

I looked at my watch. It was 0645. This I discovered was the American Reveille; the tune finished, the men doubled back to their beds. But where was I? It was a large hospital tent, full of bunk beds with sleeping soldiers. I was the only one awake, and was still fully dressed save my battle-dress jacket. For the first time I felt my right leg aching. I sat on the side of my bed, took the plaster off my leg to look at the wound. It was a wound about two inches long and about a quarter of an inch deep, as though I had been slashed with a razor blade. Today you can only see the scar if I get sunburnt. It wasn't hindering me, so what was I here for? I lit up a cigarette. It was one of my five remaining Woodbines, now very crushed. Two RAMC Orderlies enter the tent, young lads, they go around the beds looking at the labels; they woke some of the men up, gave them tablets. They arrived at me. I asked them where I was. They told me it was 144 CCS, I was labelled "Battle Fatigue". I was to see a psychiatrist that evening. Meantime there was a mess tent where I could get breakfast. I told them I didn't have my small kit. "Don't worry, lad, they've got knives and forks there."

Lad? So I was Lad now. It was a wretched time. No small kit, no towel, no soap, no friends. It's amazing what small simple things really make up our life-support system, all I wanted was for some cold water on my face. I went across

*Piles!

281

to the American Camp and from a GI (of all things smoking a cigar) I scrounged a towel. He was more than generous, he took me to his Quarter Master, who gave me two brand-new khaki-coloured towels, soap, and a razor. I'm afraid I was still in a terribly emotional state, and I started to cry "Thanks" but apparently they were aware that the Camp next to them were Battle Fatigue cases.

I wandered through a mess of tents till I found the Ablutions. It was still only 7.30, but the place was full; there was the terrible silence of a mass of people who don't know each other. I washed in silence, and the cold water made me feel a little fresher. The seat of my trousers are all sticky. Oh God, what a mess, blood, the curse of the Milligans is still working. What I really want is a bath. I'm given two different-sized pills. I ask what they are, the orderly says, "I don't know, chum." (I'm Chum now.) He knows alright, but it was early days for tranquillisers. "Take them after breakfast." I have absolutely no recollection of eating breakfast, I think that I took the tablets right away; next thing it was evening time, I'm very dopey.

"You got to see the 'Trick Cyclist'," says the young orderly. I had no idea what 'Trick Cyclist' meant. I asked. Psychiatrist? That was for lunatics. Was I one? I was to find out. In a small officer-type tent, behind an Army folding-table covered with a grey blanket sits a stern, or rather attempting to look stern, officer. He is a Captain. Middle aged, a small, almost pencil-thin, moustache. He asks me all those utterly boring questions, name, religion, etc. . . . He asks me what happened. I tell him as much as I can recall. He is telling me that it takes 100,000 shells before one soldier is killed, he ends with (and in a louder voice than before), "You are going to get better. *Understand?*" Yes, I understand. I'm back in my tent, still a bit airy-fairy in the head. I've never had mind drugs before.

I get an evening meal. There's no lighting in the hospital tents, the orderlies come round with a Tilly Lamp, and I get more knock-out pills. Next morning, "Roll Out The Barrel"; it's a great place for Battle Fatigue, a week here and it would be "Roll out the Battle Fatigue". I am to be sent back to the Regiment. I suppose they know what they are doing. Time was to prove that they didn't.

How I got back to the Battery I don't know, this was a time of my life that I was very demoralised. I was not really me any more.

Back to the Mob

JANUARY 27, 1944

The Battery are still at Lauro in the same position.

The first things I notice are the graves of those who died on the night of the fire. BSM Griffin is pottering around the graves tidying them up, they have white crosses, and the names written on them.

The tradition of putting the deceased's steel helmet on the cross still persists. One suspects that it happened at Thermopylae. I am so miserable, the spring that made me Spike

Grave of gunner killed at Lauro.

Milligan has gone. I'm a zombie. Anyone can do or say anything to me. I hear that those who had been with me on the OP fiasco had all been given seven days' leave. Why not me? As soon as our guns start to fire, I start to jump. I try to control it, I run to my dug-out and stay there. I suddenly realise that I'm stammering. What a bloody mess! The Major thinks I'm a coward, perhaps I am? If so why didn't I run from the line the first day in action in North Africa? I am aware that the date is January 27. A whole week? Where have I been? I'm on duty in the Command Post and I really shouldn't be. I manage to stop crying, but I am now stammering very badly, so I can't be of any use passing wireless messages or Fire Orders; I just copy down Sit-reps. Then they put me on the Telephone Exchange.

To add to my misery I am "Court Martialled" by the Major. I am marched into his tent by Sgt. Daddy Wilson, and I'm told I had been due for a second stripe but owing to my unreliable conduct I am to relinquish my stripe. I suppose in World War 1 the bastard would have had me shot. Mind you, he had had it in for me for a long time. I didn't represent the type of empty-minded soldier he wanted. I had been a morale-booster to the boys, organising dances and concerts, and always trying to keep a happy atmosphere, something he couldn't do. Now he was letting me have it. So I was Gunner Milligan, wow, what a world-shaker. All this despite the fact the discharge certificate from the 144 CCS had stated that "This man must be rested behind the lines for a period to stabilise his condition." I was also taking some pills that they had given me. I suppose they were early tranquillisers, all they did was make me into a zombie. I am by now completely demoralised. All the laughing had stopped.

JANUARY 28, 1944

The whole week is still very bitty in terms of remembering it. I had been told to report to the MO every morning. When he saw me, and heard the incredible stammer I had, I knew he was going to send me away from the Battery for good. In retrospect, if the idiots had just sent me back for a few weeks in the first place, I'm sure I would have been alright, but the Major, who was an unthinking bastard, loved playing God. What did he know about 19 Battery? He was a regular – a regular bastard. We weren't regulars. He was used to a life of Regiment hopping. I suppose in his career he'd been in hundreds of units, one was very much the same as the others, but for us this was not so, we'd always been in one Battery right from the start. The feeling of togetherness was something he never participated in, but we still have it. We have two reunions a year. No other mob has that going for them; we were unique. We've never heard from Jenkins. After the war, he's never been to a reunion, he didn't really belong to us. We're still together. I doubt if he is. I remember at the time thinking I'd like to order a Council steam-roller to drive over him, instructing the driver to go as slow as possible.

He lived on that one narrow plane and everyone had to be judged by that; he didn't know of deeper or higher feelings, those were areas that he could never enter. The bloody fool had got rid of someone who was deeply attached to the Battery and the lads, yet the bastard had made *me* stay at the gun position. "The noise of the guns will boost your morale," the bloody fool said. It didn't, the noise drove me mad. Came one of the saddest days in my life, I had to leave. I got up very early, I didn't say goodbye to anyone. I got in the truck, alongside Driver Wright. As I drove back down that muddy mountain road, with the morning mists filling the valleys, I felt as though I was being taken across the Styx. I've never got over that feeling.

"Do you know where I'm going?" I asked Wright.

"Yes, it's the 865 FDS."

FEBRUARY 10, 1944

MY DIARY: LANDED UP IN NO. 2 GENERAL HOSPITAL, CASERTA.

This was a real hospital, or rather they had made it so. The weather was sunny, and I was shown into a long ward with lots of windows to let in the light and air. It had a polished stone floor, the walls and ceilings painted white. Beds along the walls. Down the centre were trestle tables with books, and a few pots of flowers. Very pleasant. I was soon in bed, dressed in blue service pyjamas. This was a Psychiatric Ward with about fifty patients in. About two-thirds were under drugs, and slept most of the day. The remainder were very silent and morose. No one spoke to anyone.

All day and every day I just sat on the bed and read. I wondered if I did anything apart from that. I've checked my Letter list. I noted that I wrote to my father on January 22, to Lily Dunford on January 30, then a note "Acknowledged all mail on 30 Jan.". By chance one of those letters still exists, the one to my father. I don't mention my ordeal, but say "I pass the hours reading poetry."

By now my parents had been informed of me being a casualty. They were living at Orchard Way, Reigate, when the telegram arrived. It was stamped "OHMS. War Office". My mother had opened the door, and when she saw it she called to my father, "I can't open it." They said they felt I had been killed. Parents must have spent a lifetime of anguish as they opened the telegrams not knowing the contents.

I was to see a Major Palmer, a Psychiatrist, whom I believe invented the revolutionary deep narcosis for the treatment of Battle Fatigue. My turn came for the interview; I told him that being in hospital I was only taking up a bed space. What I needed was a job to occupy me. He looked up and said, "I appreciate that. A lot of the bastards like to malinger here as long as they can." He was a rugged-looking man with a broken nose, a relic from his amateur boxing days. I was told of a Scottish soldier who had to see him because of an "ungovernable temper". "So you lose your temper, do you?" "Aye, and I lash out." "Would you hit me?" "Yes, I would." "Well, go on and try." The Scot had lashed out, Palmer had parried and riposted with a right to the jaw, felling the Scotsman.

A novel form of Psychiatry. I wonder if it cured him. He had me posted to a Rehabilitation Camp north of Naples.

No. **W2040/M/954024.**
(If replying, please quote above No.)

Army Form B. 104—81.

Record Office,

R.A. RECORD OFFICE FIELD BRANCH FOOTS

7 FEB 1944

.... 19

SIR, ~~OR MADAM,~~

I regret to have to inform you that a report has been received from

the War Office to the effect that (No.) *954024* (Rank) *Gnr (P/A/Ldr)*

(Name) *MILLIGAN . Terence Alan* *Dvg Cl*

(Regiment) *Royal Artillery (Field)* was wounded

on the *22nd* .... day of *January* 19 *4 4* *whilst serving in the Central Mediterranean Theatre of War.*

Amendment Slip to Army Form B104—81.

It has not been reported into what hospital he has been been
admitted, nor are other particulars known, but in the event of his
condition being considered by the Medical Authorities as serious
or dangerous this office will be notified by cable and you will be y any
immediately informed. In addition he will have been given every
facility for communicating with you himself. o you.

a

fu

I am to express to you the sympathy and regret of the Army

Council.

Yours faithfully,

Rushworth

for Officer in charge of Records.

**IMPORTANT.—Any change of address should be
immediately notified to this office.**

(55827) M22108/1261 500m. P.&G. 9/39 **52-4094**   Forms/B.104—81/4

*The telegram that made my parents say,
"Blast, they missed him."*

287

MARCH 9, 1944

I'm on a lorry, with a lot of other PNs*. It takes us to a terrible muddy camp next to a small suburb called Afrigola. I was to be reception clerk that is, I sat in a tent at the entrance of the Camp, with a lot of Army forms. As the PNs came in I took down their details and put them in a file. All day long the battle-weary soldiers filed in; I was asked the same question, "What are they going to do with me?" and there was a hollow fear in each voice, some cried. God made gentle people as well as strong ones. Alas for the war effort, I was a gentle one.

Will Milligan recover? Will he get back in the big time among the Lance-Bombardier set? Above all, will he lose that stammer that makes him take four hours to say good morning? All this *and more* in Vol. 5, *Goodbye Soldier*, to be serialised in *Gay News*.

End

*Psycho Neurotics